"This book is a significant step forward in the discussion of the dynamics of church growth. Arising out of qualitative research in some growing churches in the North of England and through engagement with a number of recent academic voices, it deepens our awareness of the ecology of growth."

—STEPHEN SPENCER, Director of Theology and Implementation, Anglican Communion Office

"Rooms takes his contextual theologizing to a new level of sophistication in these pages, engaging in a dialogue not only with churches in England's North, but with contextual, practical, and decolonial theologies in the world church. In the same way that he profits from these dialogues, contextual theologians worldwide can profit greatly from Nigel Rooms's brilliant new work."

—STEPHEN BEVANS, SVD, Louis J. Luzbetak, SVD, Professor of Mission and Culture, Emeritus, Catholic Theological Union, Chicago

"As an Anglican priest and scholar, Nigel Rooms turns intentionally toward marginality and subaltern voices, gently reclaiming theology from the edges where faith is lived, contested, and continually renewed. By naming contextualization itself as 'contested,' he invites us into a more humble and attentive reimagining of the relationship between gospel and culture."

—BOKYOUNG PARK, President, International Association for Mission Studies

"We misunderstand Nigel Rooms if we think he is searching only for Northern identity. He is asking how each of our localities can be caught up in the mission of God. There is hope here for all who wrestle with the fragility of the church in overlooked contexts. But also a challenge: to find God even amidst anger and decline, and to follow Christ in ways that are not pre-packaged but patient, responsive and refreshingly convivial."

—MARK POWLEY, Archbishop's Mission Enabler for the North

"As a Northerner, I feel seen in Nigel Rooms's writing. This book presents an intricate portrait of the North and its church landscape in a way that challenges ideas of nativism and essentialism. Writing through the prism of post-colonial theology, Rooms weaves the North's unique, but subaltern, voice, contested notions of flourishing and a critical use of contextual theology. Capturing the northern identity in themes of authenticity, community, and humor, the book draws on a theology of political and cultural resilience."

—SHARON JAGGER, Associate Professor in Religion, York St. John University

Contested Contextualization

Contested Contextualization

Towards a Regional, Critical, and Post-Colonial Contextual Theology from the North of England

NIGEL J. ROOMS

WIPF & STOCK · Eugene, Oregon

CONTESTED CONTEXTUALIZATION
Towards a Regional, Critical, and Post-Colonial Contextual Theology from the North of England

Wipf & Stock
An Imprint of Wipf and Stock Publishers
199 W. 8th Ave., Suite 3
Eugene, OR 97401

www.wipfandstock.com

PAPERBACK ISBN: 979-8-3852-6503-9
HARDCOVER ISBN: 979-8-3852-6504-6
EBOOK ISBN: 979-8-3852-6505-3

VERSION NUMBER 05/04/26

To “Northerners” everywhere.

Contents

Acknowledgments ix

1 Weaving a Contextual Theology in the Twenty-First Century 1

2 An "Emic" Critique of Contextual Theology 11

3 An "Etic" critique of Contextual Theology 41

4 Contextual Theology, Essentialism, and Northern Cultural Capital 78

5 The Field Research, its Methodology and Initial Findings 111

6 Growing and Flourishing 140

7 Post-colonial Theology and the Northern Research Subjects 175

8 Towards a Regional, Critical, and Post-Colonial Contextual Theology 203

Bibliography 223

Index 229

Acknowledgments

I ACKNOWLEDGE A GENEROUS research grant from the Susannah Wesley Foundation which enabled the field research in the North of England on which this book is based. https://susannawesleyfoundation.org/

I would like to thank those who are in the background of the development and writing of this book; My researcher colleague, Elli Wort; an inspiration for the work, Steve Bevans; an anonymous peer reviewer; the copy-editor, Christopher Pipe.

1

Weaving a Contextual Theology in the Twenty-First Century

I LIKE TO THINK of working in the related fields of missiology, contextual, and practical theology as *craft*. Crafting something is based on the Aristotelian concepts of *phronesis* or practical wisdom which proceeds via *praxis*, action and reflection and *poiesis*, the production of an artefact that did not previously exist which proceeds via *techne* or skill. This book is an attempt to master the craft of contextual theology that I have chosen, or rather been called vocationally to for at least thirty years. In addition, as craft, the book aims at being a unique contribution to the field, adding "something that did not previously exist" to it. The reader will need to decide whether I have succeeded in mastering these tasks.

In 2022 I visited the world-famous Sydney Opera House in Australia and took part in the guided tour of the iconic building. The story of its creation was told as we walked around and I can relate some of it here (in my own version). An architectural competition was run in the 1950s to create the design for a new state-of-the-art Opera House. An obscure, little-known Danish architect surprisingly won the competition with his amazing, even mesmerizing design. The only problem was he had no idea how to actually build it or whether the engineering technology even existed to do so. This caused many problems and arguments and the story does not end happily, even if the Opera House is eventually built. My point here is that any great art or craft project is what we might call "emergent"—the maker has an imagination of what is possible, but the journey to making the end product is not a straight line, and much of what happens only becomes possible and clear as the project proceeds.

There is, no doubt, a lot less riding on the production of this book than the Sydney Opera House; nevertheless, my experience of creating it has been that it, too, has emerged along the way, throughout the process of its creation. The journey to its fruition in this book has been a very long one, going back to a vocation I have had within my calling to Anglican priesthood to work cross-culturally and now interculturally alongside being a lifelong disciple and learner or "reflective practitioner" (to return to *phronesis*). From the beginnings of my ordained ministry as a probationer (Assistant Curate, in Anglican terms) I have been drawn to place and context as a site of theological study and reflection. I then spent seven years working as a "mission partner" in the Anglican Church in Tanzania, which as we shall see in several places throughout the book formed something quite new in me and introduced me to the post-colonial question of the relationship of faith and culture. I was fortunate enough in the year 2000 to attend the 10th Assembly of the International Association of Mission Studies in Pretoria, South Africa. There I was introduced to missiology as a formal academic discipline and found the people who would start me on the further journey to a professional doctorate (ThD) based in what could be called the "home" of missiology in Britain, Birmingham and its University. I asked the question in my doctoral research of whether I could create an adult learning program that would help English people integrate their faith and culture.

As we shall see at the start of chapter 4, that study then precipitated a further interest in the relationship of gospel and culture in the North of England, my own place of origin. A conference and a book of essays ensued[1] and then a further call to go deeper appeared for creating a research project looking specifically at faith and culture, contextual theology in the North of England. To conduct that project, I was joined by a co-researcher, Elli Wort, and I want to acknowledge her excellent and invaluable contribution here. This volume is therefore the result of an in-depth fieldwork project which was financially supported by the Susanna Wesley Foundation[2] (with our profound, grateful acknowledgment and thanks) conducted in the North of England from 2018 to 2019. We set out with the (in hindsight) rather naïve research question: What Good

1. See Wakefield and Rooms, eds. *Northern Gospel*.

2. See https://susannawesleyfoundation.org/.

News is at the heart of flourishing churches within their communities in the North of England?

We were testing the hypothesis that there is a discernible (in actual field research data) connection between gospel and culture according to theories and models of contextual theology and/or the concept of inculturation. In doing so we were clearly within the realm of developing practical wisdom from action and reflection, plus employing the skills of qualitative and quantitative research. Our data and analysis did not reveal any direct correlation between faith and culture, but rather showed what we came to call an "accented" gospel on the basis of Bishop Pedro Casaldáliga's assertion that "the universal word speaks only dialect."[3] Such a gospel was highly nuanced, global and local, and shaped through fragility by the post-colonial and post-Christendom realities of the communities we researched. We wrote up the research in a co-authored book which we called *Fuzzy Church*[4] on the basis that one of our respondents in interview had named the porous nature of their church which was giving it life from its edges as "fuzzy." The audience for that book was practitioner-based in local churches and perhaps theologians and trainers in ecclesial seminaries. We had always set out at the start of the project to create this further work as the final "output" of it, but it proved more difficult than we had envisaged, not least because the Covid-19 pandemic intervened and Elli was unable to continue writing with me due to circumstances beyond our control. It is worth acknowledging once again, however, her presence in the background of this book, and I am grateful for her comments on the chapters as they emerged.[5] It is, though, my work alone, and I am responsible for any lack or weakness in it.

WHO THIS BOOK IS FOR AND WHAT IS IN IT

In writing *Contested Contextualization*, our audience is notably different from that of the earlier volume *Fuzzy Church*. This is an unashamedly critical missiological and theological book arising from field research. The proposed readership is therefore among those in the academy and the church who reflect at deeper levels on questions of faith and culture,

3. Casaldáliga, *Creio na Justiça*, 211, our translation.

4. See Rooms and Wort, *Fuzzy Church*.

5. Because of Elli's work on the project, I will move between the first person singular and plural throughout the book when explaining what we did and making sense of the whole.

and contextual theology. I hope, though, it is not a purely "academic" text, based as it in *phronesis* and *poiesis* by research in actual churches in the North of England. It is both an academic/reflective and a practice-based text—it lives and breathes betwixt and between those worlds. It might also serve as an interesting and suggestive model for some kinds of missiological research among scholars, students, and reflective practitioners. We wonder whether there is any equivalent study worldwide which brings quantitative and qualitative field research together with the theories and models of contextual theology and the particularity of a specific geographical region within a larger nation.

We believe, therefore, that we have an original contribution to make to critical theories of contextual theology from field research in this particular, unique location in the North of England. In this way we hope the book will have an international reach in "World Christianity" beyond the original English research context. And an initial word about that context is worth sharing here. The world is a very different place almost a quarter of the way through the twenty-first century than it was when contextual theology first found its feet at the end of the colonial period in the 1960s and 1970s (see chapter 2). England, as an ex-colonial western power, has much to answer for, yet its North, as we shall discover, has for most of its history been "subaltern" to the South of the country. It is that subaltern relationship which I believe makes it an interesting site for discussing contextual theology (and the very future of Christian faith) in the western world where Christianity is on the decline and has been for seventy or so years.

Let us return to the emergent nature of this book as craft, having set out some of our aims and hopes for it. When I was writing chapter 7, where I place the research within Robert Heaney's[6] fivefold schema for post-colonial theology, two significant things happened. First, having not been happy with the working title of the book we originally gave to the book I woke up in the middle of the night with the new title of "contested contextualization" taken from Heaney's reflections. This seemed to name the complexification of contextual theology that we had discovered in the research and which we had noted as above in *Fuzzy Church.* It also named a reality in the contemporary literature on the subject that I had interacted with in the earlier part of the book. Second, an image or metaphor for what was happening in chapter 7 emerged as I realized I was

6. See Heaney, *Post-Colonial Theology.*

"weaving" the threads of the project together into some kind of whole. I am not a weaver, I am much more of a gardener (on that craft see chapter 8); however, I think weaving is a good enough image (since all metaphors have their distinct limits) for explaining how the book has come about in this introduction along with some explanation of its contents.

We begin in the next two chapters by laying out our "tools of the trade," and at the same time asking ourselves (in critical mode) whether they are the right ones for this project. Chapter 2 establishes the traditional field of contextual theology by engaging with some history, a number of authors and two specific inculturation projects in Africa. The traditional method for this kind of contextual or practical theology is named by Graham et al. as "theology in the vernacular"[7] and connects with our discovery of the accented northern gospel from Casaldáliga. And yet, if there is to be originality in what we present in the book we need to look beyond the traditional ways of going about contextual theology and so chapter 3 engages with three authors from outside of the field who can offer us a critical appreciation of what we are attempting with some objectivity. It is here that we complexify the symbol which is "context," address a serious criticism of the concept of worldwide translatability with respect to the gospel and ask if systematic theological approaches to the western context can offer us any help. The whole book is a "critical" contextual theology, as in our title, but the critical element in the title is specifically introduced and addressed in these two chapters.

The next three chapters are the "raw materials" out of which the whole is woven. All of these build on work done in *Fuzzy Church* and the first two quote extensively from it, on the basis that readers may not be familiar with it. The regional "Contextual Theology" of our title is foregrounded in chapter 4 as we address the physical and cultural phenomenon that is the North of England. We address there the question of whether it is both desirable and, indeed possible to speak of the North and Northernness and what they might consist of. At this introductory point in the writing what is noteworthy in that chapter is that several references are made to *poiesis* in the North, via a researching stand-up comedian, a scholar of northern literature and a film depicting Northerners contesting the arrival of refugees in their poverty-stricken community. The latter two of these again emerged during the writing of the book and could not have been included if it were completed earlier.

7. Graham et al., *Theological Reflection*, 200.

Chapter 5 presents the field research, its method, analysis and results in full. It also begins the "weaving" as the threads of data are put in dialogue with what we discovered about Northernness in chapter 4. It is therefore where we really begin the complexification and contestation in the contextual theology that is forming. Some of the "tools" we uncovered in chapter 3, especially about how to conduct field research are put to use here to critique what we did and how we went about the research. In chapter 6 we introduce a whole other way of treating the research data from a not dissimilar research project on church growth in Tanzania. This adds some depth and breadth to the post-colonial claims for the book, since we engage with a reversal of the traditional flow of information, resources, and power between the west and Africa. In the chapter we do some tangential, but important, ecclesiology which affirms, thickens, and further contests our findings. Perhaps this chapter adds a distinctive element to the weave in a different colour palette to the rest.

Post-colonial theology as we employ it in chapter 7 creates the full "frame" on which the whole can be woven—and represents, more concretely at this point, the third and final element in our regional, critical, and post-colonial contextual theology. Here, as many as possible of the materials or threads from the previous chapters are brought and held together in the frame. We discover how the post-colonial and post-Christendom worlds are connected together and just how much of the deep culture of the North already provides the resources for the future of the North, its gospel and its churches. The resulting weave, as we comment at this point, is not some simply patterned piece with neat straight lines. It is a complex, contested whole which is much more abstract than immediately recognizable. Nevertheless, it may be a thing of beauty.

The final chapter is less of a formal conclusion (I explain why there) than a way of shining a light on the artefact we have created—just as a finished piece of art is often lit in a particular way in a gallery. In more emergence during the project, we employ a book in the chapter to do this illumination work, a book which is highly resonant with my own experience and the research project itself—and which I only came across while writing chapter 5. We are then able to highlight certain aspects of contested contextualization in the North of England which have been scrutinized for robustness and fruitfulness throughout the study—and therefore may prove enlightening for at least western Christianity, if not World Christianity. These are called "noticings" and are my view of what

I see in the weave of the whole book. Readers are free to work with these and anything else they see in the weave.

READING THIS BOOK

Having set out an outline of the book it is worth saying a word about approaching it as a reader. I believe it does stand together as a whole and I also recognize some readers may come to it for different reasons. Some may be more interested in what it has to say about the North of England and so may wish to go straight to chapters 4 and 7. Those interested in how we conducted field research in local churches and how that connects to their "growing and flourishing" should start with chapters 5 and 6, perhaps returning to chapter 3 to understand some of the methodological moves we did or did not make. Post-colonial thinkers may wish to engage with chapter 7 before reading more widely. Contextual theologians will want to review my understanding of the field in chapters 2 and 3 before going any further. Two other points are worth making about what is set out here.

From time to time in the book, my own life and biography necessarily feature as reflexive elements in the study. Reflexivity is a vital element in all contemporary practical and contextual theology. I was born and formed as a person in the North, and will one day rest from my labors there. I am personally and deeply engaged in the subject matter. It is, and has become more so during the writing, of lasting concern to me. In chapter 7 in particular I connect my life history with the element of the "particular" in post-colonial theology and I reference other places where I have written on this subject in relation to my privilege as a white, western, highly trained reflective practitioner.

Secondly, a note on capitalization style. I have deliberately (as the reader will already be aware) not capitalized west and western (unless in a quotation) when referring to, in particular Western Europe and North America,[8] as collectively powerful political and cultural forces in the world. This seems entirely appropriate in a post-colonial world. I do capitalize the nouns North, Northerner and Northernness in order to stress their importance in the study (also unless they are not capitalized in a quotation in which case I stay with the original). Being an adjective,

8. We might add in some aspects of countries like Australia, Aotearoa New Zealand and even South Africa to this western bloc.

northern is not capitalized. Church with a capital refers to the institution (whether the worldwide Church or a particular denominational body), and, possibly includes the local church—and that will not be capitalized to distinguish it from the larger entity.

AN IMPORTANT THREAD THAT WILL FORM THIS WORK: THE *MISSIO DEI*

However, an excursus is necessary into an assumption or thread that will become part of the whole weave of this project. We have noted that contextual theology is set within the wider frame of missiology. There is currently a broad international and ecumenical consensus in missiology on the theological concept of the *missio Dei* (not that it is without complexity and nuance). Some readers may wish to skip this section if they are familiar with both the concept and the debates around it. Various sections of this book will however make much more sense if I explain my own approach and understanding of it.

We introduced the concept of *missio Dei* in *Fuzzy Church*.[9] At its most basic level *missio Dei* contains three main ideas which also constitute one of Bosch's "paradigm shifts" in mission[10]—one that occurred in the worldwide Church in the twentieth century. First, the whole of salvation history from creation to eschaton begins and ends in God; thus, any missionary activity of the Church, global or local, is *predicated on the prior work of God*. The task of the missionary Church in any particularity is therefore to discover what God is doing and participate in that prior action. This is always an act of *discernment* and perhaps we might understand this whole book as an attempt to discern what God might be up to in the North of England in the early twenty-first century.

The requirement to join in the prior work of God (and not bypass it, ignore it, or work against it, as if our ideas and resources were more important than God's) leads us rapidly to the theological category of *participation*. Engagement with participation, I believe, significantly deepens the discussion and addresses some of the critiques of theology and action derived from the *missio Dei*. The most significant of these is, to put it rather crudely, that the *missio Dei* affirms, even baptizes any good thing that happens in the world, the local community beyond and

9. Rooms and Wort, *Fuzzy Church*, 32–4.

10. See Bosch, *Transforming Mission*.

even far from the church. In its extreme form the church becomes rather superfluous to any good works within the reign of God, most broadly defined. This question has been addressed over several decades as is illustrated in the intense debates between the missiologist and ecumenist Lesslie Newbiggin and Konrad Raiser, General Secretary of the World Council of Churches in the early 1990s[11] and later, in the work of the Protestant missiologist John Flett.[12] Here I would like to turn to the work of the British systematic theologian Andrew Davison and his book *Participation in God,*[13] which I have engaged with elsewhere.[14]

The *missio Dei* has enjoyed a broad ecumenical consensus since being critically commended by missiologists over several decades (since it was first formulated in 1952 at a Conference on International Missions in Willingen, Germany, based on some earlier original thoughts of Karl Barth), most notably the Protestant David Bosch and the Catholics Steve Bevans and Roger Schroeder in their now classic texts.[15] Bevans and Schroeder go further in a later book which sets out their own missiological project: "God is Mission. This is what God is in God's deepest self: self-diffusive love, freely creating, redeeming, healing, challenging that creation."[16] God is therefore better described as a verb rather than a noun, since from the beginning God's creative and sustaining activity is ceaseless. There is an excess of love in the community which is the Trinitarian God, who is the "act of pure being." God cannot keep God to Godself and overflows into creation, redemption and the reconciliation of all things back into God at the end of time. God moves across the border of Godself to create the universe and then the incarnate Son joins divinity to humanity in the ultimate act of salvific *kenosis.*[17] Careful as we must be not to impute human categories to God, God is then in some sense the original missionary, if the definition of missionary is one who crosses borders.

Davison uses philosophical categories and the work of Thomas Aquinas on causality (how things come into being) to state that God is

11. For example, see Goheen, "Future of Mission," 97–111.

12. See Flett, *Witness of God.*

13. See Davison, *Participation.*

14. See Rooms, "Participation, *missio Dei.*"

15. See Bosch, *Transforming Mission* and Bevans and Schroeder, *Constants in Context.*

16. Bevans and Schroeder, *Constants in Context,* 10.

17. Phil 2:5–11.

the efficient, formal, and final cause of all things, but definitely not the material cause. So, thinking about the creation of the universe, we are able to ask, "Who, or what made this happen?" (the efficient cause); "What is it formed from?" (the material cause); "Why is it like this?" (the formal cause); and, "For what purpose did this cause produce this effect?" (the final cause).[18] Christian theology has asserted over the centuries that God is the beginning, the alpha, of everything and is therefore their efficient cause. All things are fundamentally related to the character and being of God and thus God is their formal cause. And God created the universe for Godself and thus is the end, the omega of the same and therefore the final cause. Yet, while God creates out of an overflow of love (there is no *need* in God to create), God is not the material cause of creation as the creation is *ex nihilo*—from nothing. This releases the creation to be itself and at the same time to be ever and always related to God via its prior being, *participating* in God. This is the definition of the *analogia entis,* the way in which the creature derives its very being from God in every moment of its existence, how it is both at the same time like and unlike God.

Here we have a way therefore to affirm the original goodness of creation which includes human culture and distinctive regions like the North of England. This will become important as our discernment in that region proceeds. It derives its being by participation in God; by the same argument evil, brokenness, and sin, which cannot and must not be ignored, are a failure of participation. Davison sums this argument up well:

> The being of all things proceeds from God . . . all things bear some particular creaturely likeness to an aspect of his boundless perfection. God calls each creature to an active fulfilment of its destiny by being the thing he has made it to be, and evil is lack where there should be fullness in nature and in action. Evil is the failure of a person–or thing, culture, or whatever–to live up to the likeness it is called to bear."[19]

All of which returns us discernment, which is not only discerning between good and evil, but also between competing goods. We are called to discern what is the fullness of a created thing, what is the best it could be when there is nothing coming between it and the divine. This is a subtle, complex, and even contested art to which there is no simple conclusion, but a never-ending flow that participates in the *missio Dei* itself.

18. Davison, *Participation,* 42.

19. Davison, *Participation,* 239.

2

An "Emic" Critique of Contextual Theology

THIS BOOK IS CONCEIVED as a work of contextual theology. In the previous chapter we noted the background to the specific research project it is grounded in, and in this chapter and the next we attempt to offer a comprehensive introduction and critique of the subject. While questions of faith and context are as old as the faith itself as we shall see, the conscious and intentional study of the relationship between them is a relatively recent phenomenon. There are many sources for this "turn to the [contextual/cultural] subject" and in broad terms it can be seen as part of the paradigm shift that took place after the Second World War as the western world (at the very least) emerged from the ruins of the period of so-called Modernity or the Enlightenment (approximately 1650–1950) which coincided (and was connected to) the end of the colonial period in the middle decades of the twentieth century in the Majority World. Two western wars in close proximity, the meting out of industrial death and genocide alongside the liberating of subjugated peoples around the globe meant something new had to happen. The creation of the United Nations (1945) and the development of the notion of universal human rights (solidified in the Universal Declaration in 1948) also happened at the same time.

Out of all of this deeply significant change both Catholic and Protestant expressions of Church began to approach questions of faith and context in new and fresh ways. It is worth examining an example from each side of the Reformation divide. What is common between them is first, that the field of contextual theology arose from missionary *praxis*, that is, reflection on the missionary engagement of the Church as the era of colonization came to an end. The other distinct commonality worth noting is how they both draw on the social science discipline of cultural or social anthropology for their work, though this carries its own inherent tensions as well.

The Second Vatican Council (1962–65) was formative in raising a generation of Catholic missionaries, some of whom turned into missiologists in the academy and who developed a whole and coherent theological method which Graham et al. name as "theology in the vernacular."[1] Vatican II did not happen in a vacuum, however, and the very fact that it could happen at all is testament to movements that had been occurring within Catholicism for decades previously. There is not space here to review this history, but perhaps a specific example will suffice, from a largely Catholic country, Brazil, which demonstrates the forces and factors at work at the time. Irwin Leopando traces the influences on the theologian and educationalist Paulo Freire[2] to Jacques Maritain (1882–1973), who also influenced the UN Declaration of Human Rights, and Joseph Cardijn (1882–1967), who formulated what I understand to be the prototype for the method of Liberation Theology and the hermeneutical circle, "See–Judge–Act."

Vatican II becomes permissive then of a new way of doing mission theology from below.

> A more responsive approach to evangelization begins to take shape. The Council recognized the autonomy of the Church in each culture to articulate the gospel without the mediation of Western thought forms . . . Above all the Council was concerned with shaping Christian mission to meet the needs of its host cultures. The gospel was regarded as something which grew as much "from below" as it was imposed "from above."[3]

Thus, emerges what becomes the "Chicago School" of religious missionary brothers (associated with different orders such as the Society of the Divine Word and the Congregation of the Holy Spirit) who form around the pioneering work of Louis Luzbetak SVD (1918–2005). Luzbetak's book, in its original form *The Church and Cultures: An Applied*

1. Graham et al., *Theological Reflection*, 200.
2. Leopando, *Pedagogy*, 53–62.
3. Graham et al., *Theological Reflection*, 212–13.

Anthropology for the Religion Worker, framed and formed the field for others who would follow such as Steve Bevans, Robert Schreiter, Roger Schroeder, and Anthony Gittins.

Among Protestants, Eugene Nida (1914–2011) stands out as someone who embodies the twentieth-century paradigm shift we are describing here. Nida's life's work was in bible translation—a necessary task for Protestants whose existence is predicated on the Bible being read by God's people in a language (as my Anglican Reformer forebears put it) "understanded of the people." Darrell Whiteman usefully reviews the relationship between anthropology and Christian mission[4] and offers Nida as the exemplar among Protestants of this move, encapsulated by his "classic text" *Customs and Cultures: Anthropology for Christian Missions* (1954). Nida is well known for creating the "dynamic equivalence" method of Bible translation whereby translation is conducted not by translating word for word, but meaning for meaning. It is patently obvious that this is impossible without a deep immersion in the target language which in turn implies engagement and embodied knowledge of the culture, since language and culture are virtually synonymous. What emerges from this Protestant engagement is somewhat contested, especially among more conservative, evangelical Protestants who are suspicious of the social sciences. Those who are prepared to engage are sometimes called out as barely Christian, as Whiteman notes[5] was the case for Charles Kraft with his important work *Christianity in Culture* (1979). The work of Paul Hiebert (1932–2007) from the Mennonite Brethren tradition is also worth remarking on here as it has been deeply influential in missiology over several decades and is still regularly cited today. Protestants have generally referred to the work of engaging faith and culture as contextualization whereas some Catholics prefer the theological neologism "inculturation."[6] Two more recent examples from both traditions can be offered: the evangelical mission scholar W. Jay Moon uses contextualization as the frame for his book offering the principles and practices for developing *Intercultural Discipleship* (2017) and Australian-based Catholic Gerald Arbuckle reinforces the arguments for a radical inculturation in the context of postmodernity in his work *Culture, Inculturation and Theologians: A Postmodern Critique* (2010).

4. See Whiteman, "Anthropology and Mission,"– with his helpful historical diagram on p. 68.

5. Whiteman, "Anthropology and Mission," 81.

6. Rooms, *Faith*, 5–6.

Contextual theology has therefore been established across a wide ecumenical consensus over the past seventy or so years. This chapter and the next are designed to offer appreciation and critique of the field first of all from within (in an emic fashion, in this chapter) and then from without (the etic, in the next chapter), that is, from theologians not formed in or utilizing a missiological frame through their own *praxis*.

The first task in a critical appreciation of contextual theology is to locate the method in the whole sweep of Christian thought from the time of the NT. Such material is freely available and we will simply offer a summary overview here helped by Graham et al.'s description[7] and the documentary sources reproduced in their subsequent book from 2007, *Theological Reflection: Sources*, and Robert Hunt's *The Gospel among the Nations: A Documentary History of Inculturation* published in 2010.

THE VERY MIXED HISTORY OF INCULTURATION IN CHRISTIANITY

The "way" described in Acts 9:2 begins as a sect of Judaism after the death and resurrection of Jesus and the coming of the Holy Spirit. The new faith is understood by its followers as something to be given away across cultural boundaries by the apostolic or "sent" embryonic "church."[8] This is the self-understanding of the community who had gathered in Jerusalem from many nations and languages and heard the words of God in their own tongues (Acts 2:8). The ultimately persuasive argument in the so-called Gentile controversy (a deeply divisive issue based on strong adherence to cultural notions of purity) is that the Spirit was recognized as at work beyond the received and accepted boundaries of the Jewish faith.[9] A centrifugal missionary religion is born, without much of a center. If the message of the saving work of Jesus' death and resurrection is to be heard in the known world, it will need to be communicated in creative ways which take account of context and culture. A good example of this is found in Acts 17. Thus, according to Graham et al.:

> The earliest disciples found themselves shaping their message according to the audiences among which they found themselves. But the question remained, of how far the unity of all

7. Graham et al., *Theological Reflection*, 200–12.

8. See John 20:21.

9. See Acts 10:47; 11:18.

> Christians . . . could be modified in the face of a diversity of cultural settings, and how far the distinctiveness of any given context should shape Christian doctrines and practices.[10]

Robert Hunt notes that the NT is written in *koine* Greek—the malleable language of the Roman Empire that facilitated intercultural relationships in commerce, politics, and religion at the time.[11] Yet the embryonic churches of the NT are called to stand against culture too, both Gentile and Jewish,[12] and thus develop a distinctive culture of their own. He concludes:

> The challenge of the church to be at once a distinct human community (and thus one that possesses its own culture) while affirming God's universal providence for and presence among the nations, and then living as a sign of God's intention that all humans be gathered into the reign of Christ, can be seen as a key theme of early church history.[13]

We never escape this tension within inculturation or contextualization as the classic text of Andrew Walls, "The Gospel as Prisoner and Liberator of Culture," demonstrates. His suggestive image of the academic alien from another planet with a periodic research grant to study Christian faith longitudinally across the centuries offers up the "indigenizing" (assimilation, becoming of the culture) and the "pilgrim" (distinctive, being separate from the culture in order to transform it) principles.[14] Where the emphasis is put is a matter of constant debate as contemporary controversies around the place of LGBTQIA+ people in the church amply demonstrates.

Returning to the early church we noted in our previous book how Christians in the Roman Empire were observed by those outside the faith such as in the Epistle from Mathetes to Diognetus[15] which we quoted in large part there. The indigenizing/pilgrim tension is picked up in these phrases in the Epistle: "They [Christians] find themselves in the flesh, and yet they live not after the flesh. Their existence is on earth, but their citizenship is in heaven." And questions about how to engage with the

10. Graham et al., *Theological Reflection*, 204.

11. Hunt, *Gospel*, 7.

12. See 1 Cor 8–10; Titus 1:10–16.

13. Hunt, *Gospel*, 8.

14. Walls, "Gospel as Prisoner," 17–28.

15. Rooms and Wort, *Fuzzy Church*, 56–7.

prevailing philosophy and religion in the empire continued to deepen. Both Graham et al.[16] and Hunt contrast the approaches of Justin Martyr (ca. 100–165) and Tertullian (ca. 155–220) to the employment of philosophers such as Plato within Christian thought:

> Justin Martyr, *Apology II, xiii*
> For all writers [of philosophy] through the engrafted seed of the Word, which was planted in them, were able to see the truth darkly; for the seed and imitation of a thing, which is given according to capability, is one thing, and the thing itself, of which communication and imitation are given according to His grace, is another.[17]

> Tertullian, *The Prescription against Heretics, Chapter VII*
> Away with all attempts to produce a mottled Christianity of Stoic, Platonic and dialectic composition! We want no curious disputation after possessing Jesus Christ, no inquisition after enjoying the gospel! With our faith we desire no further belief.[18]

Even Justin Martyr's intentions are to argue for the superiority of the Christian faith by turning "the arguments of their non-Christian partners against them." However, further along the pilgrim-indigenizing spectrum is the theologian Origen (185–254), who is unafraid of appropriating hierarchical Platonic thought forms into his understanding of the Trinity.

> Origen, *On First Principles, Fragment 9*
> The God and Father who holds the universe together, is superior to every being that exists, for he imparts to each one from his own existence that which each one is; the Son, being less than the Father, is superior to rational creatures alone (for he is second to the Father); the Holy Spirit is still less, and dwells within the saints alone.[19]

Such hierarchical assertions were surpassed by later Trinitarian theology (though their vestiges hang on in many ways among contemporary Christians), but what this shows is the inescapable embedding of Christian faith within culture. Today among the more conservative traditions within the Church we still hear echoes of Tertullian, who is named as the

16. Graham et al., *Theological Reflection*, 200–1.

17. Hunt, *Gospel*, 37.

18. Hunt, *Gospel*, 38.

19. Graham et al., *Theological Reflection*, 205.

"Key Figure" in Bevans and Schroeder's "Type A Theology" (which has a "negative" theological anthropology and is suspicious of culture).[20] Yet for me such a position is ignoring the Word made flesh from the beginning offered to us John 1:14. As Graham et al. put it, "The understanding of early Christian writers of the inescapably culturally rooted nature of the gospel thus represents an important and enduring source for styles of theological reflection that seek to embody cultural particularity and diversity."[21]

The arrival of the Christian faith at the heart of the Roman Empire in the fourth century changes everything for the relationship of that faith with the new cultures it encounters. When this period of history is reviewed in books about Christian mission it is customary to largely pass over the many and varied shameful and, let's face it, downright cruel and evil episodes in what was done to others in the name of Christ as Christendom expanded. Instead, the focus is on those few figures who stand against imperial power and forced conversion, looking for a way to engage hearts and minds through culture and persuasion. It is hard, on the other side of that history, to avoid that approach in this book as well, but before we engage with the "beacons of light" it behoves us to lean into the darkness, for we cannot understand the importance of a postcolonial approach to Christian mission without engaging with Imperial Christianity. Or, as my late friend and mentor, John Hull, would put it, "Christianism"—the all-powerful ideology of the triumph of Christianity over all things. As Robert Hunt posits in this period, "mission attentive to engaging a culture was largely overwhelmed by a new type of imperial mission that sought to destroy and replace such cultures."[22]

The destructiveness of Christianity takes time to develop, but the first significant step is taken by Emperor Theodosius (347–395) who ends freedom of religion in the Roman Empire by making Christianity

20. Bevans and Schroeder, *Constants in Context,* 37. For a long time now I have found this typology most helpful as it demonstrates the length and breadth of the Christian missiological "playing field" and names the necessary "fault lines" between different positions on the pitch (to extend the sports analogy) throughout history. We must accept that broadly conservative (Type A), liberal (Type B), and liberationist (Type C) standpoints are all valid (this is the point of giving them letters to move away from being pejorative about any of them). We can, therefore generate dialogue and debate between the three types, and we will never finally all come to unified agreement. Bevans and Schroeder, in my view, combine elements of all three types in their proposal for mission as *prophetic dialogue.*

21. Graham et al., *Theological Reflection,* 207.

22. Hunt, *Gospel,* 17.

the only faith allowed within it. In the first centuries of the new alliance between Rome and Christianity different attitudes to mission prevail, sometimes even in the same leader, as Anton Wessels shows in his important work on historical inculturation in Europe. He notes[23] how Pope Gregory the Great (ca. 540–604) initially supported the use of violence against the so-called Pagans or, as we might put it, adherents of European Traditional Religions. Later in a well-known edict, preserved for posterity by the historian, the Venerable Bede,[24] he encourages Augustine, missionary to the Anglo-Saxons and first Archbishop of Canterbury (d. 604), not to destroy the temples of the people but to assimilate them into the faith as Christian places of worship. Yet a century or so later Boniface (ca. 675–754) in a papal mission from England to Germany destroys any vestige of the old ways in a desire to abolish them altogether,[25] although Alcuin (ca. 740–804) stands firmly against such practices and somewhat prevails.[26] It is hard not to conclude, however, that the power of the (Roman) sword, even if it wasn't physically present on the bodies of these missionaries, was never far away as a threat which backed them up. Only when earlier missionaries such as Patrick (ca. 385–461) stepped beyond the boundaries of the *"Pax Romana"* in places such as Ireland did they do so without the protection of the Empire. It is little wonder European Christians find evangelization problematic after so many centuries of the Church–State settlement.

The "Christianization" of Europe is virtually complete by around 1000 CE when Scandinavia finally joins the movement.[27] We place inverted commas around "Christianization" since, as contemporary commentators pointed out, it is all very well converting people by baptism (at the point of a sword) and compelling them to attend worship, but this does not capture their hearts and their minds, as Wessels states, quoting the Venerable Bede.[28] Yet it is probably no coincidence that from this point onwards the dark forces of destruction of the other take an even more sinister turn. Converting people from their traditional religions seems relatively straightforward in this period, but when Christianity comes up against Judaism and Islam the task is much more difficult and

23. Wessels, *Europe,* 11–12.

24. Wessels, *Europe,* 12.

25. Wessels, *Europe,* 10.

26. Wessels, *Europe,* 100.

27. Wessels, *Europe,* 103–4.

28. Wessels, *Europet,* 3.

the impulse to resort to violence so much the stronger. The Crusades (1095–1291) against the Muslim world with the aim of "recapturing" the Holy Land, while not directly relevant to our subject, entrench violence as a systemic response to people who will not convert to the Christian faith. This is not the place to rehearse that history; suffice to say that that violent reflex is taken far beyond Europe in subsequent centuries and has often been quoted to me throughout my life as a substantial reason not to believe in the Christian God.

The violent reflex reaches its zenith in mission to the Americas, beginning from Spain and Portugal with the Portuguese Henry the Navigator (1394–1460) and the Italian/Spaniard Christopher Columbus (1451–1506). Columbus is sponsored by the King and Queen of Spain, who in turn are charged by a Papal Bull from Alexander VI in 1493, quoted in large part in Hunt.[29] Columbus, his ships and discoveries are mentioned by name and while there is an expectation of instruction in the faith for the people in these new lands (in what we might call the small print) the overall purpose is clear:

> You, as behoves Catholic Kings and Princes . . . propose to subject and reduce them to the Catholic faith. We therefore . . . exhort you . . . to bring these people to the Christian religion, and to let no pains and labours deter you . . . We constitute you [over all these lands and people] . . . with full, free, and entire power, authority and jurisdiction.[30]

If ever there is a *carte blanche*, there it is in black and white. Many books have been written about the genocide so perpetrated on such peoples as the Aztecs, Mayans, and Incas. Once again it is the dissenter who shows up this evil policy for what it is. Bartolomé de las Casas (1484–1566) stands almost alone in accepting the prior religiosity of the American peoples and working with it—advocating against their enslavement. Hunt quotes his writings extensively and this extract sums up his approach:

> One way, one way only, of teaching a living faith, to everyone, everywhere, always, was set by Divine Providence: the way that wins the mind with reason, that wins the will with gentleness, with invitation. It has to fit all people on earth, no distinction made for sect, for error, even for evil.[31]

29. Hunt, *Gospel*, 68–70.
30. Hunt, *Gospel*, 69.
31. Hunt, *Gospel*, 72.

Ultimately Las Casas's arguments and actions founder on the money, power, and privilege that this new world showers on its colonizers. Graham et al. offer a damning line of his that echoes down the centuries of Christian enslavement, "I left behind me in the Indies, Jesus Christ our God, scourged, tortured, crucified, not once but a million times."[32] James Cone could not agree more with that assessment of what happens when the Christian church engages in slavery, none other than the re-crucifying of Christ.[33]

Picking up the theme of the inherent racism in these policies for forced conversion and slavery, Willie James Jennings begins his book on the origins of race in Christian theology by retelling a scene from the life of Henry the Navigator when the first major shipment of slaves arrives in the Southern Portuguese port of Lagos. In a showpiece event on August 8, 1444, 235 slaves are paraded as an example of Portuguese colonial power, divided up, and sold as "black gold."[34] Jennings goes on to quote extensively from the account of the day by the Royal Chronicler (named as Zurara), where he shows sympathy and even writes of his tears for the plight of the slaves who he thinks of as "sons of Adam." Nevertheless, the deeply Christian nature of the ritualized way the day unfolds and Zurara's racial categorization of those being sold means that "Zurara deploys a rhetorical strategy of containment, holding slave suffering inside a Christian story that will be recycled by countless theologians and intellectuals of every colonialist nation."[35] We will return to Jennings's critique of contextual theology in the next chapter, for the moment we note once again a heinous evil conducted while offering "conversion" to the enslaved.

Other beacons of light stand out in this period, though, as we noted above, they are few and far between. Just as with the Jewish faith and Islam, Christian mission is much less fruitful in the East and this gives birth to remarkable experiments in contextualization especially from the Jesuit Order, though these would eventually be shut down conclusively. Bevans and Schroeder[36] name and discuss these Jesuits in chronological order:

32. Graham et al., *Theological Reflection*, 211.

33. See Cone, *Cross*.

34. Jennings, *Christian Imagination*, 15.

35. Jennings, *Christian Imagination*, 20.

36. Bevans and Schroeder, *Constants in Context*, 183–92.

- the Spaniard Francis Xavier (1506–52) in India and mainly Japan—though it is only in Japan where he truly begins to respect the local culture;
- the Italian Alessandro Valignano (1539–1606), who continued Xavier's work in Japan;
- the Italian Matteo Ricci (1552–1610), who worked exclusively in China;
- the Italian Robert de Nobili (1577–1656) in India; and finally,
- the Frenchman, Alexandre de Rhodes (1591–1660) in Vietnam.

These missionaries were variously effective if counting numbers of converts, but all of them left a viable community of new Christians in the places they lived. Some worked in the higher echelons of their chosen societies, others in the lower; all learnt the language, wore the clothes and ate the food of the people they shared the Christian faith with. Nevertheless, the borders of this contextual engagement in the "test case" of Ricci's work in China became known as the "Chinese Rites Controversy" and the final word on the subject came from the Decree of the Sacred Congregation for the Propagation of the Faith in Rome in 1645 with a resounding "no."[37]

We could continue with this this review of missionary methods with Protestant expansion, the "Scramble for Africa" and the destruction/conversion of the First peoples in North America. However, such histories are well rehearsed elsewhere[38] and the overall lesson for this writer, having reviewed this timeline once again, is that inculturation is a "minority report" in the history of the Christian faith. To put it another way, of the three types of Christian theology outlined on a table I have long found helpful,[39] Type A, sourced in Tertullian emphasizes the expansion of the institution of the Church, often crushing any dissenting voices. This raises the question about our research as to whether Types B and C might have found their time. Or are we still crying in the wilderness?

37. See the document reproduced in Hunt, *Gospel*, 73–6.

38. See, for instance, Bevans and Schroeder, *Constants in Context*, 206–38; Bosch, *Transforming Mission*, 239–345.

39. Bevans and Schroeder, *Constants in Context*, 37.

CONTEMPORARY EXAMPLES OF "THEOLOGY IN THE VERNACULAR"

We have established the validity of the field of contextual theology and briefly examined the various approaches to the relationship of faith and culture across the history of Christianity. Our concern in the research we undertook in the North of England was to root our understanding of how faith and culture are integrated in what was happening on the ground in actual churches. We suggest therefore that it would be useful to offer three current examples of theologians working with the theological method called "theology in the vernacular," from Graham et al., and then to examine two grass-roots inculturation projects in detail.

Robert Beckford

As an important example of "theology in the vernacular" Graham et al.[40] cite the work of Robert Beckford, a Black British contextual theologian, from a Pentecostal background and now Professor of Black Theology at the Queen's Foundation in Birmingham. They excerpt a section of his 1998 book *Jesus is Dread* where he engages in dialogue with the Rastafarian faith of Bob Marley. Beckford asks what Christians might learn from Marley while being openly critical of some of his stances and beliefs. He concludes with a question which would seem to inform the rest of his subsequent theological endeavor:

> Although Rastafari claims to be qualitatively different from European theology, in reality Rastafari is bound to the traditional English-Christian religion, because it uses the same manuscript traditions and sources. Despite this aberration, Marley challenges us to question the usefulness of the Christian religion for Black diasporan subjects—namely, how can we reconstruct the Baldhead religion [i.e. white English Christianity] so that it has relevance in contemporary Black Britain?[41]

Thus, Beckford now works at the intersection of "the fields of theology, cultural studies and politics."[42] Beckford would not consider himself a theologian of mission, but we place him here in this "emic" chapter, not

40. Graham et al., *Theological Reflection: Sources*, 400–10.

41. Graham et al., *Theological Reflection: Sources*, 409.

42. Queen's Foundation, "Prof. Robert Beckford."

least because of his concern for a Black British apologetic for Christianity which nevertheless radically explores the boundaries of the faith. A great example of his reconstruction project which draws on the methods of inculturation is the "Jamaican Bible Remix" album Beckford created with musicians, producers, and the UK Bible Society in 2017.[43] Using the Bible Society's Jamaican patois translation of the New Testament from 2012 and mixing it with Black urban music from Britain, Beckford claims to create a "powerful sonic fiction" which is a "social, political and theological commentary" on Jamaican diasporic life in the UK. In working with the Bible translated into the Jamaican vernacular in this way Beckford states:

> Translation is much more than grammar and syntax, it is also about communicating a people's worldview, their history, their hopes and aspirations. I guess you could say we see language as being redemptive. To say the Jamaican language is redemptive is to affirm the ways in which Africans who were captured found ways of keeping their language and their culture alive.

We note here again that language and culture are virtually synonymous and therefore redemption, even salvation, is found in the performance of the vernacular within a Christian idiom.

Wonhee Anne Joh

In conducting our research in Northern England and placing it alongside Robert Heaney's introduction to *Post-Colonial Theology* we noted the *coloniality* of the whole region in its historical subservience to the South of England and the *hybridization* that is possible in such circumstances. We therefore connected post-colonial theology with the project of contextualization, something which is also clearly evident in Beckford's work. Our second contemporary example of a contextual theologian picks up this relationship in the specificity of developing a post-colonial theology of the cross. Heaney dedicates two chapters of his book to working with Wonhee Anne Joh's understanding of the work of Christ, which represents for him (and us) a concrete example of post-colonial hybridization.

43. The full album is available at https://www.canterbury.ac.uk/arts-and-humanities/school-of-humanities/religion-philosophy-and-ethics/research/jamaican-bible-remix.aspx. The subsequent quotes about the project are also found in Beckford's introduction to the work on this page.

Joh is a Korean-American currently working at Garrett Evangelical Theological Seminary in the USA as Professor of Theology and Culture.

Heaney engages with Joh's major work from 2006, *Heart of the Cross: A Postcolonial Christology.* The book, he explains[44] revolves around two Korean concepts which are virtually untranslatable into English: *han* and *jeong.* Once again, we note the relationship between language and culture. *Han* is a form of suffering born of oppression, or simply the experience of life in this world which leads to "unresolved resentment." It provides the human person with energy for the possibility of destruction *and,* interestingly, construction. It is something found in the powerful and the powerless.[45] *Jeong* is almost the opposite of *han* and expresses a complex form of love found in relationship and arising out of "in-betweenness." Relationships characterized by *jeong* are life-enhancing and (in another connection to Beckford's understanding of language) redemptive.[46]

Utilizing these words, deeply formed as they are in Korean experience, society, and culture, enables a complexifying of the nature of suffering and the binaries of oppressor and oppressed. Thus, the cross can be re-imagined away from traditional notions of sacrifice, self-denial, and suffering that have particularly affected women because of the inherent patriarchy in the classical approaches of the tradition. The cross can therefore be read now politically as a site, "of deep *han* and deep *jeong,*"[47] an understanding which also critiques approaches such as Moltmann's which lead to metaphysical interpretations of inner Trinitarian life. It is the Empire rather than the will of the Father that crucifies Jesus. Heaney quotes Joh at length on the way Christ subverts the empire on the cross:

> The spectacle of crucifixion, which long functioned for *Pax Romana* to beat down courage and resistance, now becomes the center of another narrative about power, a story that displaces Rome . . . Rome is rendered by its own cross of torture an interim power. The spectacle of the Roman cross is now wielded against terrorizing Rome. This is to steal the show.[48]

Thus, Heaney can conclude:

44. Heaney, *Post-Colonial Theology,* 90.
45. Heaney, *Post-Colonial Theology,* 94.
46. Heaney, *Post-Colonial Theology,* 95.
47. Heaney, *Post-Colonial Theology,* 102.
48. Heaney, *Post-Colonial Theology,* 103.

> Jesus, in the midst of colonization, exists in the "in-between" demonstrating *jeong* to foreigners, compatriots, collaborators, and the voiceless. The way of the cross does not only destabilize the binaries of Christ and colonized, it transgresses and destabilizes the simple dualisms of colonized/colonizer, friend/enemy, liberator/oppressor associated with many revolutionaries.[49]

Redemption through the demonstration of *jeong* on the cross is a project of integrative love which joins power and compassion in the divine and human.

José De Mesa

Our final contemporary example of inculturation is found in the work of José De Mesa, a Filipino lay theologian who is now an emeritus professor of theology at De la Salle University in Manila, Philippines. He narrates "Inculturation as Pilgrimage" in his Louis J. Luzbetak Lecture from the year 2000, reproduced in the collection of lectures edited by Steve Bevans.[50]

Without absolutizing culture, De Mesa reverses the usual order of faith/mission and culture in the dialogue of inculturation and prioritizes culture as the primary guide to the task. The task is one of pilgrimage, however, which importantly emphasizes the fluid nature of culture and the way in which inculturation, by definition, is an unfinishable work. Traditional approaches and even Liberation Theology are simply inadequate to reach the people. Thus, "Using culture as a guide includes pinpointing of issues, questions, and concerns that are relevant in the local situation together with the way that culture looks at such questions."[51] De Mesa therefore calls for reappropriation of the tradition driven by the local culture and which requires fresh cultural categories of which De Mesa proposes four for the Filipino context[52]—not unlike the concepts of *han* and *jeong* in our previous example. Starting with the original missionary translation of the Lord's prayer, De Mesa draws out these four fundamental themes for a Filipino inculturation. They are that God's will (*loob*) be done, the importance of home in the sense that God's Kingdom

49. Heaney, *Post-Colonial Theology*, 106.

50. Bevans, *Mission and Culture*, 5–34.

51. Bevans, *Mission and Culture*, 11–12.

52. Bevans, *Mission and Culture*, 17–20

has to arrive there (*mauwi*), the everyday concrete need for daily rice (*kanin*) instead of bread, and never being left alone (and therefore overcome by temptation) but to remain in community with God and each other (*huwag iiwan*).

De Mesa explains how he overcame his European and American epistemological formation and the hegemony of western thought forms by deeply entering into the experience of his people at a time of great stress and oppression. He asks where God is and what God wills in the midst of such struggles and so arrives at the foundational importance of the word for "will" (*loob*), a particular version of which "denotes a beauty that wells deep within the self and that which is not only ethically good, but winsomely good as well."[53] Here is the heart of his Filipino theology which draws disciples into the divine will to become like God and therefore has echoes of divine *theosis* comparable to the Eastern Orthodox theological tradition.

De Mesa then outlines the implications of his deep personal engagement with his own culture. He claims that the primary purpose of inculturation is to "facilitate the Christian experience of God within and through the instrumentality of culture."[54] God's presence is both discernible in the here and now within the local culture and offers a way of making sense of and speaking about our experience of God in familiar categories. For De Mesa inculturation also relativizes all theological formulations and western categories are shown up for what they are—embedded in culture too. His final point is one we have made already that inculturation is about the close relationship of language and culture and thus the importance of the vernacular (literally "born in the house") is once again emphasized.

It is worth noting here an inspiring development of De Mesa's thought in the work of Antonio Sison who takes inspiration from him in his book on indigenous inculturation. In the book Sison examines the theological significance of cultural artefacts and practices in Africa, Mexico, and The Philippines to great effect. He demonstrates that language is not the only way into a study of inculturation—we must also take seriously *poiesis,* the crafting of material objects and practices.[55]

53. Bevans, *Mission and Culture,* 21.

54. Bevans, *Mission and Culture,* 23.

55. See Sison, *Art.*

ECCLESIOLOGICAL INCULTURATION PROJECTS IN AFRICA

Having reviewed three theologians engaging with faith and culture we now turn to examining in more detail the work of practitioners of inculturation on the ground with a specific people. While there are many to choose from, for example the field research of Laurenti Magesa[56] or the collected Christological essays in Schreiter,[57] we identify two examples here not least because they both have trajectories that are not limited to their common African context. Vincent Donovan and Claude Boucher are examples of western Catholic missionaries immersing themselves in the questions of inculturation among the Maasai of Tanzania and the Chewa of Malawi respectively. How effective they were as westerners in a post-colonial world will be one of the questions we can put to their work.

Claude Boucher Chisale

We will take Boucher's work first, largely because there is more to be said about Donovan's and placing them alongside each other interrogatively should also be helpful. Claude Boucher is a White Father (Missionary of Africa) who has been in Malawi for the majority of his ministry since 1967. The book we are using as source material[58] claims on the back cover that he is "adopted into the Chisale clan" and "initiated into the secret *Nyau* society of the Chewa and is recognised locally as a Chewa chief."

In 1985 Boucher Chisale worked with another artist, Tambala Mponyani, to create the "*Missio Banner*" with the pedagogical objective of informing German Catholic parishes about inculturation as constituting the contemporary "concept of mission"[59] during the 150th Anniversary celebrations for Ludwig Missionsverein, now known as Missio Munich. The original banner remains at the Missio Headquarters in Munich, while reproductions have been created and given many uses.[60]

56. See Magesa, *Anatomy of Inculturation*.

57. See Schreiter, *Faces of Jesus*.

58. See Boucher, *Gospel Seed*.

59. Boucher, *Gospel Seed*, 1.

60. The banner can be viewed on the internet by visiting the site of the KuNgoni Art Craft Centre: http://kapmalawi.org/work_boucher_chisale_claude_missio_banner.html.

Boucher Chisale disavows pre-Vatican II universalizing missionary theology in favor of the "incarnational" approach of inculturation which takes the contribution of local cultures utterly seriously—"Christ came to perfect not to destroy."[61] Thus, the local purpose of the banner is to "invite Malawian Christians into the mystery of life and death as understood through the gospel message and spelled out in a hidden manner in the richness of their own cultural symbols and rituals."[62]

The banner, it seems to this author, is a work of genius, though not without critique, as we shall see. The genius lies in the visual depiction in one place of the interaction of the Christian story and Chewa/Malawian culture and in utilizing both the narrative mode of communication from Malawi in proverbs and stories which generate meaning[63] alongside the cycle of the Church's Liturgical Year with its seasons.[64] Thus, after the cruciform focus at the center of the banner is dealt with, the year is divided into four seasons covering Advent to Christmas, Lent, Easter, and the gift of the Spirit following Pentecost. It is easy to see how the banner then becomes a pedagogical move for anyone viewing it.

At the center of the banner is Christ depicted as both crucified and risen with the image of a maize seed (maize is the staple diet of Malawian subsistence farmers)—this Jesus is the "heart of the gospel message."[65] The three persons of the Christian Trinity are also present at the center of the picture.[66] The novel use of a Malawian mask for God/the first person of the Trinity is a fascinating facet of the work (though there may be hints here of the popular confusion of the whole of God with the first person of the Trinity). It seems masks function somewhat like icons in Malawian traditional spirituality.[67] Included at the center are both non-human animals and the ancestors as collaborators with God, offering a truly holistic grounding to the theology being demonstrated here.

A two-way relationship between Christianity and Malawian culture is envisaged on the banner, "suggesting Christianity is enriched by having

61. Boucher, *Gospel Seed*, 2.

62. Boucher, *Gospel Seed*, 3.

63. Boucher, *Gospel Seed*, 4.

64. Boucher, *Gospel Seed*, 17.

65. Boucher, *Gospel Seed*, 5.

66. Boucher, *Gospel Seed*, 16.

67. Boucher, *Gospel Seed*, 13. See also Sison, *Art*, where the author discusses in depth the use of masks in African culture through the particular *Hekima Christus* altarpiece mural from the artist Engelbert Mveng in Nairobi.

it roots in Malawian soil" and that "God has prepared the Malawi soil to nurture the seeds of the gospel . . . He walks with his people of Malawi, leading them through their culture and history to the fullness of revelation in Christ."[68] It is possible therefore to read the banner through Walls's indigenizing and pilgrim principles. The vast majority of the banner would seem to be indigenizing, blessing the traditional aspects of Chewa culture that are compatible with Christian faith, including all the life-cycle rites of passage for birth, coming-of-age, child-birth, marriage, and death.

Some "pilgrim" principles are elucidated from time to time especially during the Lenten period (a "Journey back to God's values"[69]), and utilizing Gospel stories such as Zacchaeus and the parable of the prodigal.[70] The case of the suspicion of witchcraft around elderly women who become neglected is dealt with via the story of the revelation of the risen Christ to Mary Magdalene, who is assumed to be elderly and without a husband.[71] Other elements of witchcraft are also questioned and overcome by naming Christ as "the only *Sing'anga* who can help Malawians to rediscover the meaning of trust in God and in each other!"[72] *Sing'anga* is the Chewa word for the "diviner" (Boucher Chisale's translation) role which contains elements of shamanism. However, Christ as healer is complexified by Cécé Kolié in his essay in *Faces of Jesus in Africa*.[73]

Which brings us to three critiques of this project since direct comparisons of "this" (e.g. *Sing'anga*) in the local culture to "that" (e.g. Christ the healer) as an aspect of Christian faith, while tempting are more often than not, in our experience now, derived from an essentializing of both sides of the faith–culture continuum. As we discovered in our research in Northern English churches there was really only one direct reference to a "this equals that" equivalent between culture and faith. As the exception, it proved the rule that disavows this possibility.[74]

Essentializing, among other things, "fixes" culture in time and space, reducing and simplifying it to certain accepted aspects of it, while overlooking its dynamism over time, as well as its complexities and

68. Boucher, *Gospel Seed*, 17.

69. Boucher, *Gospel Seed*, 52.

70. Boucher, *Gospel Seed*, 62–5.

71. Boucher, *Gospel Seed*, 84–5

72. Boucher, *Gospel Seed*, 112.

73. Schreiter, *Faces of Jesus*, 128–50.

74. Rooms and Wort, *Fuzzy Church*, 74.

contestations. This is the other side of the beauty and pedagogical value of a visual image such as the *Missio Banner*. It is unchangeable and fixed in 1985 and perhaps even further back in memory—in the book the cultural practices being described are often referred to in the past tense, so it is unclear how many are still in continuous use. We have stated clearly that culture and therefore inculturation is a fast-moving dynamic phenomenon and it is hard to capture this constant movement in a work of this nature.

There is only one reference in the book to a historical and political change in the Malawian context, which came about when the colonial government in the 1930s banned the "poison ordeal" for divining who was a witch.[75] The ordeal has obvious connections with medieval European methods of doing the same (which resulted, more often than not, in the death of those being tested). It is hard to escape therefore a limited and backward-looking view of "culture" here which sets the "culture" in some imagined "traditional" village setting and which again is hardly contested. Nowhere do we see a breeze-block house, petrol-driven transport, reference to family planning, deforestation for agricultural land, the nation state, democratic institutions, global economic forces (for instance, the ubiquitous presence of the Coca-Cola company or its equivalents from China) and other aspects of being in a contemporary global and globalizing world.

Finally, it is hard to escape the feeling that what we are offered here is a largely western gaze on the majority Chewa culture (about 30% of the population). Given the above critiques, Boucher Chisale's project is not entirely a decolonial one. Indeed, there are at least seven other tribes in the country[76] and we do not know what contestation there is about what is presented here from both within and beyond the Chewa people.

Vincent Donovan

Vincent Donovan's (1926–2000) approach to inculturation within evangelization among the Maasai people has had a life of its own way beyond its initial implementation for less than a decade from the mid-1960s in Northern Tanzania. This is due to the enormous impact of his book[77] in

75. Boucher, *Gospel Seed*, 106.

76. Boucher, *Gospel Seed*, 7.

77. See Donovan, *Christianity Rediscovered*, originally published by Orbis in 1978

the churches of the west, both Protestant and Catholic. I need to declare my personal involvement here in the trajectory of Donovan's book which I first was introduced to during my ordination training in the late 1980s (I still have the copy which is severely annotated and dog-eared now). It is also important to connect Donovan's approach to its origins partly in the work of the Anglican missionary Roland Allen (1868–1947), who, as many have commented (including Allen himself!), was decades ahead of his time in anticipating how ministry and mission might be organized away from expensive structural arrangements.[78] I worked in an Anglican Diocese in Tanzania for seven years (from 1994 onwards) which covered parts of the land on which Maasai lived and herded their cattle, including the places Donovan and his Spiritan colleagues evangelized in. I wondered for myself what the long-term results were of Donovan's work, given that I never once heard him or his work talked about. I noted his inclusion as an example of the "anthropological" model in Bevans's first 1992 edition of *Models of Contextual Theology* (revised and expanded in 2004). I used Donovan's book in sermons and other teaching, and returned again and again to its simple but profound writing—who can fail to be moved by the description of losing and finding faith encapsulated by the hunting lion as God?[79] I noted how the Maasai as a people group seemed to unconsciously represent something to westerners which was strangely attractive, perhaps because of the way they (at least in our imaginations) held on, as best they could, to their traditional life and culture, were resistant to conversion over many decades, and indeed, despite their belief in a supreme God, had no interest in life after death and traditionally left their dead to be consumed by wild animals.[80] I think this is partly how Donovan's work came to be connected with doing mission and evangelism in the "hard ground" of post-Christian western society.

---

and available in several reprints and new editions. I work with one from 1982 published by SCM Press.

78. See Allen, *Missionary Methods*.

79. Donovan, *Christianity Rediscovered*, 61–4.

80. There is certainly evidence for such attractiveness in how the "first evangelization" movement to the Maasai came about among the Spiritans. They attracted the maverick and perhaps tougher, even heroic, American brothers who were up for the challenge such as Fr. Eugene Hillman (b. 1924), a contemporary of Donovan. How much the power and privilege of gendered whiteness is at play here is a moot point, as we shall see in the work of Hodgson, *Church of Women*, 88–9.

I wonder also if some deep nostalgia for what westerners gave up centuries before means we are drawn to these exceptional people[81] (however essentialist our perceptions might be of them). Between 2004 and 2006 the British Broadcasting Corporation (BBC) used Maasai young men in their traditional dance as an "ident" on UK television—a very short film to connect one program to the next.[82] I suggest this choice is part of the same phenomenon, since I doubt whether other African tribal dancing would be used in the same way. There is something exotic and other about the Maasai which is attractive to westerners, as Donovan himself notes at the start of his letter to his bishop explaining his new evangelistic approach.[83]

While Donovan's approach may be familiar to many readers, we do need to briefly summarize it here. Beginning with the initial letter, he sets out his dilemma as a new missionary sent to the Maasai. The prevailing *modus operandi* in the 1950s and 1960s for what is today named as the Congregation of the Holy Spirit, or Spiritans for short, was the mission station—a static place providing education for children, healthcare, and worship space, a classic "centripetal" ("come to us," and we might add colonial and civilizing) model of missionary endeavour. Hodgson[84] calls it the "School Approach" and as such it is a long-term project of educating people into the faith from a young age so that in time generations of educated Christian adults can emerge to lead in the community. Donovan is impatient of it and counts no fruit in terms of converts after seven years of operation. Despite much activity, no evangelism is taking place, in his view. Discussion of God, or even accepting Christianity, simply does not happen with the Maasai.

Donovan resolves to leave the static mission station and be with the people as an out-and-out evangelist and nothing else, according to Allen's proposals which he claims are found in St. Paul; moving on from the embryonic Christian community before its pastoral need "chokes" the evangelist.

81. On other levels the Maasai are exceptions. They are traditionally nomadic, herding cattle to where there is grass to eat, rather than living in settled communities conducting arable subsistence farming. They are a Nilotic ethnic group in contrast to the majority Bantu tribes of sub-Saharan Africa and thus they speak an entirely unrelated language to many of their neighbors, which means the *lingua franca* of Tanzania, Kiswahili, is also quite foreign to them.

82. See PRES BITS, "BBC One Ident 2004 to 2006."

83. Donovan, *Christianity Rediscovered,* 14.

84. Hodgson, *Church of Women,* 115.

This movement evangelizes the evangelist, not least because the western "faith" Donovan carries with him is hopelessly inadequate to connect with the lived experience, spirituality, and beliefs of the Maasai. Many of the Bible's origin stories, Donovan discovers, arise from an agricultural community, not a nomadic cattle-based one (for instance, Cain killing Abel[85]). Original sin is unintelligible in this society in its absolute sense following St. Augustine. Donovan has to lose the faith he has brought from the west that Jesus is the one who has dealt with sin and find it again in relation to how the Maasai live their lives. How Donovan achieves this in the short time he is with the Maasai occupies the rest of the book. Some "villages" (essentially fairly mobile, temporary settlements or *boma*) accept the new faith and are baptized and receive the Mass regularly as a "whole" community; others reject the message as Donovan has now crafted it and he learns like all good evangelists simply to walk away. In relation to the history of conversion during Imperial Christendom, Donovan's learning is worth repeating: "no [version of] Christianity has any meaning or value, if there is not freedom to accept or reject it."[86] It is important to note that this decision to be Christian or not is taken by the male elders of the community in conversation with Donovan on behalf of the whole community. His approach was to those males with the power to make such a decision in what he understood to be a communitarian society.

Two further studies demonstrate that Donovan's work was a short-lived experiment on the ground in Tanzania, though for other reasons it developed a life of its own in relation to mission in the post-Christendom west. John Bowen[87] visits the site of Donovan's work with the question, as a Protestant, "What happened next?" He meets Donovan's successor Spiritan missionaries, interviews them, and participates in a local Mass. Inevitably his report is somewhat superficial, but he is able to conclude "that things did not unfold as Donovan had hoped, though the underlying principles continued to be honored."[88] In an echo of my own church's wrestling with the tension between the institution and "fresh expressions" of church, Bowen notes that Donovan's ideas, in the longer term, were not acceptable either to the Church or to the Maasai. Bowen seems unaware of a much more important, extensive and yet earlier anthropological

85. Donovan, *Christianity Rediscovered*, 57.

86. Donovan, *Christianity Rediscovered*, 108.

87. See Bowen, "What Happened Next?"

88. Bowen, "What Happened Next?," 81.

study of Spiritan Evangelization among the Maasai by Dorothy Hodgson. This study is much more critical and fruitful for our own work. Hodgson worked among, and then researched as an anthropologist, both the Spiritan missionaries and the Maasai from 1985 until 2000, so her work represents a large and longitudinal study which generated a great deal of ethnographic data using multiple methods.[89]

Hodgson notes early on in the work (and as a woman herself) a neglect of gender analysis in mission studies in general and the way in gender relations are never simply related to "local factors" given the realities of national, capitalist and global forces at play in every place.[90] Her work therefore stands over against both Donovan's communitarian approach to Maasai conversion solely through powerful males and much contemporary writing on Maasai culture which claims an overt resistance to Christianity for various reasons, "Not only are these arguments simplistic, essentialist and ahistorical, but they are premised . . . on an understanding of 'Maasai' that is not just homogenous but deeply androcentric."[91] For instance, she is able to show clearly how the position of the Maasai in Tanganyika/Tanzania in its colonial period during the twentieth century reshaped the place of men and women in their society quite profoundly,[92] which leads to the gendered nature of spirituality among the Maasai that the Spiritans over time encounter. And in addition, as we have noted throughout this chapter, "Maasai religious beliefs and practices, like their cultural practices and social relations, are and always have been diverse, dynamic, and historical, even before colonial and/or missionary encounters."[93] What is difficult to read in her work are anthropological descriptions of "female circumcision"[94] without any sense in the whole book that they also amount to genital mutilation in feminist thought, which has to be, on the evidence here at least, one of the limits of "pure" ethnographic methods.

In chapter 2 of her book Hodgson presents three researched portraits of Spiritan Fathers evangelizing the Maasai from different generations, none of which, surprisingly, is Donovan (probably because his stay was in fact so short) though some are contemporary with him. His work

89. Hodgson, *Church of Women*, 16.

90. Hodgson, *Church of Women*, 3–4.

91. Hodgson, *Church of Women*, 6.

92. Hodgson, *Church of Women*, 13.

93. Hodgson, *Church of Women*, 14.

94. Hodgson, *Church of Women*, 55.

is dealt with in some detail in the next chapter, which discusses methods of evangelization.[95] She notes how the tougher male missionaries met the stereotypical tough and resistant male Maasai and took them on in a masculine manner[96] which led to "an unwillingness to consider seriously the interests and talents of women."[97] Rather their approach was based on essentialist tropes which the Fathers even name as "Maasai-itis"—that the Maasai were "so special, so unique."[98]

Hodgson describes three evangelistic approaches over the period of Spiritan work with the Maasai from the 1950s to her present. We have already described the "School Approach," which Donovan critiqued. Hodgson calls Donovan's evangelistic efforts the "Boma Approach"[99] and she offers a serious critique of it by analyzing the journals and writing of the evangelists:

> Despite the rhetoric of "communities," actual implementation of the *boma* approach reflected the gendered assumptions and concerns of the missionaries . . . the first step of the *boma* approach was to meet with the elder men of the homestead . . . and the influential male leaders, were targeted.[100]

Nevertheless, even at this point there is evidence that more women than men take an interest in the new faith and its instruction. Some even took up leadership roles in the new churches, challenging the perceptions of all the men involved.[101] Hodgson concurs with Bowen that it is largely the institution that kills off this innovation.[102] Evangelization does not however stop, as the "Individual Approach" now emerges from political changes occurring in a new socialist Tanzania and the predilection for westerners to individualize. Essentially anyone, any individual, is invited to instruction in the new faith in what is a fairly *ad hoc* and unsystematic

95. Hodgson, *Church of Women*, 125–39.

96. Hodgson, *Church of Women*, 89.

97. Hodgson, *Church of Women*, 107.

98. Hodgson, *Church of Women*, 97.

99. Hodgson, *Church of Women*, 125. A boma is one way of describing the collection of mobile dwellings in which groups of Maasai live together and herd their animals from. They are communitarian units which can be approached by a single missionary as Donovan did.

100. Hodgson, *Church of Women*, 134.

101. Hodgson, *Church of Women*, 136–8.

102. Hodgson, *Church of Women*, 139.

process.[103] Such an individual approach suits the western missionaries both ideologically and pragmatically and it works!

> And the church did flourish, but not in the form the missionaries desired. With the transition to the individual approach, the gender difference in interest . . . became vividly apparent. Now that anyone was free to attend religious instruction, regardless of school enrolment or *boma* residence, women flocked to the classes.[104]

The "church of women" therefore emerges, much to the consternation of almost everyone concerned apart from the women themselves, leaving a serious critique of previous attempts at inculturation. Hodgson names the virtual inseparability of culture and religion and the ubiquitous blind-spot around gender of the Spiritan missionaries as well as the fact that "their concepts of Maasai culture and religion were also deeply ahistorical and essentialist, conveying little sense of the historicity, dynamism, and diversity of Maasai beliefs and practices."[105] "Pilgrim principle" discontinuities around the arbitrariness of Eng'ai (the God of the Maasai) remained unresolved even as Hodgson wrote[106] and this author also noted a complete absence of any discussion in Hodgson of the place of the Bible in Maasai Christianity and very little engagement with the nature of the Trinity. It is however in the testimonies of the converted women who obey the innate desire of their hearts for God (which they name *oltau*[107]) that something new and beautiful emerges in discovering altruistic love. Hodgson quotes a convert, who is not a million miles away from some of our Northern English research subjects in *Fuzzy Church* who were new to the faith, "Before, you either loved or didn't love a person. Now, you love them as you love yourself . . . The big thing we have learned in church is love."[108]

Hodgson concludes:

> In many ways, therefore, the Catholic Church has enabled Maasai women to create an alternative female community beyond the control of Maasai men. Although Maasai men occupied

103. Hodgson, *Church of Women*, 139.
104. Hodgson, *Church of Women*, 140.
105. Hodgson, *Church of Women*, 143.
106. Hodgson, *Church of Women*, 144.
107. Hodgson, *Church of Women*, 154.
108. Hodgson, *Church of Women*, 167.

> positions of formal power within the church . . . women found their presumptions of bureaucratic power irrelevant if not laughable. Women were much more interested in coming together to learn, to pray to Eng'ai, and to talk to one another than in the formal hierarchies and obligations of church bureaucracy. It was the spirit, not the structure, of the church that appealed to them.[109]

To put this in theological terms, the very thing that scuppered Donovan's work—the institution—could be bypassed by the actual missionary work of the Holy Spirit among those who were receptive to her invitation, the women of the Maasai. And presumably this is not the end of the story, since we write another twenty or so years since Hodgson completed her field work, and stories of the continuing conversion of large numbers of Maasai to Christianity continue to emerge from the region.

Hodgson discusses the successes and the contestations of inculturation in a final chapter, noting with us that inculturation necessarily creates fuzzy boundaries: "the borders between the church of the Catholics and the church of the Maasai, between 'culture' and 'religion,' were often blurred and sometimes contested."[110] The result is highly complex and allows hard questions to be asked such as: "Is inculturation perhaps just a form of colonial "cultural preservation," a strategy to keep the Maasai 'traditional' in a world of rapid modernization?"[111] (something we noted was also probably happening in the creation of the Chewa *Missio Banner*). So once again the project of inculturation is messy and unfinished:

> The dominant meanings and manifestations of "being Maasai" and "being Catholic" in everyday life have changed and will continue to change . . . because of the continuing prosaic and poetic struggles of men and women believers and non-believers, missionaries and catechists, to define the terms and outcomes of the encounter. Although religious change and conversion are always processes of becoming, they are neither linear nor unidirectional.[112]

These two examples of attempts at inculturation in concrete African contexts have been mightily instructive. We have noted essentializing tendencies in both of them and how God the Holy Spirit seemed to work

109. Hodgson, *Church of Women*, 187.

110. Hodgson, *Church of Women*, 251.

111. Hodgson, *Church of Women*, 254.

112. Hodgson, *Church of Women*, 255.

around those in at least one of them. They have complexified the nature of inculturation in many and varied ways which is instructive for our own project in the investigation of how contextual theology is properly "contested." They lead us, also, to consider some deeper interpretive questions within the study of contextual theology.

THE HERMENEUTICS OF CONTEXTUAL THEOLOGY

At root the question of faith and culture is one of how we understand the relationship between the universal and the particular. I addressed this in my doctoral and subsequent research on the possibilities for the integration of faith and culture in England[113] and it is worth repeating some of my assertions here.

Hans-Georg Gadamer in his seminal and classic work *Truth and Method* makes the most important "post-modern" move in recovering the particular over against the hegemony of the universal in the Enlightenment. False universals such as the western colonial project[114] can be reimagined by focusing on the particular, without losing the sense that the horizons of each particularity can be expanded in relation to any other particularity[115] and therefore in some sense reach towards an overarching universal. Lamin Sanneh's work on the *translatability* of the gospel[116] is a good example of this—with translatability being the universal element in his schema which takes every particularity utterly seriously. In this way interpretation of each particularity is therefore possible in a universal manner: "all reality is hermeneutical."[117] Interpretation of any culture is always possible, and begins, according to Thiselton,[118] by "asking what it is to stand in the shoes of the other and to listen in openness."

Here is the starting point of the decolonial project in the way we reimagine the relationship between the universal and particular. Yet it is only the starting point, since it is not so easy to stand in another's shoes and truly listen without bringing our own blind spots and tendency to

113. See Rooms, *Towards a Pedagogy*; *Faith of the English.*

114. See Gorringe, *Furthering Humanity.*

115. See Thiselton, *New Horizons.*

116. See Sanneh, *Translating.*

117. Rooms, *Faith of the English*, 60.

118. Thiselton, *New Horizons*, 28.

essentialize what we see at almost every turn.[119] We underestimate the complexity of the particular at our peril; we need to complexify the particular in an anti-essentialist way. We will return to these themes in the next chapter.

In addition, we have learnt that the interpretation of cultures is not static but dynamic, and therefore unfinished. Theologically it is a part of what it is to live "between the times" in the improvization of the Christian faith in the fourth act of the drama of salvation.[120] Neither is interpretation any kind of linear process from "here to there" or from "this to that." Rather, it is much more like a complex unending spiral which we can join at any point, but in which our understanding will only ever be partial. Nevertheless, it seems the gospel, the good news of God in Jesus Christ, will find a way by the ceaseless activity of the Holy Spirit.

It is worth noting that Robert Schreiter in his review of the "future" of missiology in a further Luzbetak Lecture from 2010 largely concurs with these conclusions in relation to the inculturation project. He first notes how even the concept of culture itself has been "essentialized" in the era of globalization.[121] We have remarked how globalization was absent from the Malawian Missio banner. The global forces creating a gendered space for the spirituality of Maasai women to flourish needed to be uncovered to understand what was happening to them. We also note with Schreiter that different emphases can be placed on the universal and particular when conducting "intercultural hermeneutics" alongside opposition to the violence of colonizing forces in the hegemony of empires in the past and today.[122]

119. We might have had occasion in this chapter to refer to Henning Wrogemann's extensive work in *Intercultural Hermeneutics*, published in 2016, since it covers much of the same ground with some very rich case studies especially on the ground in Africa. However according to Terry Muck, "Intercultural Hermeneutics," 194–202, and others it remains within a German and western paradigm unprepared to engage with the work of Bosch, Bevans, Kraft, Walls, and Sanneh to name but a few scholars of missiology. Neither is there any explicit discussion of essentialism in cultural theory. Once again, we recognize the difficulty of stepping into the shoes of the other.

120. Wells, *Improvisation*, 54.

121. Schreiter, "Missiology's Future," 280.

122. Schreiter, "Missiology's Future," 281.

SEEKING A REGIONAL THEOLOGY OF INCULTURATION IN THE NORTH OF ENGLAND

Having reviewed inculturation in historical perspective and looked at multiple examples of it, we are ready to connect this chapter with the research we undertook in the North of England. We think our project is somewhat unique (no doubt other studies are available) in the trajectory we have covered here. We are bringing the faith and culture question to bear on a relatively "subaltern" region in the western world, the North of England. We wished to investigate the relationship between gospel and culture in a distinct area that is often ignored and denigrated. Since inculturation is often portrayed idealistically and theoretically in the literature, we felt that this required actual field research on the ground in local Christian communities.

We justify our approach as a specific example of what Sedmak calls "regional theology."[123] He outlines the approach thus: "The theological imagination tries to discern deeper layers of meaning and challenge in a social reality. It tries to read the signs of the times to become conscious of the struggle to realize deeper values and the struggle for a full and happy life."[124]

Finally, we connect our project with how Tim Gorringe sums up his theology of culture in his major book on the subject, *Furthering Humanity.* Culture is understood by Gorringe as "the human task"[125] realized between the particular of the incarnation of both Christ and the church in a place, such as the North of England, and the universal nature of the translatability of the gospel which is also that Christ.[126] We expect that by examining in detail one particular place or region as a site of contextualization of the gospel this study will be in a dynamic and two-way relationship with the universality of the same gospel as it is found in every culture and place. Out of this dynamic will emerge the contestation of contextualization, as we shall see in the next chapter when discussing a critique of translatability.

123. Sedmak, *Doing Local,* 111.
124. Sedmak, *Doing Local,* 112.
125. Gorringe, *Furthering,* 4.
126. Gorringe, *Furthering,* 100–1.

3

An "Etic" critique of Contextual Theology

We turn in this chapter to engage with the necessarily fewer number of scholars who offer a critique of contextual theology from outside of the discipline of missiology *per se*. It is also worth noting that the boundaries of the emic and etic here are not entirely discrete and our choice of interlocutors may blur this distinction in at least one or two cases.

TAKING ON PRACTICAL THEOLOGY—COURTNEY GOTO

We begin with Courtney Goto as her work confronts head-on even the very notion of context in theology and is perhaps the most serious critique to date that needs to be engaged with. Goto is an Asian-American emerging scholar in the broad field of practical theology (and that particular version of it found in the USA) based, at the time of writing, in the Boston University School of Theology. I have argued elsewhere that missiology and practical theology can be treated as allied fields, at the very least,[1] while there are clear distinctives as well. Both, it seems to me, are concerned with *praxis*, or reflection on human experience which is always embodied in place and time. Thus, it is entirely appropriate that Goto in her 2018 book, *Taking on Practical Theology: The Idolization of Context and the Hope of Community* notices the ubiquitous employment

1. Rooms and Ross, "Practical Theology and Missiology," 144–47.

of context in practical theology knowledge production. In the book she attempts a full deconstruction of the notion and how its assumptions are related to preserving existing power dynamics with an eye to a reconstruction with much greater awareness of its dangers. It is worth noting at this point that the book is addressed mainly to the (American) Practical Theology academy as a "community of practice."[2] This does not mean that what Goto claims is true is not relevant for reflective practitioners of Christian ministry and mission on the ground elsewhere, just that her main audience is what we might call *professional* practical theologians who make a career from their employment working in the field in educational institutions.

Goto's book sets out to unmask the unconscious assumptions or "gods," as she names them, when researchers go about their studies. This is why she claims context can become an idol. Since, she claims, "the notion of 'context' has been made one of the most powerful gods of our discipline," her aim is to ask "how our use of the term maintains privilege and inflicts harm."[3] While practical theology as a discipline has been developed in the white western world,[4] in working with the notion of context Goto is also clear that her critique extends to any engagement with an "other" across a boundary and it is therefore just as apposite in the field of missiology,[5] which has been arguably a more global enterprise (though still largely dominated by white western scholars[6]). Goto states openly that racism is her point of departure for the discussion of context which reflects her social location[7] and connects her work to that of Willie James Jennings who we will engage with next.

Goto gives several examples from within the academy of the problem with idolizing context as she sees it.[8] Perhaps the two most serious of these for our purposes and research are where a researcher, "mistakenly treats her contextual analysis as the reality to which the symbol

2. Goto, *Taking on Practical Theology*, xviii.

3. Goto, *Taking on Practical Theology*, xv.

4. Goto, *Taking on Practical Theology*, 2.

5. Interestingly Goto references the Catholic missiologist Robert Schreiter's work as unmasking "the historic practice of adopting western Christianity as the universal norm for theology" (*Taking on Practical Theology*, 3n6).

6. See, for instance, Reddie and Troupe, *Deconstructing Whiteness*.

7. Goto, *Taking on Practical Theology*, xix.

8. Goto, *Taking on Practical Theology*, 5.

context points"[9] and where the researcher is unaware of their reflexivity whereas, "in reality he is making over the data to fit his 'context.'"[10] Thus, Goto defines the overall problem as theologians idolizing, "context by taking as normative their own cultural, theological, gendered, and/or disciplinary frame of reference, all the while believing they are being helpful and even attentive to context."[11] The researcher has not recognized their own, "power to define the other as well as define reality *for* the other from one's privileged standpoint."[12]

Goto understands context as a "disciplinary symbol"[13] which contains epistemological, normative, and methodological assumptions which go unquestioned. Often in our everyday use of the word in speech and writing we are wont to treat it as more of a sign than a symbol, but that is to miss the complexity of polyvalency that a symbol brings and reduce it to the one thing that the sign represents. While we imagine that context refers to something "out there," we can easily miss what it refers to inwardly in ourselves as reflexive people; "the symbol *context* continues to open us up differently over time, constantly challenging, affirming, and remaking our interpretations of context."[14] Actually, on reflection with Goto here, I think this has been true of my work on the contextual theology of Northern England for much of a whole decade now and certainly throughout this research project. The meaning of the "context" which is the North has developed and deepened, and indeed this a further reason for writing this book, beyond the original reflections in *Fuzzy Church*. Missing this aspect of the symbol means ignoring "how each of us brings different inward (subjective) experiences to contextual analysis, creating variation between and among the ways that we perceive, interpret, and discuss context."[15] Symbols therefore have a much deeper referent within those who employ them and as such they become shared and assumed quasi-religious commitments within the discipline. Therefore, "although the meaning of context is often treated as self-evident, shared, and

9. Goto, *Taking on Practical Theology*, 5.
10. Goto, *Taking on Practical Theology*, 5.
11. Goto, *Taking on Practical Theology*, 5.
12. Goto, *Taking on Practical Theology*, 5, her emphasis.
13. Goto, *Taking on Practical Theology*, 8.
14. Goto, *Taking on Practical Theology*, 9, her emphasis.
15. Goto, *Taking on Practical Theology*, 13.

without need of reflection, *context* is not a sign but a complex symbol that cannot be taken for granted."[16]

Given the religious nature of symbols they can lead to idolatry if we forget that every symbol has its limitations, for it points to something greater than itself[17]—thus, "when we fail to reflect critically on a symbol, we fail to detect its limitations, and that is idolatry."[18] Further implications of the idolatry of context are that it becomes made in our own image; "we need 'context' in a form we can manage, manipulate and translate for our own use as scholars."[19] Also, context offers unequal power to those who are in control of it—in this case the contextual researcher over against those they are researching who are forced to see themselves in terms of the researcher's idolatrous view of them. The idolatrous symbol and the symbol makers displace the symbolized for the sake of maintaining the *status quo*.[20] Goto's project is one of de- and re-construction, a "breaking" of the symbol of context[21] so that its limitations may be understood and it can therefore be revised and employed in new and creative ways.

Goto sets her study within the paradigm shifts in epistemology and hermeneutics from the Modern period onwards, something we noted towards the end of the previous chapter. She understands her work as continuing this movement especially as it relates to the "new paradigm" emerging from engagement with race, class, gender, intersectionality, and postcolonialism.[22] Her stance as a practical theologian is to take up the role of prophet and tactician[23] and she notably references John Hull alongside Steve Bevans and Roger Schroeder as participating in this prophetic tradition within practical theology.[24] Tactics are about questioning the "regnant paradigm" in one's academic work and writing from the margin—and anyone, whether marginalized or mainstream, can take up this position; "one can make an ethical choice to stand in the blurred boundaries of being an insider and an outsider to multiple

16. Goto, *Taking on Practical Theology*, 11, her emphasis.
17. Goto, *Taking on Practical Theology*, 11.
18. Goto, *Taking on Practical Theology*, 12.
19. Goto, *Taking on Practical Theology*, 13.
20. Goto, *Taking on Practical Theology*, 14.
21. Goto, *Taking on Practical Theology*, 14–17.
22. Goto, *Taking on Practical Theology*, 52.
23. Goto, *Taking on Practical Theology*, 54.
24. Goto, *Taking on Practical Theology*, 54–5, n5.

groups in order to challenge oppression."[25] The research which forms the basis of this book certainly makes that choice—in a divided England we have chosen to be biased to the North,[26] a region characterized by marginality in relation to the whole. Goto states her position as a person with advantages and disadvantages in the work of prophetic tactics because of being an Asian American.[27] Yet, "members of dominant groups . . . can, in fact—on moral as well as intellectual grounds—seek to widen their horizons"[28] as they become allies with marginalized people.[29] Crossing boundaries has the potential to transform the boundary crosser, however initially powerful they may be (evidence for which we uncovered in the research itself).

With this background (or even a form of context[30]) for the project we now turn to the heart of Goto's work—a case study in the question of context in practical theology. Goto differentiates between a typology of three approaches to context she discerns in the literature alongside three common, yet often hidden strategies for crossing boundaries and studying context.[31] But first Goto discerns four ways the term context is employed in routine usage.[32] First as *social milieu* which is the "big picture" perspective and can be examined from multiple perspectives and disciplines. It is largely the definition that we began our project with when addressing the North of England as context. Second, context is used a "*framing device*" when one subject is discussed in the terms of another frame of reference. Context is also read as the "*background story*" as a way to describe how a particular intervention came about as is often the case in the Introduction to a particular work. Goto comments on all these three usages thus, "the theorist attempts to discern or, in the case of frame, to place important factors 'behind' lived experiences under investigation, as if what were behind were distinguishable or separable."[33] Goto questions how distinct we can make context, which leads to the fourth usage of context as a "*locus of concern*" in a particular time and place.

25. Goto, *Taking on Practical Theology*, 59.
26. Wakefield and Rooms, *Northern Gospel*, 35–50.
27. Goto, *Taking on Practical Theology*, 77.
28. Goto, *Taking on Practical Theology*, 69.
29. Goto, *Taking on Practical Theology*, 80.
30. Goto, *Taking on Practical Theology*, 83.
31. Goto, *Taking on Practical Theology*, 83.
32. Goto, *Taking on Practical Theology*, 87–89.
33. Goto, *Taking on Practical Theology*, 89.

The focus on time and place here eliminates the distinctions inferred by the other meanings, "a particular place/time has its own tightly woven historical/cultural/religious/aesthetic/political/economic integrity that resists being separated into parts."[34] It is this fourth definition that we have come to after the emic critique in the last chapter and the complexifying of the North that emerged during the research, while recognizing that we, with other practical theology researchers, "slide easily back and forth between and among the multiple meanings of *context*."[35]

Goto ends up then in the space between the classic polarity, from the discipline of ethnography in cultural anthropology, of participant and observer, the emic and the etic. We know this is an unresolvable polarity which requires constant negotiation but does result in Goto being able to delineate three approaches to context within the bounds of the polarity and which are discernible in the guild of practical theologians. They are the critical objective, critical subjective and critical intersubjective approaches. It is helpful here to address each of these in turn in relation to the research we conducted in this project.

Critical Objective

Goto's definition here is an "attempt to *locate* lived experiences in a faith community, discerning how a practice, a situation, or a problem arises *in situ*."[36] What then happens is that the researcher attempts to situate the data collected in the context, "within recognizable patterns and systems that explain why people act and believe the way they do."[37] There is a movement from the micro to the macro, or the particular to the universal, via "categories of analysis"[38] generated by the researcher in the academy working in an interdisciplinary fashion. Goto problematizes this approach of moving from smaller to larger containers and we recognize there are elements of this approach in how we understand Northernness within local, regional, and national boundaries, though our approach fits more closely with the second of Goto's proposals below. We did indeed, in *Fuzzy Church*, bring Fox's categories of authenticity, community, and

34. Goto, *Taking on Practical Theology*, 89.
35. Goto, *Taking on Practical Theology*, 89, her emphasis.
36. Goto, *Taking on Practical Theology*, 93, her emphasis.
37. Goto, *Taking on Practical Theology*, 93.
38. Goto, *Taking on Practical Theology*, 94.

humor, which for us describe the *Gehalt* of Northernness from her research to make further sense of our data—and we will further nuance them in the next chapter. Yet Fox is a Northern feminist researcher who belongs in the North, and sits firmly outside the Church, thus creating a "fuzzy" edge even within this approach. And we employed Heaney's five aspects of post-colonial theology[39] to illuminate the othering of the North in the past and present.[40] Heaney is an insider to the Church and coloniality as a Christian Irishman, but an outsider to the North. We will further develop his work in chapter 7.

Critical Subjective

Here the attempt is to elevate "categories of analysis (i.e. in the form of themes, symbols and stories) that are particular to the faith community, which can then be analyzed."[41] In addition, Goto claims that "the themes that emerge from one faith community are not necessarily transferable to any other,"[42] which we think is true at a "surface" (perhaps more sociological) level, while our work assumed that at the deeper levels of belief and behavior (perhaps more anthropological) there are commonalities that can be usefully discerned. Goto also claims here that in both these first two approaches the researcher's context tends to be played down or taken as neutral or more objective, though I think we could disagree here. We located ourselves and our personal histories within the Northern context and we are not about to leave it for any other. Two important interlocutors in *Fuzzy Church,* Heaney and Fox, locate themselves and their studies in very concrete and particular fashions, Fox especially as a Northern feminist stand-up comic and poet.

It is no surprise that Goto locates the origins of this approach in the contextual theology of missiologists like Steve Bevans[43] and she defines it thus: "critical reflection on practices of people traditioning Christian faith in light of their culture, history and identity."[44] In referencing another of

39. See Heaney, *Post-Colonial Theology.*

40. Rooms and Wort, *Fuzzy Church,* chapter 6.

41. Goto, *Taking on Practical Theology,* 95.

42. Goto, *Taking on Practical Theology,* 95.

43. Goto, *Taking on Practical Theology,* 95, n19, though it is perhaps notable that Goto does not name the relationship between contextual theology and missiology, a crucial point of departure perhaps between practical theologians and missiologists.

44. Goto, *Taking on Practical Theology,* 95.

the Catholic "Chicago School" of missiologists, as I have termed them, Robert Schreiter says, "the researcher attempts to perceive and elevate the faith community as a site of local wisdom, revealing its unique point of view."[45] Particularity is foregrounded in relation to the universal which is kept in the background and our project is clearly set in this tradition. Goto stands largely against universalizing tendencies in practical theology research (see her chapter 4) and while we understand the pitfalls, this project wishes to hold together the particular and universal in a nuanced way as we noted in the previous chapter. I also wonder whether there is another departure from Goto worth noting here between practical theology and missiology. Perhaps Goto is missing the emphasis in missiology on the *missio Dei,* as outlined in chapter 1 and thus the requirement for discerning the presence and activity of God who *is* mission within each particular context. While the perichoretic "dance"[46] of the Trinity[47] discovered and discerned as particular people in a particular time and place participate in that dance, such discernment is a further more universal dimension in addition to the local faith community as a place of wisdom on its own terms.

Critical Intersubjective

This third approach goes one step further in engaging those being researched in the research itself, "all participants in the research process practice critical awareness of themselves, others, and their interaction as they discern context."[48] Co-creation and co-construction occur between all parties in the project. Thus, "knowledge emerges 'in between,' as participants attend to differences and overlaps in what they know, how they know it, what they value, and what they are discovering."[49] In contrast to the employment of "bracketing" researcher bias in reflexivity especially in the critical subjective approach here, in co-creation, "multiple worlds collide and assumptions are upended, confirmed, and interrogated by

45. Schreiter, *Constructing Local,* 96.

46. Davison prefers the more accurate translation of the Greek word *perichoresis* as "making room for" (which is not unknown in the beauty of dance of course). See Davison, *Participation,* 57, n51.

47. Bevans and Schroeder, *Prophetic Dialogue.* See especially their chapter 1 where they offer some very suggestive images of participation in the dance of God.

48. Goto, *Taking on Practical Theology,* 97.

49. Goto, *Taking on Practical Theology,* 97.

all knowers."[50] It is here that our research can be seriously called into question by Goto's critique. We defined the research questions and took them to the communities identified by leaders in Church bodies as being where "something is happening." While some of the research methods were largely open-ended (for example, use of pictures to provoke conversation, participant observation in worship events) we analyzed the data that was collected and presented it as a report and a book. It was not co-created via analysis or interpretation with the participants, though sharing the material in different ways at the end of the of the project has been surprising and illuminating as we have received positive feedback such as Christian Northerners being "seen," often for the very first time. Thus, while we may have taken some "baby steps"[51] towards the critical inter-subjective approach we have to admit a limit to our research at this point. Nevertheless, our research journey has helped us to see clearly with Goto that "all communities are hybrid, multiple and fluid to some degree"[52] and therefore to treat our findings with a proper degree hermeneutical suspicion and note their "provisional, partial nature."[53]

Addressing "Nativism" in Research

Goto deepens her critique and the idolization of context in chapter 5 of her book, finding elements of nativism in the work of contemporary practical theologians who employ variations of all three of the above approaches. Goto warns, "research that reveals the situation of the other in the utmost detail can sometimes drift into a form of colonialism called 'nativism' where the 'natives' are subjected to a colonial gaze and used by the elite for their own purposes."[54] In addition, "the way that the 'native' comes to be understood is too often in terms of the assumptions, theories, concepts, categories, desires and wishes of groups that experience privilege most of the time."[55] Nativism can occur despite the best intentions of the researcher to allow the marginalized other to be seen and have their

50. Goto, *Taking on Practical Theology*, 97.
51. Goto, *Taking on Practical Theology*, 98.
52. Goto, *Taking on Practical Theology*, 108.
53. Goto, *Taking on Practical Theology*, 126.
54. Goto, *Taking on Practical Theology*, 135.
55. Goto, *Taking on Practical Theology*, 148.

voice heard, and in the process "unwittingly harm" the subjects.[56] Goto is also concerned as to who benefits from the research, asserting that it is more often than not the academy and the researcher that does so. Goto then engages with the radical scholars Rey Chow and Gayatri Chakravorty Spivak, who question the possibility of any privileged person undertaking research with those different from themselves and avoiding colonialism.[57] They emphasize the gulf of difference between researcher and subject and accept *untranslatability.* At this point in Goto's project she herself finds the limits of her own critique of researching context, when stating her disagreement with Chow and Spivak: "they virtually undermine the whole project of research and call in to question their own role as academics, since any research is predicated on learning about who is other and depends on being understood by others."[58] In other words the possibility of crossing a boundary into another's world for their good is not finally anathematized. Perhaps there may not be a direct relationship, but there is at least an analogous one between this question and the God who leaves the life of heaven and is born in the creation according to the Christ-hymn in the Epistle to the Philippians. A theology grounded in the *missio Dei,* in some sense can also, therefore help us here. It is God who crosses boundaries as the divine missionary who self-limits and self-empties in *kenosis* through creation and salvation and while this is fraught with danger for all parties, we should remember that the cause is the surfeit of divine love that cannot help but cross the boundary of Godself. Perhaps research conducted out of love (in the *amateur,* the one who operates out of love) would be at least one criterion for assessing the credibility of contextual research, without being naïve about the nature of that love.

It is important, however, to take these critiques of colonialism and nativism seriously, particularly as they relate to "interpretation and representation" and which Goto desires to hold together in interrelationship. In terms of interpretation or hermeneutics we discussed both its importance and difficulty (especially in any final way) in the previous chapter and we should rightly address representation here. Representation is "an intellectual and aesthetic project of portraying the other for an audience to encounter, engage, and respond"[59] and even positive

56. Goto, *Taking on Practical Theology,* 148.

57. Goto, *Taking on Practical Theology,* 150–51.

58. Goto, *Taking on Practical Theology,* 151–52.

59. Goto, *Taking on Practical Theology,* 153.

representations can harm. We have certainly attempted to interpret our data collected in Northern churches where "something is happening" and wish to represent Northernness and Northern Christians to a wide readership. Whether we have colluded with colonialism in the process is a question we will need to return to in a later chapter. We will have to be aware that any representations we produce are "symbols that may point to reality with some accuracy but bear the imprint of their makers as all symbols do"[60] and therefore we will need to "guard against privileging the researcher's assumptive world."[61]

In addressing nativism, Goto suggests the requirement for the researcher to go beyond engaging simply with their own reflexivity. Rather the following questions need to be asked:

> Who defined the research problem? For whom is this study worthy and relevant? Who says so? What knowledge will the community gain from this study? What knowledge will the researcher gain from this study? What are the likely positive outcomes from this study? What are some possible negative outcomes? How can the negative outcomes be eliminated? To whom is the researcher accountable?[62]

These questions go somewhat beyond nativism *per se* to wider issues of what we might call "extractive" colonialism, where the natives are exploited for what they can offer to the academic world. While it is tempting to dive into answering these questions for our research project right here, they are probably best left until chapter 5 where we address methodology.

Going further in Critical Intersubjectivity

Goto has a further critique in Chapter 6 of "recruiting and training insiders" in the critical intersubjective approach, not least because this contains the inherent danger of doing "epistemic violence" to the research subjects as they are co-opted into the world of the outsider researcher in a further unconscious colonizing move. In doing so, both sides may be unable to "think critically, for example about hybridity, translocality,

60. Goto, *Taking on Practical Theology*, 153.

61. Goto, *Taking on Practical Theology*, 161.

62. Goto, *Taking on Practical Theology*, 161–62.

interstitiality, racism or colonialism."[63] Since this goes beyond the methods we employed, it is not the place to comment further here, though Goto's reflections on the importance of mimicry in postcolonial thought in relation to the position of research subjects will need to be returned to in chapter 7.

Nevertheless, after (for our purposes) a digression about how her work affects teaching in the academy in her chapter 7 Goto's overall proposal is to advocate for developing a Critical Intersubjectivity which she places in capitals to distinguish it from that version which has been subject to her critique. It is in this space that the reconstruction of context as a useful concept in practical theology can take place.[64] Ultimately, she suggests a two-way process between researcher and subject at the boundary between them. Suggestively, this position is not unlike the finding in our research in Northern churches where "something is happening" that what made that something happen is the relationship between insiders and outsiders at the boundary of what we called "fuzzy" churches. So Goto can elaborate on this space further, "Even more radical would be for co-researchers to examine the context not only of the insiders but also of the outsiders, being attentive to tensions, overlaps, and what emerges in the encounter between these assumptive worlds."[65] We will therefore return to this question in chapter 5, since we can demonstrate from the research data that critical intersubjectivity can be found at the fuzzy or porous edges of the churches we investigated.

Concluding Comments on Goto's Critique of Context

We have engaged at length with *Taking on Practical Theology* as it is directly relevant, from an etic perspective, to our project. We have located our method within Goto's critique and found its clear limits, where we are found wanting. No doubt if we took on the task again (and had more time and resources) we could approach it quite differently. Nevertheless, we have learnt, or even been conscientized about, *humility* with regard to our conclusions about the Northern context which can only be contingent and symbolic in time and space. We have noted how there are many questions about our method that require responses, at the very least, if

63. Goto, *Taking on Practical Theology*, 177.

64. Goto, *Taking on Practical Theology*, 228.

65. Goto, *Taking on Practical Theology*, 230.

not final and complete answers. We will return to these later in the book. We find hope in the liminal fuzziness of "Intersubjective Space" where we believe God is to be found, perhaps more than anywhere else.[66]

THE LIMITS OF TRANSLATION—WILLIE JAMES JENNINGS

Race as a question deeply informs Goto's stance and arguments in her book while not being its sole focus, the next work we engage with places race front and center. Willie James Jennings[67] seeks to uncover the theological roots of race and racism in the Christian project since its inception, claiming that the "Christian imagination" is deeply infected by forces that lead to the supremacy of whiteness and a colonial stance towards the other.

Jennings is currently the Associate Professor of Systematic Theology and Africana Studies at Yale Divinity School, which places him firmly in the etic position in relation to missiology and contextual theology. Like Goto, he is writing from within and for the American theological academy, though his goals are also much wider than that. His work only tangentially intersects with our concerns in this book, yet there is another line of thought which makes this tangential engagement crucial to our subject. This is not least because we have to reckon with the race question at some point in the project. It would be all too easy to collude with the agenda of white male colonial supremacy and bypass or ignore it. In the previous chapter we noted the tendency in the historiography of missions to pass over the dark and even downright evil episodes that characterize much of the missionary enterprise. Jennings faces this reality head-on in setting out his research question.[68] Given the potential of Christianity, as it expands, to exhibit "its own deep wisdom and power of joining, mixing, merging, and being changed by multiple ways of life to witness to a God who surprises us by love of differences," why is it that instead, "the intimacy that marks Christian history is a painful one, one in which the joining often meant

66. For a full discussion of how God may be more "available" to humanity in liminal spaces, see Carson et al., 221.

67. See Jennings, *Christian Imagination.*

68. Jennings, *Christian Imagination,* 9.

oppression, violence, and death, if not of bodies then most certainly of ways of life, forms of language, and visions of the world?"[69]

Jennings's method is to focus deeply on the life and works of four characters from the medieval and/or colonial history of Christian expansion between the fifteenth and nineteenth centuries in the first two parts of the book which represent his diagnosis; *displacement* and *translation*. He deals in fine detail with primary texts from each character which provide strong evidence for his arguments. In the third part he moves to his proposal for a new *intimacy* in communion between peoples. It is not possible to do justice in a short summary here to the fine theological work that is demonstrated by Jennings, but we can only do our best to present his argument as faithfully as possible before working with the points at which it affects our own.

The book opens with a fifteenth-century primary text written on the arrival of some of the first African slaves in Portugal at the very beginning of the colonial project. Needless to say, theological reflection is required of the Court Chronicler (Zurara) to make sense of this Christian innovation, the buying and selling of black human beings. Quickly Jennings's main thesis emerges: that it is the theological mistake of supersessionism[70] that is behind the justification of such racist acts. Supersessionism, put crudely, is the replacement of Israel in the history of salvation by the Church, and in this case the white, European, male Church which becomes the defining characteristic for true Christian identity. All other converts have to conform to this ideal, "because it [the Church] had jettisoned Israel from its calculus of the formation of Christian life, created a conceptual vacuum that was filled by the European."[71] Here and elsewhere through subsequent centuries (as Jennings notes in later chapters) it is clear that white Christian nations (e.g. Great Britain, the USA, and South Africa) thought of themselves as Israel entering their promised lands in their colonizing projects, so that "supersessionist thinking is the womb in which whiteness will mature."[72] Slavery (and other colonizing practices) separates colonized people and their identity from land and geography, meaning that "native identities, tribal, communal, familial, and spatial, were constricted to simply their [slave] bodies, leaving behind the very

69. Jennings, *Christian Imagination*, 9.

70. This is Jennings's spelling—it is also sometimes supercessionism in the literature.

71. Jennings, *Christian Imagination*, 33.

72. Jennings, *Christian Imagination*, 36.

ground that enables and facilitates the articulation of identity."[73] Thus, in a further move outlined throughout the book, race takes the place of having a geography, "without land functioning as identity signifier, racial designations historically understood and politically activated continue to be compelling sensible ground on which to envision collective agency."[74] There is, therefore, no true community which provides its people with identity and within which God can dwell without place. Displacement is complete when the Church replaces Israel and race replaces land.

The point at which Jennings intersects most clearly with contextual theology is in his section on "translation" and in particular when he examines the life and work of the Anglican Bishop John Colenso among the Zulu people in colonial South Africa in the mid-nineteenth century. Colenso was a missionary whose self-appointed task was that of translation, both of the Scriptures and Christianity, into the Zulu and Nguni language systems.[75] In the translation process at his residence and printing house, Bishopstowe, he pioneered an indigenous involvement in the work that was almost unprecedented at the time.[76] Yet along with his friend and collaborator Theophilus Shepstone (a British South African colonial administrator who eventually ruled the whole colonial area) he was also implicated, at least in the early years of the work, in the translation of "native worlds into European hegemony," as form of "nativism." In fact, "Colenso brought Christianity into vernacular languages, and Shepstone used vernacular languages to bring the natives into colonial existence."[77] The two would eventually fall out and separate (at the same time as Colenso's well-documented fall from "orthodox" grace in the eyes of his Church), but at first, they were together in a project of native education through mastery of the language on the basis that "where the British educated head goes, the native bodies will follow."[78] The theological aspects of the Colenso case study are important for Jennings:

> For it is precisely [Colenso's] theological vision, along with the full development of the white supremacist state, that destroyed the spectacular trajectory of the Bishopstowe mission station. That theological vision also exposes much of the architecture of

73. Jennings, *Christian Imagination*, 43.
74. Jennings, *Christian Imagination*, 63.
75. Jennings, *Christian Imagination*, 125.
76. Jennings, *Christian Imagination*, 131.
77. Jennings, *Christian Imagination*, 125.
78. Jennings, *Christian Imagination*, 132.

> modern-day white, Western theological engagements with non-Western Christians. Equally important, Colenso's reflections show the ambiguous inner logic of strategies of contextuality . . . Bishop Colenso's thought reveals the deeply contorted ground on which translation of the Christian world had been forced to proceed.[79]

The case of Shepstone and Colenso is an important one as it demonstrates the complexities and unintended consequences of missionary work tied up with colonialism. What starts out as a proper immersion in the language and culture of people groups, turns into a thorough co-opting of that knowledge of indigeneity in the white power base, an exercise in nativism. Jennings claims Shepstone, aided by Colenso's theological support, simply used his profound knowledge of African languages and social systems "to gain full control of the African."[80]

Jennings notes a "flight to the universal" in Colenso's theological work. His argument is complex and bears more scrutiny than we can offer here.[81] Colenso inevitably brought his theological formation in English/European Enlightenment theology to his task which affected his theological anthropology, his understanding of the place and authority of the Bible and indeed the whole "science" of understanding religion itself, beyond Christianity. Colenso developed a positive understanding of the place of Zulu religion and the people's eternal destination (this became part of the heresy accusations against him). This was "a powerful and revolutionary act given the prevailing missionary and theological sentiments of his day."[82] Yet he joins the whole movement Jennings discerns of those who disconnect the life and beliefs of indigenous peoples with their land, which is controlled and operated by and for the benefit of the colonialists.

In addition, Jennings also finds a version of supersessionism in Colenso's *Commentary on the Book of Romans* in which the particularity of Israel, and the Jew, becomes what can be described as an unhelpful ethnocentrism and is trumped by a universal; "the true spirit of the gospel." So, "Colenso's first major hermeneutic move is to place all peoples under the fundamental problem, ethnocentrism."[83] The result of this is that, for

79. Jennings, *Christian Imagination*, 132.
80. Jennings, *Christian Imagination*, 126.
81. Jennings, *Christian Imagination*, 132–50.
82. Jennings, *Christian Imagination*, 135.
83. Jennings, *Christian Imagination*, 140.

Colenso, "Israel loses any historic trajectory of liberation, any political hope born in the past that should shape the present."[84] Jennings notes a "massive blind spot" in this argument since while Colenso counts the English settlers as analogous to the Jewish nation, they have enormous influence to refashion "a people's way of life for theological reasons."[85] Colenso's universalism goes further and "folds all humanity into righteousness, not damnation," which develops "theological sameness in all people"[86] and demonstrates Colenso's embeddedness in both the German Idealist tradition and Enlightenment romanticism.[87]

Jennings summarizes the complexities and hidden dangers of Colenso's theology in an important paragraph:

> The bishop drew on the biblical story to fill in his description of God the Father and thereby render at times an exquisite picture of divine love. But at the same time, Colenso's vision evacuated Christian identity of any real substance. All theological identity is essentially the same, Jewish, Christian, or Zulu—an internalized struggle of the religious consciousness to hear the word of love and acceptance from God the Creator-Father and his son, Jesus, and to follow the dictates of the moral universal inherent in all people. What looks like a radical antiracist, antiethnocentric vision of Christian faith is in fact profoundly imperialist. Colenso's universalism undermines all forms of identity except that of the colonialist.[88]

So, for Jennings this is clear evidence that universalism and colonialism are deeply intertwined, and results in a theology which universalizes "the earth, that is, to free it from particular ways of life."[89] He can further comment on the vacuity of this missionary enterprise which is, "by its proper nature boundary crossing, but this universalist vision reduces the power and presence of the very things it claims to grasp, the particularities of African peoples."[90] Ultimately the paucity of Colenso's theology is exposed: "Colenso, like many of his contemporaries, was unable to perceive what was being asked of him as a [white European] theological teacher in the

84. Jennings, *Christian Imagination,* 141.
85. Jennings, *Christian Imagination,* 141.
86. Jennings, *Christian Imagination,* 143–44.
87. Jennings, *Christian Imagination,* 144.
88. Jennings, *Christian Imagination,* 145.
89. Jennings, *Christian Imagination,* 146.
90. Jennings, *Christian Imagination,* 146.

new world of Africa. Grasping the inner logics of both worlds required a depth of intimacy that Colenso lacked."[91] Colenso's theology is not finally about the African, but rebounds to its English progenitor's interests by a utilitarian co-opting of the Zulu voice. We can be clear, then, that Colenso's translation is not a simple one-way street. Jennings has shown the complexity of what is coming back from the context to the white missionary, read as it through European lenses and supporting colonial power. The opportunity for a genuine two-way street (or intersubjectivity in Goto's terms) characterized by "concurrency" which "describes the possibilities of cultural inner logics being joined together, to the possibility of freedom in the transgression of boundaries"[92] is missed in Colenso's collaborative work with his African partners.

This analysis leaves Jennings with a question about translation which directly connects here with the work of missiologists Lamin Sanneh and Andrew Walls, both of whom may be familiar to readers of this book, since they have made major contributions to questions of contextualization. He asks pointedly, "What is the translation of a Christian world supposed to create?" and he answers his own question clearly: "Centrally, translation should beget Christian agency."[93] We will claim in chapter 6 that the Christian project in Africa can have a reverse agency and impact on understanding our research churches in the North of England, and engage with post-colonial agency in chapter 7. Yet it is the shape of that agency that really matters—Colenso was able to partially create it, but it was a distorted agency proscribed by the colonial missionary which resulted in "isolating and reductive forms of Christian agency."[94]

Jennings rehearses critically the work of Sanneh, and then Walls, since both directly address the translation question. Once again, the full argument cannot be reproduced here but we shall need to engage particularly with Jennings's serious criticism of both scholars. One of the issues in the background of the discussion is the different academic "world" that Sanneh and Walls operated in, since he notes their scholarship is often overlooked by both postcolonial theorists and theologians—it is too positive for some and too radical for others.[95]

91. Jennings, *Christian Imagination,* 150.

92. Jennings, *Christian Imagination,* 154.

93. Jennings, *Christian Imagination,* 155.

94. Jennings, *Christian Imagination,* 155.

95. Jennings, *Christian Imagination,* 323, n.25.

In missiology Sanneh's approach to translation[96] is well-known and we referred to it in chapter 2. He asserts that the universal element in the missionary enterprise is the translatability of the gospel—it can cross any boundary. In relation to translation in Africa, Sanneh is known for being positive about the "unintended consequences" of translation on the continent, one of which Jennings notes is "the formation of black agency and cultural being."[97] Hidden within the Bible, and the Christian faith that comes with it, are means to resist and even overcome the oppressor, as witnessed in the national Independence movements of the twentieth century.[98] Jennings, along with others, accuses Sanneh, however, of a universalizing tendency which overlooks how Bible translation missed other possibilities for translating "profane" African cultural artefacts (such as in the Malawian *Missio* banner discussed in chapter 2) and therefore introduces the sacred/secular divide into Africa where it did not exist before.[99] This is related to the universalizing supersessionism that Jennings discerned in Colenso and he also finds in Sanneh since he "theorizes a historical Christianizing process through the idea of a universal humanity that transcended Jewish particularity,"[100] which Sanneh traced back to a reading of St. Paul. I believe, however, that Sanneh is holding together the universal missionary nature of Godself active in history with the cultural and contextual particulars of the places where that work is witnessed; he has, in Jennings's words, "discerned in his historiographic imagination an animated theological essence that moves through time from one cultural situation to another."[101] While Sanneh makes no reference to the *missio Dei* in *Translating the Message,* Jennings would seem to have discerned it in his work in any case as this, "animated theological essence." Sanneh could therefore have, I suggest, perhaps unconsciously, intuited a sense of the *missio Dei* throughout his work.

It is at this point that I want to make a tentative interjection borne of my own experience working as a priest and "mission partner" (not evangelizing missionary *per se*) in Africa. I discerned what I have come to call an "African epistemology" with regard to how knowledge of the presence and activity of God was apprehended by the Tanzanian Christians

96. See Sanneh, *Translating.*

97. Jennings, *Christian Imagination,* 155.

98. See also Jennings, *Christian Imagination,* 157.

99. Jennings, *Christian Imagination,* 322, n116.

100. Jennings, *Christian Imagination,* 155.

101. Jennings, *Christian Imagination,* 157.

I was alongside for seven years, which certainly questioned, and in some cases broke down, many of my western, Modernist, liberal assumptions about the world and God's relationship to it.[102] My experience was that the Africans I lived and worked alongside carried God's missionary nature, the *missio Dei,* as we described it in chapter 1, as an assumption in their imaginations, since we are talking of Christian imagination with Jennings. It was something my colleagues lived in their daily experience, from their first prayer on waking, to the prospect of taking any journey by motorized vehicle, to giving thanks for God's leading, guiding, and safe arrival at the end of another day. They were so much more "porous" in their "social imaginaries" to God's presence in their world than my "buffered" western self, to use Charles Taylor's terminology.[103] In reflecting on my time in Tanzania, I recognize that. while I could have my imagination transformed by my contact with Africans, my own western theological formation constantly denies this reality. I wonder how difficult it is for anyone working in and from the west to fully grasp this reality, which is why I am sympathetic with Sanneh here, as an African working in a western academic paradigm looking for novel language (translatability) that describes the remarkable adoption of the Christian faith in so many particular African cultures, ethnicities and by extension, nations. Jennings is rather accusing Sanneh of not being sophisticated enough in his historical analysis (on western intellectual terms) when it comes to the development of the nationalisms that overtook the colonial project, "Modernity, and one of its signature realities, cultural nationalism . . . demand a slower, more studied reflection than Sanneh allows."[104] Maybe so, but I do not believe referencing a so-called African epistemology is here a retreat into simple piety, knocking down the discussion with appeal to God, or in fact a similar co-opting of an African reality into a colonial project as Colenso's work demonstrated. Neither, I hope, is it another form of essentializing the African, though I recognize that my tentative hypothesis rests on personal experience and not much else. Rather, I am suggesting that a porous African epistemology is radically open to God being at work despite our human limitations, or even the colonial project. Nevertheless, such an epistemology stands over and against me and yet I also recognize the danger of the appeal which may gloss over another of Jennings's criticisms that Sanneh "does not attend carefully to . . . the

102. Rooms, "God and My Whiteness," 137–47.

103. See Taylor, *Secular Age.*

104. Jennings, *Christian Imagination,* 157.

translating of native worlds into the old worlds of Europe."[105] This is a question that we shall return to in chapters 6 and 7 where we take data from how churches grow in Tanzania and translate it back to the west.

Jennings treats Walls's work slightly differently, equating translation with incarnation,[106] and he appreciates the indigenizing and pilgrim principles which we also referred to in the previous chapter. Again, he notes Walls's views on the place of Israel where the book of Acts demonstrates that the "movement out of Israel is the movement toward the universal"[107] and the place of language as the medium of that movement in cross-cultural communication. So, while Jennings values what Walls and Sanneh affirm he thinks they do not go far enough and he wants to peel away further layers of the act of translation such that he has a "deeper concern" with regard to "the translation of multiple worlds simultaneously."[108] He wishes to add the, "greater tragedies of frustration and confusion" caused by translation to their analysis.[109]

More seriously, as we have seen, Jennings accuses Sanneh and Walls of "a subtle form of supersessionism."[110] His argument is that any translation of Christian language such as in the Bible occurs "inside Israel's house," which is "a space where people are joined in worship and where ways of life come into the communion of the common, of eating, sleeping, and living together."[111] Thus, the problem can be stated:

> By drawing the incarnation so tightly inside translation they [Sanneh & Walls] eclipse a deeper historical movement with its concomitant theological scandal. Christians are, through Jesus Christ, brought into the story of Israel, which is indeed God's story. What is at stake is not simply particularity and certainly not the dialectic between the particular and the universal, but rather the scandal of particularity.[112]

Since this critique cuts across the hermeneutical comments we made on the particular-universal polarity (or dialectic) in chapter 2 it needs to

105. Jennings, *Christian Imagination,* 157.
106. Jennings, *Christian Imagination,* 158.
107. Jennings, *Christian Imagination,* 158.
108. Jennings, *Christian Imagination,* 159.
109. Jennings, *Christian Imagination,* 159.
110. Jennings, *Christian Imagination,* 159.
111. Jennings, *Christian Imagination,* 160.
112. Jennings, *Christian Imagination,* 160.

be addressed here. Jennings's focus becomes clear when he develops the implications of his stance:

> Israel's particularity bound up in Jesus means that his scandalous particularity is the means through which Christian faith acquires its social and political materiality. That social and political materiality draws our imaginations not first to the translation of the gospel message but to the joining of peoples in the struggle to learn each other's languages in the process of lives joined, lives lived together in new spaces, and constituting a new history for a new people.[113]

Jennings can therefore discern the heresy of docetism[114] here, since the universal translatability of the gospel in his view takes little account of the embodied and earthy implications of new Christians being joined to Christ.[115] Further, adoptionism[116] is also present which ignores or underplays, "a genuine historic entrance of the divine into space, time and body," thus missing "the way divine entrance is imagined among peoples" via "real presence and real relationship," all of which is therefore tragic.[117] In conclusion then:

> Unfortunately, the universal (bound up in docetism) and the contextual (bound up in adoptionism) are currently the dominant options for the contemporary theological imagination. They are two sides of the same coin, the one enabling the other, and neither finding its way to a Christian theology that of necessity creates intimacy.[118]

There is a parting of the ways to be found here, a fundamental difference between approaches and just as we noticed a limit to the research in question in this book in Goto's work above we have another limit here. The research has focused on the relationship between faith and culture, and what Jennings suggests is that this simply does not go far enough. While I wonder whether the work of Walls and Sanneh is as seriously flawed

113. Jennings, *Christian Imagination,* 160–61.

114. The denigration of Jesus' humanity as a kind of illusion, elevating therefore his (universal) divinity.

115. Jennings, *Christian Imagination,* 166.

116. A theological position which understands that Jesus was born only as a human, and it was at some later point that he was "adopted" by the Father as the divine Son of God.

117. Jennings, *Christian Imagination,* 167.

118. Jennings, *Christian Imagination,* 167.

as Jennings makes out (and also whether I am qualified as a missiologist and practical theologian to decide that), and how Jennings understands Christian *catholicity* in relation to the particularity of Israel, I recognize that the research we presented in *Fuzzy Church* did not foreground political and social issues first and foremost, though we brought some of these to bear when thinking of the "coloniality" the North of England suffers.[119] We will redress some of this lack of engagement in the next chapter. Perhaps we could understand this parting of the ways by reference to Bevans and Schroeder's typology of approaches to Christian mission.[120] It seems to me we are at the boundary or fault line here between "Type B" theology where we could largely place the work of Walls and Sanneh and the liberationist "Type C" theology where we can clearly position Jennings. Another example would be John Hull's approach to mission, which Goto also referenced. Hull has a very similar standpoint to Jennings, arguing as he does from a liberationist perspective.[121]

What then is this intimacy which Jennings is seeking as his response to the deficiencies of Walls and Sanneh? It seems it is a complex notion related to his use of the word "communion" and which is formed by overturning the supersessionist heresy. Jennings addresses his approach to supersessionism by reviewing the Jesus event and the beginning of the Church in the book of Acts in his chapter 6. His conclusion about the Jewish Jesus and what was happening through him is this:

> Rather than follow a historical construct that posits the Jesus movement as simply a reform movement in Judaism or follow a vernacularization thesis that isolates the gospel message into its essential components, which were then re-seeded in the cultural/ethnic matrices of various peoples, Roman, Hellenistic, and so forth, I suggest an advent of a new form of communion with the possibility of a new kind of cultural intimacy between peoples that might yield a new cultural politic.[122]

He suggests that as Cornelius, the Roman centurion, receives the Spirit in front of St. Peter there are new possibilities for countering hegemony, renewing Israel and overcoming violence by the introduction of "a new

119. Rooms and Wort, *Fuzzy Church*, 48–50.

120. Bevans and Schroeder, *Constants in Context*, 37. See the earlier discussion and footnote in chapter 2; the three Types are properly both differentiated and held together as valid approaches to Christian mission.

121. See Hull, *Towards the Prophetic*.

122. Jennings, *Christian Imagination*, 265.

reality of belonging that drew together different peoples into a way of life that intercepted ancient bonds and redrew them around the body of Jesus and in the power of the Spirit."[123] Thus Jennings believes this new possibility exists between the circumcisers' desire to make the Gentiles "fully" Jewish and an imagination where the two communities exist alongside one another in parallel without the one really "touching" or meeting the other in intimacy. A version of this is exhibited in Acts 15:28–29 where certain Torah cultural rules are recommended for the new converts. Thus, according to Jennings, the embryonic Church is unable to live out fully[124] the possibility of a truly "biracial humanity"[125] held out by the conversion of Cornelius and his family, which eventually leads to segregation. Essentially the Church has never lived up to its calling even from this early moment.[126]

Jennings then uses the Epistle to the Ephesians to outline his approach to this "new cultural politic" via an anti-supersessionist theology. It is the Gentiles who were "far off" and are now "brought near and incorporated into Israel"[127]—the two become one (although this is not at the expense of either, for they both find their full place in relation to Christ). If there is any kind of supersession (and it is hard to think of Christianity without some form of it[128]) it is found at this point.

> It is not the usurpation of the people of God, Israel replaced by the church, but of one form of the Torah drawn inside another, one form of divine word drawn inside another form–that is, the word made flesh . . . Just as Torah formed Israel's identity, establishing human life in the presence of God, so Jesus intends the formation of new humanity in his presence, listening to his speaking through the Spirit. This new biracial humanity, Jew and Gentile (metaphorically speaking), would be the basis for peace.[129]

123. Jennings, *Christian Imagination*, 269.

124. Jennings, *Christian Imagination*, 270–71.

125. Jennings, *Christian Imagination*, 272.

126. Jennings, *Christian Imagination*, 271.

127. Jennings, *Christian Imagination*, 272.

128. See Meyer, "Ineradicable Supersessionism." Indeed, Jennings's argument is predicated on Jesus being the promised Messiah from within Judaism, which implies an inevitable discontinuity or break with the majority of adherents of the Jewish faith who still await their Messiah.

129. Jennings, *Christian Imagination*, 272.

Supersessionism equates, in Sam Wells's approach, to the analogy of salvation history being like a "Five Act Play," to imagining oneself in the wrong act. The Acts are: Creation—Israel—Jesus—Church—End/Eschaton. In the current time we are properly in Act Four, the Church and we can see easily the mistake of thinking we are in Act Two, Israel, which is firmly now in the past. Such a misreading of our current state, Wells states, leads quickly to violence and the requirement for on-going sacrifice as if Jesus had not rendered this redundant, and Jennings would agree.[130] What the nature and shape of Act Four is like is what is up for grabs, once we have made this theological move.

This new space (cultural politic) created in Act Four is extremely vulnerable to "critique and ridicule," its announcement of new ways of being together in Christian kinship "cannot be verified," and the life of Jesus the Messiah is the "slender thread that holds Gentiles inside Israel as authentic not exclusive inheritors of its legacies."[131] There is real unease and discomfort here in the complexities of new citizenship.[132] It is, as we might say in the contemporary Church, a new intercultural reality that is being held out before us here, which is a much more fraught two-way street in contrast to when the traffic flows in only one direction.[133]

There are two ways in which Jennings's approach here might be critically appraised. The first leads to the second. Translation has its foundation in language and ideas and thus potentially leads to the abstraction of Jesus from the person who is the embodied promise of God. The Christ is available to the church by the presence of the Spirit (of that same Jesus) in the here and now of Wells's Act 4. Translation is therefore a necessary, but secondary task to the apprehension of the Christ, who is the promise, which is now and not yet. The "gospel" therefore is not static information about Jesus, the gospel is Jesus, dynamically enacted in every moment by the Spirit.[134] It is therefore always embodied and in some broad sense sacramental (as baptism and Eucharist would demonstrate). In the same way God is much more an active verb than a static noun if we adhere to the notion of the *missio Dei* as outlined in chapter 1. Perhaps a focus on the promise rather than the gospel might help us here, in the conditions of pluralism

130. Wells, *Improvisation*, 56.

131. Jennings, *Christian Imagination*, 272.

132. Jennings, *Christian Imagination*, 273.

133. For example, see Gittins, *Living Mission*.

134. Jennings, *Christian Imagination*, 270.

and postmodernity as Gregory Walter[135] notes. Walter draws on cultural anthropology and postmodern philosophy to examine the nature of gift which he suggestively relates to the biblical notion of promise, returning to the original promise to Abraham. There is a sense in which promise becomes a kind of universal which permeates Judeo-Christian history (it perhaps inhabits or even drives all five Acts of the play), but which does not suffer the supersessionist critique that we have been dealing with here in quite the same way since it is contiguous across Israel and the Church (if, as we noted above, one holds to Jesus as the Messiah). Walter is clear that the biblical promise is "double and extended gift"[136] which encompasses the several kinds of gift available to humanity, including some of their darker elements. The double nature of the promise as gift is the space between the initial offer and its fulfilment, "It [the promise] consists of four matters: the initial gift, the trust or distrust of the one promised, the field created by that trust and the extension of the gift between the pledge and its fulfilment, and the fulfilment itself."[137]

There are at least three implications of this which are fruitful in this discussion. First, time in the "field" between the pledge and its fulfilment (between Act 3 and Act 5) becomes God's time, and since all time is present to God, "God's promise has no closure or completion."[138] Thus, "promise permits the emergence of new time by granting possibility and therefore agency to those who trust in the promise."[139] We note the use of agency here which has a clear connection to Jennings's use of it. Liberation arises and the sacramental nature of all things emerges when all time (and space) is God's. Second, the Spirit who is given in the field of the promise (in Act 4) in order that, that same promise might be embodied in God's people is a weak power which is "a power that is open to the other, welcomes the new, and does not attempt to preserve the present in the face of the past or the future."[140] Here we note another connection with the theme of humility that has been emerging in this study and possibilities both of anti-racism and finding a future for churches after Christendom in late-modernity. Finally, embodiment here takes us to both the Eucharist as the place where Jesus is most fully present and the

135. See Walter, *Being Promised*.

136. Walter, *Being Promised*, 6.

137. Walter, *Being Promised*, 35.

138. Walter, *Being Promised*, 37.

139. Walter, *Being Promised*, 37.

140. Walter, *Being Promised*, 49.

embodied practices of *phronesis* and *poiesis* which complexify intimacy and communion within the *missio Dei* since God's presence by the Spirit is so often strange and a hidden mystery. Christian life in Act 4, as we are grafted into Israel and can sit now on the "front porch" as God's people, is characterized by the craft of "welcoming the stranger"—who is both God and the other.

What Jennings, therefore seems to be describing, in his call for intimacy (despite the limitations of that notion as we have understood it) is a vision for intercultural Christian community[141] which surely must be affirmed. As a practical theologian and missiologist, I am looking for the lived experience in the here and now that encapsulates and feeds back to theological stances and, apart from some suggestions about housing and where we choose to live,[142] Jennings's proposals for concurrency, communion, and intimacy are thin, while he does not apologize for the potentially idealistic nature of his analysis.[143] What concurrency and intimacy in the Church as part of Israel actually looks like today will have to be left to others it seems—I suggest Gittins's[144] and Kwiyani's[145] recent works are an excellent starting point as they are concrete ways to live out intercultural *phronesis* and *poiesis*.

I do want to affirm the theme emerging here, however. I think Jennings's imagination of Christian mission as the joining of the Gentiles into the new community of Christ the Messiah with all its inherent vulnerability is one of the ways we might find appropriate humility in mission in the west now the post-Christendom Church has lost the power she once had. And it is interesting to note that humility was how we concluded from Goto's critique of context earlier in this chapter. We do need alternative theology to reverse the colonial mindset so prevalent still in the Church today which says that we have something that those who are not "signed up" do not. We are indebted to Jennings for exposing the deep-rooted nature of this distorted imagination in the Christian faith.

141. In contrast to "multicultural." I prefer "intercultural" as "multicultural" is more like the two separate lanes on a highway than the genuine possibilities for intercultural intimacy that a "two-way street" affords.

142. Jennings, *Christian Imagination*, 287.

143. Jennings, *Christian Imagination*, 288.

144. See Gittins, *Living Mission Interculturally*.

145. See Kwiyani, *Multicultural Kingdom*.

THE GOSPEL IN THE WESTERN CONTEXT—GERT-JAN ROEST

For our third conversation partner in the etic critique of contextual theology we turn to Gert-Jan Roest, a Dutch Reformed theologian (and practitioner) from the Netherlands. His book, *The Gospel in the Western Context: A missiological reading of Christology in dialogue with Hendrikus Berkhof and Colin Gunton* is a development of his PhD thesis. We place it in the "etic" category as it is an avowed work of, and engagement with, systematic theology in the Reformed tradition, while the author describes himself as a church planter and pastor[146] in Amsterdam and the book references missiology in the title. The book appears in a series entitled "Studies in Reformed Theology," published by Brill, and not in a series dedicated to missiology. There are several reasons for engaging with this work. It addresses the "Western context" which is related in many ways to the context of study in this book. It engages with gospel and context (or faith and culture) and so is thoroughly connected to our contextualization project. Finally in the book as a whole and in this specific chapter it is hoped that dialogue with an approach to contextualization from systematic theology may offer fresh insight. Roest's research question arises in the highly secularized environment which is the author's location: "How can I re-tell the story about Jesus in such a way that people in this city [Amsterdam] will rejoice in what God has done? How does one go about contextualizing the gospel [in this context]?"[147] The initial question is therefore definitely related to our own, but the method of answering it is quite different, and might therefore be instructive.

Roest turns almost immediately from the particularity of his residence and ministry in Amsterdam to the universalized "Western Context," characterized by a post-Christendom reality for the church, a complex postmodernity in society and the post-Christian nature of people in the street.[148] The work addresses this "reality" from systematic theology, and in particular the theology of one Dutch and one English Reformed theologian, Berkhof and Gunton respectively, while noting that they also both have an ecumenical orientation.[149] They are chosen because they are modern systematic theologians who "have consciously

146. Roest, *Gospel*, 1.

147. Roest, *Gospel*, 4.

148. Roest, *Gospel*, 12–14.

149. Roest, *Gospel*, 20.

related to the Western context, and they live or have lived within the Western context."[150] Berkhof, Roest claims, was much more influenced by liberation theology which drew him away from "a traditional orthodox position" whereas Gunton remained "firmly within the Chalcedonian parameters."[151] Here we could subject this approach to the critique of Goto; a white male interrogates two other white males on the universal nature of the "dominant culture" in the west in a deliberate move which diminishes "diversity in the Western context."[152] This approach is, at the very least, open to Goto's critique of the idolatry of context, since the polyvalency of the symbol is being treated largely as one thing. Nevertheless, the study is performed by a church-based theologian utilizing "dogmatics and theological hermeneutics" from within the discipline of systematic theology[153] and it is this aspect of the work which we trust will bring an etic critique to questions of faith, gospel, and culture.

It is to Christology, understood as both the person and the work of Christ,[154] that Roest turns immediately within systematic theology to address his subject which is the obvious and natural move, one which we made ourselves in our research and was affirmed above in this chapter. In a further articulation of the research question he asks, "What are the contours of a contextualized gospel for the Western world at the beginning of the 21st century?"[155] and he expects a reading of the western context (starting from the work of the two chosen theologians) and Christology to provide the answers via a contextualizing of Christology. Thus, the work as a whole, attempts to "bring questions that have arisen on the mission-field back to Western systematic theology,"[156] that is, questions of contextualization or inculturation. Berkhof and Gunton are also employed because they are two systematic theologians who have taken their location in the western world seriously as a source and "discussion partner" in contrast to others who rather ignore it.[157]

150. Roest, *Gospel*, 19.

151. Roest, *Gospel*, 21. Whether there are such limits (and where they might be) to "orthodoxy" is a moot point. We refer readers once again to Bevans's and Schroeder's three types of theology.

152. Roest, *Gospel*, 15.

153. Roest, *Gospel*, 16.

154. Roest, *Gospel*, 17.

155. Roest, *Gospel*, 21.

156. Roest, *Gospel*, 23.

157. Roest, *Gospel*, 23.

One realizes immediately a limitation of Roest's study in our missiological and practical theology terms in that it does not complete a full cycle of the hermeneutical circle (we could note a similar critique of Jennings's work too, in a different kind of book). Yes, the research begins with experience in secularized Amsterdam and takes this to a highly sophisticated theological reflection, but there is no field testing in further action of the "contextualized gospel" that is created through the study.[158] Nevertheless, there is surely something to learn here about the theology of contextual theology. What is being attempted in Roest's study is a systematic theology of contextual theology rather than contextual theology itself, which is conducted in ongoing process by *praxis* (action and reflection) in the field. Roest's is a view from 30,000 feet, as it were, rather than from the "balcony" (over the "dance floor" where the action is taking place).

Context is defined from Hoedemaker as "a junction of religious, cultural and social histories which becomes the soil for a deliberate believing stance of Christians, from which inherited and more or less taken for granted ways of thinking are fundamentally criticized."[159] This is a definition of context, we note from within the Christian community, rather than separate from it, something which Roest returns to from time to time noting with Berkhof that the church is always embedded within its society and culture and influenced by it.[160] On the other hand, not allowing the context to be defined on its own terms could be problematic. This definition also imagines the context as "soil" into which the gospel/church is inserted as seed (Roest uses this metaphor extensively later in the book and I have long had critical disagreement with it). In Goto's categories this is context as *social milieu* and, given the definition and method employed by Roest, he utilizes a largely "critical objective" approach to context, in Goto's terms. There is good evidence for this throughout the study where the universal, high-level aspects of the culture/context of the west are delineated. It is not that Roest is unaware of a wide range of particularities in the west, just that he is prepared to bypass them for the

158. It is reassuring to note that Roest developed his work beyond the extant study with further publications in his native Dutch. See his publication website: Bookfish, "Boeken van Gert-Jan Roest."

159. Roest, *Gospel* (in translation), 8, 298.

160. For example, Roest, *Gospel*, 126.

sake of focusing on the "dominant culture."[161] In this way he rather elides context and culture.

It is worth describing, in summary, Roest's method. In turn, in Parts 1 and 2 of the book, both Berkhof and Gunton's *corpus* are read in relation to two questions: their method and content of "reading the Western context," and the method and content of their Christology. These four categories are then evaluated (in a rather positive/negative binary fashion) by the researcher before bringing that evaluation to Part 3. In the final section of the book the importance of the gospel is reiterated and described in relation to a modified method and content for reading the western context, drawn from but not exclusively dependent on, Berkhof and Gunton, utilizing other interlocutors.

What do we learn, in brief summary, from Berkhof and Gunton? Berkhof, "engages the Western context from a down-to-earth anthropocentric-historic angle"[162] which for this reader resonates with Bevans's anthropological model of contextual theology.[163] He takes the human condition seriously via discerning the "sense of life" in people and society and relates that to the human Jesus. Gunton has a more critical take on the west, especially since the Enlightenment introduced new forms of idolatry (that is, the replacement of God[164]). His Christology, as is well-known, is fully Trinitarian and he develops an important understanding of "relational ontology."[165] Perhaps his is a more synthetic model of contextual theology, with elements of the countercultural (in Bevans's terms).

Roest's research question remains after his interaction with Berkhof and Gunton around "What are the contours of a contextualized gospel for the Western world at the beginning of the 21st century?"[166] He finds both theologians wanting on this question, with Berkhof over-emphasizing context at the expense of the gospel, whereas Gunton, while placing the gospel at the centre of both the content and method of theology, "stays so much in the intellectual realm that the 'sense of life' [from Berkhof] and the pain and suffering in the context remain at a distance."[167] The project for the third part of the book is precisely a theological interrogation

161. Roest, *Gospel,* 15.
162. Roest, *Gospel,* 262.
163. See Bevans, *Models,* chapter 5.
164. Roest, *Gospel,* 239.
165. Roest, *Gospel,* 194.
166. Roest, *Gospel,* 262.
167. Roest, *Gospel,* 263.

of the relationship between "gospel and context." I think this is possibly where a significant contribution of Roest's work lies and I will attempt to outline his approach here.

The question of the relationship between gospel and context/culture is at the heart of the task of inculturation or contextualization. Thus far in my journey with this question I have relied on Andrew Walls, Kwame Bediako, and Lamin Sanneh (notwithstanding Jennings's observations on Walls's and Sanneh's work rehearsed earlier in this chapter).[168] We are clear that there is no isolatable or supra-cultural "core" of the gospel, as in the outdated idea of the "kernel and the husk" (hinted at above with the related metaphor of the seed inserted into soil). Roest agrees,[169] drawing on Walls, without being aware, seemingly of Bediako and Sanneh and the concept of translatability, as the commonality that allows the gospel to travel (or, indeed, Jennings's critique of their approach). Nevertheless, Roest adds some theological depth to this position with regard to the *mystery* which is the ultimately unknowable presence of Christ,[170] the importance of the Spirit joining the Son as the "two hands of God" (following Gunton and before him Irenaeus) and "eschatological reserve" since, following Hoedemaker, "only when all cultures have processed and contributed their reception of the gospel, will the essence of the gospel become clear."[171] I am grateful to Roest for these insights.

If there is no isolatable kernel of the gospel, the question remains what unity is there in the many gospels that arise out of many cultures? There are several answers to this question and Roest synthesizes them usefully. I have usually quoted Walls's classic essay where he states that the continuity we observe through Christian history is "continuity of thought about the final significance of Jesus, continuity of a certain consciousness about history, continuity in the use of the Scriptures, of bread and wine, of water."[172]

Then I have stayed with Bediako and Sanneh's notion of the translatability of the gospel, though clearly Jennings has questioned even this in relation to the scandal of particularity, and we need to take his critique seriously. It is worth noting that Bevans and Schroeder's six *constants* in their

168. Rooms, *Faith*, 4–14.

169. Roest, *Gospel*, 274.

170. Roest, *Gospel*, 268.

171. Roest, *Gospel*, 271.

172. Walls, "Gospel as Prisoner," 21.

classic missiological text, that we have referred to several times[173] mirror and expand somewhat Walls's proposals for a continuity here: Christology, ecclesiology, eschatology, soteriology, anthropology, and culture.

Roest's argument proceeds as follows: beginning with Walls's corpus where he discerns four "points of coherence" within the gospel;[174] worship of the God of Israel; the ultimate significance of Jesus Christ; God is active where believers are;[175] believers constitute a people of God transcending time and place. These might be equivalent in some ways to the six constants of Bevans and Schroeder; ecclesiology in the church incorporated into Israel (cf. Jennings), plus being the people of God; Christology, soteriology, and eschatology in the ultimate significance of Christ and the transcendence of time and place; anthropology and culture in "where believers are."

Roest then turns to compare this analysis with the work of Ted Campbell,[176] who investigated shared understandings of the gospel across Christian history and the wide range of denominations in that history. In a suggestive (though seemingly academically unconnected) comparison with Walls's schema, Campbell offers three "clusters of interrelated meanings"[177]—the basic narrative of Jesus' life, death, and resurrection (which can be told in a myriad of different contextual forms); how God brings about human salvation through Jesus; and the importance of all this being "according to the (Hebrew) scriptures."

For Roest, these three clusters become, in an interesting metaphorical move, the "common DNA of the gospel that is proclaimed in many different contexts," which could perhaps be compared to Sanneh's concept of translatability. They are then further summarized by Roest as the "the gospel-narrative, the gospel-frame and the gospel-salvation" and are pictured diagrammatically with all three clusters centred on "the mystery of Jesus Christ in our midst"[178]—a reference back to his conclusion from Gunton. I believe this central element of mystery could be fruitfully compared with the *missio Dei,* as outlined in chapter 1, if it were placed in a Trinitarian frame which encompassed all of creation. For me, the "our" in

173. Bevans and Schroeder, *Constants in Context,* 33.

174. Roest, *Gospel,* 276–77.

175. It is unclear whether Roest, as a Reformed, confessional theologian can envisage God being where believers are not.

176. See Campbell, *Gospel in Christian Traditions.*

177. Roest, *Gospel,* 279.

178. Roest, *Gospel,* 285.

"the mystery of Jesus Christ in our midst" needs to be taken further. The "our" is all people, believers or not, the "world" in biblical terms. Christ, by the Spirit is present and active before any engagement with the gospel.

Roest then develops a "gospel-centred model for reading the context"[179] via further interaction with "Third World"[180] theologians and theologians from the *Gospel and our Culture* network that arose in the 1990s, mainly in the USA, to continue the work of Lesslie Newbigin in the west. In a diagram[181] Roest attempts to show how a contextual gospel can arise by asking three questions and making three moves that correspond to his three clusters of meaning in the gospel. The questions are:

- What is the worship and meta-narrative in this context?
- What kind of salvation is needed and visible in this context?
- What life-style is visible in this context?

The corresponding moves are:

- Interact with the context in light of worshipping Israel's god, the Creator of the world, and responding to his gracious claim (gospel-narrative).
- Interact with the context in the light of the promising news about the new creation (gospel-salvation).
- Interact with the context in light of a cruciform spirituality (as seen in Jesus) (gospel-frame).

At this point I believe we reach the limit of Roest's study for the current research for several reasons. First the context is being read solely through the gospel and therefore (in Roest's method) the church which rather eliminates the agency of the context (*contra* Jennings again). The movement here is mostly one-way and ignores the need for listening and dialogue (unlike Goto's intersubjectivity). In addition, the proposals become somewhat all-encompassing[182] and subject to the critique that if mission is everything then it might also be nothing.[183] I don't believe Roest's approach to how God is present and active in the world largely

179. Roest, *Gospel*, 314.

180. His nomenclature taken as self-disclosure from some time past.

181. Roest, *Gospel*, 315.

182. Roest, *Gospel*, 316–21.

183. Bosch, *Transforming Mission*, 511.

or wholly through the Church is adequate in the light of a participative understanding of the *missio Dei*. Roest states, "The church has, therefore, to discern the context in the light of the *missio Dei*. By regularly reading the Scriptures, the church can discern and respond to God's future breaking into the present."[184] But where, in addition to the Scriptures, is the listening to the experience of individual people as well as society and culture as a whole *on their own terms*—since all the creation participates in God's (missionary) being? Yes, there are some helpful proposals in what Roest describes as emerging from such a task, such as being anti-imperialist, prophetic, and using imagination and the arts. Yet overall, I realize in reading Roest that because of how I understand the *missio Dei*, I am more committed to the anthropological model of contextual theology than perhaps I had previously thought, even if some aspects of the countercultural will need to be engaged with eventually.

A further critique of this work is with regard to the next move Roest makes: he turns to a Christian philosopher of the west who he thinks can do the heavy lifting of reading the context for him, namely Charles Taylor. I like Taylor's work and think it contains much wisdom for us, but to rely wholly on it, as Roest does here, is problematical for me as we shall see. His reasons for doing so are that Taylor's work is discussed by philosophers and theologians[185] (which no doubt it is), but this doesn't mean that it can bear the weight of what is being asked of it here.

What happens next is that four "options" drawn from Taylor's understanding of the west now being in the "Age of Authenticity" are used to describe the "Western context."[186] They are: Christian faith; exclusive humanism; new and alternative spiritualities; and anti-humanism under the inspiration of Nietzsche. There is a footnote which states that Islam in Europe is also a "force to be reckoned with,"[187] but no reference is made to other world faiths that are very present across the west. There are many ways to understand western society beyond these four, mostly philosophical categories. For instance, the Sinus group in Germany identifies at least ten categories or sociological "milieus" in western countries on a sophisticated grid between social class and a position on the spectrum

184. Roest, *Gospel*, 295.

185. Roest, *Gospel*, 332.

186. Roest, *Gospel*, 335.

187. Roest, *Gospel*, 335, n.16. It is unclear therefore whether Roest understands Islam as a threat or a potential partner in a religious approach to society.

of tradition/modernization/reorientation.[188] The Australian longitudinal Church Life Survey[189] identifies a significantly large group of people in Australia (also a highly secularized nation) who are not people of faith, but neither are they in any other of Taylor and Roest's categories. They are in fact quite open to questions of faith, while not actively exploring "alternative spiritualities."

Clearly some people do exist in these four high-level categories, yet for me they oversimplify and essentialize the west while at same time seem to lead Roest to treat the prevailing context largely as a threat.[190] There is a great deal of Walls's pilgrim principle here and very little of the indigenizing which receives only brief attention.[191] Thus, Roest's conclusion to his research question, the "contours of a Western gospel" addresses these four categories with the three elements of the gospel narrative, salvation, and frame leaving the reader with equivalent high-level proposals including a long confessional statement aimed at the group of spiritual seekers.

At the end of this interaction with Roest, his work has proved to be largely a foil to addressing contextualization, contrary to the hopes I had when setting out and choosing to study his work. I should not be so surprised, perhaps, that an approach to contextual theology from systematic theology and which is interdisciplinary with essentially only philosophy is inadequate for our purposes. Some resonances have been discerned between mine and Roest's approaches, but we separate over the breadth of the *missio Dei*. There has been a confirmation and theological thickening of understanding about a *mystery* at the heart of the *missio Dei* and what is continuous in the diversity of the gospel. In addition, we have discovered how the gospel and culture question can only be resolved at the end of time and gained some insight into the bigger questions of the secular age in the west. While there remains a residual feeling at the end that God's world is much bigger than the Church may currently imagine.

188. See Sinus, "What Are Sinus-Milieus®?"

189. See https://www.ncls.org.au/.

190. I do not know, but I do wonder if this perceived threat is another effect of the breaking of Christendom, where it is simply hard to accept that the church in the west will have a much smaller space in society than it once did.

191. Roest, *Gospel*, 358.

IN CONCLUSION

Our three interlocutors in this chapter have given us much to think critically about in this project. They have thickened considerably our understanding of the possibility of a postcolonial contextual theology for the North of England. They have further warned us against essentialism and nativism, treating context and culture in reductionist and universalizing ways. Context is a complex symbol rooted in the particular. Culture and cultural change with the gospel are not linear, but messy and fuzzy especially at the boundaries or in other words; diverse, dynamic, hybrid, multiple and fluid. Nevertheless, the God of mission is at work through the Spirit who is able to operate among us despite our human essentializing tendencies. The gospel is embodied in the mystery that is Jesus Christ, rather than a set of ideas or hegemonic power plays. All of which leads us to the place of humility and "eschatological reserve" in relation to the promises of God begun in the particularity of Israel and extending to the whole earth. On the way the importance of land, place, and Christian agency are affirmed; all of these have been found to be fundamental in this research. We turn then to the land, the people and the culture of the North of England in the next chapter.

4

Contextual Theology, Essentialism, and Northern Cultural Capital

BUILDING ON THE WORK we did on the North in *Fuzzy Church* this chapter addresses the questions raised by our critique of contextual theology in chapters 2 and 3 of this book in relation to the specific instance of the North of England. We make particular reference to avoiding essentialism in contextual theology and defend our approach in *Fuzzy Church* to mining for the *Gehalt* of the North, or in other words what constitutes "northern cultural capital."

This book is the culmination of a long-standing project in contextual theology. I began with doctoral research exploring the question of inculturation in England which resulted in *The Faith of the English* in which I noted, in one particular chapter, how the English myth of Robin Hood both encapsulated English culture and negotiated the liminal space between the North and South of England where I was living at the time, in Nottinghamshire.[1] Having been born and raised in the North, in East Yorkshire this generated a curiosity about the lack of theological reflection on my home region in theological literature. A number of people from across the North gathered and collaborated together to produce an initial collection of essays on the theme of *Northern, Gospel, Northern Church* in which I wrote a chapter arguing for a "bias to the North" on a similar basis to the call from liberation theologians for a "bias to the

1. See Rooms, *Faith,* chapter 4, 73–92.

poor."[2] This proved to be a further impetus to the current research project which resulted in the book *Fuzzy Church*, the precursor volume to this one. This current chapter needs to be written at this point for this book, but it is not starting off with a blank sheet of paper. I do not wish to be accused of self-plagiarism, but assuming that some readers are coming to this book without being familiar with these previous publications, I do need to rehearse some of their arguments here.[3] Hopefully I will also be able to deepen and broaden them by placing the material in dialogue with what we have discovered about contextual theology in chapters 2 and 3 as well as fresh literature on the North which I have not interacted with before, namely Alex Niven's *The North Will Rise Again*. I therefore hope to make a further original contribution to a contextual theology of the North of England by weaving together some older and newer threads.

THE PLACE, THE LAND, THE GEOGRAPHY—AND ITS CULTURE

We remarked in the previous chapter that Willie James Jennings noted the importance of land and agency for the subjects of contextual theology. This is where we begin, with defining the physical boundaries of the North, which we covered in *Fuzzy Church*.

It is worth noting that physical geology and geography plays its part in the creation of the North. As Russell[4] points out, the vast majority of land over 2,000 feet in England is found from Derbyshire northwards. The Northern, Eastern, and Western borders of the North are fairly simple to note given the Scottish border and extensive coastlines. More problematic is where the Southern boundary lies. Overall, the nature of the land in the South and East of England and its associated weather patterns make it suitable for certain types of agricultural land use and settlement which are different from those to the North and West. Rivers too make significant barriers, at least in historical perspective. In my own view the River Trent is an important marker of the N–S divide, though others work with the Mersey–Humber axis. For example, Russell distinguishes

2. Wakefield and Rooms, *Northern Gospel*, chapter 2, 35–50.

3. Thus, I will be transparent in this chapter and quote (sometimes extensively) from previous material where it forms a starting point of departure for the argument. I will occasionally edit or adjust the quotations lightly for use in this book.

4. Russell, *Looking North*, 22.

between the "far" and the "near" North and plumps for "seven counties" roughly north of the Humber–Mersey line.[5]

In the book *Northern Gospel*, we quoted human geography demographics from Danny Dorling and others which clearly show a sociological North–South divide in England along many categories (e.g. birth rates, education, poverty, health, life expectancy, etc.).[6] While ten years have passed we know that those have been years of Government-led austerity which have only exacerbated the divide despite initiatives around the "Northern Powerhouse" and "Levelling up" of which more later. Dorling claims that the demographic divide runs along a line between the Bristol Channel and the Wash and I pointed out[7] that this is virtually contiguous with the Roman road, the Fosse Way which still runs (in large parts) in a straight line from Exeter to Lincoln (and which therefore places Cornwall, at least notionally, in the North). Thus, the physical and human geography of England are deeply intertwined with its history right back to the first Roman invasion. Apparently, the Fosse Way acted as an early boundary for the Romans against the North, just as the much stronger Hadrian's Wall did later against the Picts and the Scots, much further North.

On the question of the boundaries of the North, Niven, interestingly, agrees with my earlier conclusions:

> For the purposes of this book, I have assumed that the English North begins on the Scottish border and ends somewhere in the northern Midlands. This is broadly in line with the old medieval idea that when you venture into "England North of the Trent"–that is past the river which circles the southern tip of the Pennines–you are entering another land entirely to the more settled, more recognizably English parishes of the London-centric South.[8]

Yet there remains a complexity here about the North. In the earlier phases of this project, I found myself running workshops on the North-South question in the Church, and as I noted in *Northern Gospel*, this often resulted in objections to defining the North—and even its existence at all—from the workshop members:

5. See his map, Russell, *Looking North*, xii.
6. Wakefield and Rooms, *Northern Gospel*, 3–10.
7. Wakefield and Rooms, *Northern Gospel*, 40.
8. Niven, *North Will*, xv.

- the North can't be defined as it is relative—for example Sheffield is in the South if you are a Geordie [from Newcastle]
- there are massive regional and local variations in the North so you can't lump it all together in one
- in any case there is poverty and deprivation in the South too so why are we just focusing on the North?
- while we are at it there are plenty of places that are well off and more 'Southern' while being in the North–just think of Harrogate!
- or is it just an English class thing and much less to do with the geographical North?[9]

There is no doubt that there are huge internal and micro-regional differences, rivalries, and even perhaps hatreds across the North. Niven's approach to this actuality is instructive. As a native of the North-East (he was born and brought up in the rural hinterland of Newcastle) he locates his narrative there while backing the argument up with stories from across the region. He argues that "the North will only ever get to where it needs to be by embracing concrete forms of pan-regional community."[10]

We will follow this line of thinking consistently in the book, treating the North as an entity, a given reality which is rooted in history and physical geography, but is not limited to those categories. The next step is to realize that the region creates what we came to call Northernness out of its people and its culture. The notion of Northernness emerged from some steps I first made in *Northern Gospel* following the broadcaster, writer, and cultural commentator Stuart Maconie. After the conversations about the existence of the North noted above had settled down:

> what emerges [from those conversations on the existence of the North] is something that we might call a "consciousness" of the North which contains all sorts of elements including geography but ranging much more widely into attitudes, values and culture. A possibility might even emerge of understanding the North as a verb rather than a noun such that it is about a dynamic formation in the Northerner rather than some static geographical notion.

There is fluidity and dynamism in the idea of the North which is not restricted to a specific place. Maconie agrees in his conclusion:

9. Wakefield and Rooms, *Northern Gospel*, 41.
10. Niven, *North Will*, xv.

> I'm not sure that northernness is geographical. It's philosophical . . . northernness is a cast of mind, not a set of co-ordinates . . . It's about realising that the best place to drive a Range Rover is Cumbria not Islington. It's about embracing that life is short and work is hard and that London is not the answer to everything.[11]

We therefore come to a dynamic cultural understanding of the 'North' which is geographically based, created through beliefs, attitudes, and values and expressed in a myriad of ways.[12]

Thus, the context of the North as the starting point for a contextual theology is here defined, in Goto's terms (see chapter 3), as *social milieu* and *locus of concern*. It includes both a "cast of mind," an imagination, and a particular marginalized geography. And to this we add a fluid, dynamic definition of culture (see chapter 2), knowing now that context and culture are related but different, and culture is made up of ever-shifting beliefs, attitudes, values, behaviors, and lived experience. In this work I take it as a given that culture includes cultural expression through music, literature, and the arts, but is not reducible to these things. This, however, is where Niven largely concentrates his energies when referring to culture (alongside the politics of the region), as we shall return to later.

We have noted the rather blurred southern boundary to the geographical North and I noted how important this is in both *Northern Gospel* and *Fuzzy Church* in forming the culture of the North. This is because social anthropologists demonstrate that culture is formed at its boundary[13] and that much of what is said and written about northern culture is either from the South or developed in relation to the South (see particularly the table from Russell[14] reproduced in part in *Fuzzy Church*).[15]

Having reviewed the land and place of the North and started a discussion of context and culture we are ready to dive deeper into the critical questions that are raised when discussing the culture of the people of a region such as the North.

11. Maconie, *Pies and Prejudice*, 337.
12. Wakefield and Rooms, *Northern Gospel*, 42.
13. Wakefield and Rooms, *Northern Gospel*, 42.
14. Russell, *Looking North*, 37.
15. Rooms and Wort, *Fuzzy Church*, 41.

NORTHERN CULTURE—ESSENTIALISM, NATIVISM, AND THE POSSIBILITY OF *GEHALT*

Let us begin in our description of Northernness with a list of ten characteristics Russell outlines as "Northern self-identity" as noted above:

- Independent
- Blunt/straight talking
- Hardworking/physically tough
- Competitive
- Practical/productive
- Careful with money
- Friendly/Hospitable
- Proud of roots and identity
- Meritocratic/egalitarian
- Humorous/witty[16]

In *Fuzzy Church* we discussed these characteristics in relation to data from our research.[17] We added honesty to blunt/straight-talking and thought "being authentic" was also present in our research subjects' values. We noted evidence for the strength of roots and identity, friendliness and hospitality among them and its extension even into the formation of community.

Yet we also had to deal with the accusation from scholars such as Karl Spracklen that there is no escape from essentializing northern culture in this enterprise of Russell in outlining northern self-identity[18] because such a task reifies or unhelpfully sets in stone the North's own

16. Russell, *Looking North*, 37. While this list might look like an overall positive set of attributes (even generic), they are placed over against both how the South sees them and how the North views the South in Russell's book. Many have real negative connotations in English culture as a whole. Three examples, which are important for how they will develop in this chapter are: "blunt / straight talking" is seen as "rude / lacking in social graces" from a southern perspective and southerners are perceived for the North as "evasive / duplicitous"; "proud of roots and identity" easily becomes "parochial" and southerners are perceived to be "cosmopolitan / rootless"; being "humorous / witty" is thought of as "crude" humor in the South whereas Northerners think of their compatriots as "quick-witted but overly fond of *double-entendre*."

17. Rooms and Wort, *Fuzzy Church*, 42.

18. Rooms and Wort, *Fuzzy Church*, 44.

view of itself when, he, Spracklen, believes this has been constructed by the more powerful southern voice.

> There is a hegemonic performativity imposed on the north by people with cultural power in the south of England, people who control policy-making, industries and popular culture . . . The hegemonic centre contrives culture to keep the north of England as dark as colonial depictions of Africa, a dangerous and savage place filled with post-industrial victims.[19]

Therefore, Spracklen claims that Northernness is essentially a "made up" thing constructed from "various myths and invented traditions"—it is a *simulacrum,* something which has no origin or truth behind it at all. Following the postmodern sociologist and thinker Baudrillard he states, "The north has no essential existence in this framework because all we can ever know and share are the myths and narratives that allow us to construct and reproduce the simulacrum."[20]

We then noted how Spracklen has to account for the reality of Northernness, even in his own experience while still believing that it has no real substance, it is a simulacrum. For this he employs[21]

> magic and superstition [closely allied in his mind to religion and a form of Paganism]:
> Northernness is a form of sympathetic magic, which Northerners choose to perform, albeit through the constraints of hegemonic cultural formations and the symbolic boundaries and invented traditions of imagined community.[22]

And he makes therefore this, in our view, rather sad conclusion, since it cannot result in any transformative action:

> But we have no choice. We know we must continue to perform because without the performance of northernness, the north of England, the simulation and the imagined community, will collapse. Our northernness is our equivalent of the pagan cycle of the seasons. If we do not perform the rituals of the north, the sun will not rise tomorrow. So we go about our daily business of being northern.[23]

19. Spracklen, "Theorising Northernness," 13.
20. Spracklen, "Theorising Northernness," 10.
21. Rooms and Wort, *Fuzzy Church,* 44.
22. Spracklen, "Theorising Northernness," 14.
23. Spracklen, "Theorising Northernness," 14.

Suggestively, Alex Niven's review of the political and cultural (in the sense of the creative arts) history of the later twentieth century in the North is summarized in his own words as "Ruin and Revival," which is the title of the third part of his book.[24] He also notes a cycle between moments of real creativity and flourishing in the North through modernist and futurist movements in the 1960s and 1970s and urban renewal in cities only to see them fall into ruin and die very soon after their inception. He concludes:

> As we have seen already, northern history is defined by a sort of endless back and forth: between surging, energetic bursts forward into a future way in advance of the conservative norms of English culture . . . and equally drastic recoilings into a radically bleak psychic and actual landscape . . . And so the blend of victimhood and hopeless dreaming is compounded in a seemingly endless and inescapable cycle.[25]

Perhaps we were too quick in *Fuzzy Church* to dismiss this cycle of "boom and bust," this performance of the "pagan cycle of the seasons" in the cultural life and history of the North and we need to lean into the dread darkness and difficulty it represents a little more. Maybe it is another form of essentialism to gloss over, in naivety and sentimentalism even, such deep challenges to real long-lasting change and the possibility of a future in the North. Niven is nothing but realistic throughout his book, yet on the penultimate page[26] he admits to being a practicing Catholic as well as a committed socialist. There has been very little hint of this faith position up to this point, but it does help to explain his additional commitment to a future for the North, stating that "some form of prodigal hopefulness—or at least vaulting ambition—is quite simply the only way to go."[27]

It is this faith position that also led us to disagree with Spracklen in *Fuzzy Church*. Even if we did move too swiftly towards it, we argued strongly for a position between "the essentialist and the evacuated simulacrum,"[28] using the PhD research of Kate Fox[29] to bridge that gap.

24. Niven, *North Will*, 171.
25. Niven, *North Will*, 282.
26. Niven, *North Will*, 288.
27. Niven, *North Will*, 288.
28. Rooms and Wort, *Fuzzy Church*, 45.
29. See Fox, *Stand Up*.

Fox researched her own profession (that of northern feminist stand-up comic and poet—a "performance artist" in her own words). In her research she develops the notion of the "Northernness effect" which we described thus, in relation to the other interlocutors we have been working with:

> Certainly, Fox agrees, from solid evidence in her in-depth research interviews with Northern performance artists, with both Russell and Spracklen with regard to how, what she terms the "Northernness effect" is created via: ". . . a classed and gendered cultural imperialism by which the [Northern] region is stigmatised and Othered in relation to the more socially and economically powerful South of England.[30]"[31]

Fox, by digging deeper into the research interviews, developed the concept of "northern capital" as a form of cultural capital which is defined as the ability to inspire and be inspired. She was then able to name the content of that capital as the values of "authenticity, community, humour and lack of pretension." We then noted:

> It seems that Fox is onto something here beyond essentialism (while remaining critical of it[32]) by noting the values embedded in northern capital. They are clearly connected with Russell's list but somehow lie deeper within the experience and meaning of Northernness.[33]

Fox's delineation of Northernness along these four values allows her (and us in our reading of her) to do several things. The first is to find the strength for holding together both *affirmation* and *resistance* in herself as a performance artist and here we can connect with chapter 2 again around the classic work of Andrew Walls and which we also noted in *Fuzzy Church*:

> Thus, we might discern here a need, which I uncovered some years ago when first studying the relationship between faith and culture for what we could call a creative relationship in the tension between "affirmation and resistance." These are the two words we noted above that Kate Fox uses[34] for her response

30. Fox, *Stand Up*, 55.

31. Rooms and Wort, *Fuzzy Church*, 45.

32. Fox, *Stand Up*, 58–59.

33. Rooms and Wort, *Fuzzy Church*, 45.

34. Fox, *Stand Up*, 109.

> to the intersectional experience of subjugation as a northern, working class woman, but they correlate closely, I would suggest with Andrew Walls's indigenising and pilgrim principles.[35]

We might also suggest that the tension between the indigenizing and pilgrim principles is not unlike the difference between the anthropological and countercultural models of contextual theology from Bevans. Certainly, there are many things (even many evil, perhaps sinful, things) that must be resisted within and with-out the North itself, particularly when it turns against itself, as we noted from Niven. To return to our participatory understanding of creation from chapter 1, evil exists when some aspect of being is not true to itself, which is why, for example, essentialism, as a failure to see the full truth of a people, place or culture, must be resisted.

Second, and developing this theme, the double-edged nature of northern capital (or culture), understood in this frame, allows the unmasking of nativism (which we referred to in chapter 3), which can actually be resisted. We gave an example of this in *Fuzzy Church* based on the popularizing of the northern sport of Rugby League on television in the UK in the 1960s and 70s.[36] Fox offered two good further examples of resistance which we wrote about in *Fuzzy Church*:[37]

> Fox suggests that if we consciously and authentically "come out" as northern, that allows the possibility of "re-signifying" the labels that are thrust upon us from the outside[38] thus changing the nature of the othering discourse "from within."[39] This is the same move the gay community made in adopting the initially pejorative term "queer" for themselves so that it changed its meaning altogether and became a cause for joy and celebration among the community.

Second, and perhaps an extension of re-signifying, is what Fox calls "talking back."[40] If we are authentic, true to ourselves, our culture and our context then it is possible to call out what the other sees in us and projects onto us in their othering. We can name it for what it is, to hold

35. Rooms and Wort, *Fuzzy Church*, 50.
36. Rooms and Wort, *Fuzzy Church*, 46.
37. Rooms and Wort, *Fuzzy Church*, 51.
38. Fox, *Stand Up*, 101.
39. Fox, *Stand Up*, 105.
40. Fox, *Stand Up*, 104.

it up for examination and scrutiny. Once again this is not to retreat into chippiness but is an assertive move which reaches towards inclusivity and equality.[41]

Third, Fox is able through *affirmation* of Northernness to discover a reconciling space between herself and her audience, which I believe is extendable to the fraught relationship between North and South in England. Here is what we said in *Fuzzy Church* about this:

> Fox allows for the possibility of inhabiting the space between ourselves and the other differently. Fox notices the liminal, or "betwixt and between," trickster nature of her public performances and, by paying attention to that space between, realises that a new kind of performer-audience relationship can emerge. One which is characterised by a decision she notes, on the part of one of her interviewees to "love the audience.[42]"[43]

We have been able, then, via Fox's work, to find a space for understanding and working with Northernness between essentialism and nativism and the evacuated simulacrum. We have learnt that Northernness really matters to all sorts of people and it has real-life effects, even economic effects. It matters also, then, that we reach towards what it consists of and how to understand it. So far, the content of Northernness in authenticity, community, humor, and lack of pretension has been mined from an emic researcher, Fox, who is open to the etic.

We need to justify this approach further. For this we turn to Clive Marsh's use (in his book, *A Cultural Theology of Salvation*) of Tillich's concept of *Gehalt*. We only briefly touched on this in *Fuzzy Church* by introducing the idea. First, however, we affirmed a theistic stance towards the world, which is clearly related to a participatory understanding of creation—the sense that we have often come back to in this book—that all things ultimately derive their being from God, in every moment of their existence. We can claim that culture, like Northernness,

> is indwelt by God and redeemable for God's purposes. Our approach to culture then, theologically, following Max Warren, is to take off our shoes, for it is holy ground. This is not to essentialize it, but neither is it to treat it as a form of magic.

41. Fox, *Stand Up*, 51.

42. Fox, *Stand Up*, 103.

43. Rooms and Wort, *Fuzzy Church*, 51.

> Northernness, we believe, cannot be a "simulacrum" with no contribution to make to God's promises and purposes for the world.[44]

I believe is worth saying a little more about the holiness of culture here. It is not the fulness of, say, the "holy of holies" in the Jerusalem Temple, but it is the possibility that we might be able to discern God within culture. I have often referred to a double negative assertion of Michael Oleksa which gives a helpful sense of this stance towards culture: "we can never be sure Christ is not."[45] This discernment of God's presence in culture therefore requires humility, time, patience, and careful sifting of possibilities, something we are attempting in this book. And then we introduced Marsh's work which further theologizes the possibilities here:

> Clive Marsh . . . undertakes the task of looking for the meaning of salvation through historical and contemporary cultural artefacts and in doing so he updates Paul Tillich's theological method to help him. . . . our task is to do a very similar thing with Northernness to that which Marsh does with, say, the USA TV series *Breaking Bad* and *The Big Bang Project*: discover what Paul Tillich called the *Gehalt* or "depth-content" within it and how that connects with the kingdom of God and the gospel of salvation. This requires us not to be simply *extracting* meaning[46] in the essentializing manner we have seen happening, but rather to take off our shoes, listen carefully and critically and discern the God-givenness of Northernness. This, in Marsh's terms, is to ask, "How does what is being interpreted [in our case Northernness] help us better discern and fashion human action in anticipating the kingdom of God which is yet to be?"[47] The kingdom, Marsh points out, has a future orientation which we could add inevitably leads to action. This is what is missing in magic which only leaves us with more of the same.[48]

Paul Tillich (1886–1965) is well known as a theologian of culture, especially in his earlier work, before he moved to the USA in the 1930s. He rather went out of fashion in the later twentieth century as the concerns of liberation theology and neo-Orthodoxy after Barth criticized

44. Rooms and Wort, *Fuzzy Church*, 47.
45. Quoted in Bevans and Schroeder, *Constants in Context*, 297.
46. Marsh, *Cultural*, 40.
47. Marsh, *Cultural*, 42.
48. Rooms and Wort, *Fuzzy Church*, 47–48.

his overly "accommodationist" and "liberal" views of culture.[49] Marsh attempts to recover critically his approach and develop it away from its origins for a postmodern study of (more popular) culture and cultural artifacts. Tillich was working with the theological meaning of the arts (and particularly the visual "high" arts), which in this book we take to be a subset of a much larger understanding of culture. Marsh's description of Tillich's schema is worth reproducing here with the caveat that he immediately states that this is an over-simplified presentation:

> we must note the importance of three key terms for Tillich: form (*Form* in German), content (*Inhalt*) and "depth content" (*Gehalt*). With respect to fine art or literature, it could be said that depth-content is what it is "really about." Its form is more the means by which the self-presentation of a work (its content) achieves the communication or transmission of its depth-content.[50]

Depth-content (*Gehalt*) is more complex than what an artifact is "really about" since it must not be separated from both form and content, as somehow the most important thing about the piece of art which leaves behind the art itself. Marsh wishes to expand the scope of Tillich's project to a much broader set of cultural projects, particularly popular televisual ones and he desires to move away from an understanding of *Gehalt* as simply "the religious or theological meaning expressed within a work of art or popular culture."[51] Marsh is committed to a helpful description, in our missiological terms of the *missio Dei* and the basis for the theological method of his project (and indeed ours):

> if we are to take seriously the presence and activity of a lively, creative, future-oriented God within the midst of the human realm (the consequence of a commitment both to incarnation and to the presence of God's life-giving Spirit in the world), then we cannot constrain God's presence, or our perception of that presence, to specific practices or aesthetic social locations.[52]

Thus, Marsh wishes to affirm the ontological possibility of God's presence in culture (specific practices or aesthetic social locations) and then move beyond Tillich and define *Gehalt* as the identification of the "*theological*

49. Marsh, *Cultural*, 37.
50. Marsh, *Cultural*, 38.
51. Marsh, *Cultural*, 39.
52. Marsh, *Cultural*, 40.

trajectory which any work can be shown to contain"[53]—with the emphasis also on the word "any," I suspect. Whether this leaves the project still open to the "liberal" critique is a moot point, yet the focus for me here is on *discernment,* which while never certain is also not naïve. Marsh can then further describe his theological method in relation to seeking *Gehalt* as depth-content as theological trajectory in, say, a popular television series:

> A meaning (one of many possible meanings) thus results from the interaction between the series as "text," the theological interpreter as one who brings theological materials to bear on the series, and the interaction which happens between interpreter and text, in the light of broader cultural discussion about the series and the theological tradition within which the interpreter sits.[54]

For a practical theologian like myself, what is suggestive here is how close this description of theological method is to the way in which Graham et al. offer the method of Whitehead and Whitehead (for theological reflection in Christian ministry) also as a development of the original work of Tillich in their chapter, "Speaking of God in Public: Correlation."[55] They too are taking Tillich beyond Tillich when utilizing correlation as a theological method. The Whiteheads place the "ministerial concern" (or "text" in this case) in a triangle between Christian scripture and tradition, human experience and culture/society in the wider world. This is theological and spiritual *discernment* which we have noted as a key motif of this project of contextualization and leads us to discerning Northernness between essentialism/nativism and the evacuated simulacrum.

Marsh then further describes how he understands theological trajectory in the content of *Gehalt* by placing it within the "kingdom of God and gospel."[56] The effect of this is that first the kingdom brings a future, eschatological perspective to discernment (and the concomitant theological hermeneutics of the project) which leaves us in the "now and not yet"[57] of Wells's Act 4 of the drama of salvation we referred to in chapters 2 and 3. He also notes the consequent need for provisionality in the making of conclusions from such discernment, or, in other words, for

53. Marsh, *Cultural,* 40, his emphasis.

54. Marsh, *Cultural,* 41.

55. Graham et al., *Theological Reflection,* 161.

56. Marsh, *Cultural,* 41.

57. Marsh, *Cultural,* 42.

"eschatological reserve" which we discovered was a requirement of this project in chapter 3 from Roest.

Marsh utilizes the work of Tim Gorringe in *Furthering Humanity* (as we did in chapter 2) to bring "gospel" within the purview of seeking *Gehalt*. Gospel in Gorringe's terms is precisely his book's title—the "furthering of humanity" itself in human justice and fulfilment since his definition of culture is simply "the name of that whole process in the course of which God does what it takes . . . to make and to keep human beings human. Culture in this sense is, under God, 'the human task.'"[58] Another way of putting this is what many have called, more recently "flourishing life."[59] Thus, Marsh is able to definitively move beyond Tillich and seek:

> the *Gehalt* which grasps hold of glimpses of the kingdom of God or the gospel–sought from a dialogue with any product of human culture and seeking to capture that which lies between the object being interpreted and the vision of humanity yet to be–may derive from anything humans produce, and come from anywhere.[60]

It seems that in conclusion Marsh affirms much of what we have already discovered about the work of contextual theology in chapters 2 and 3—namely that it is grounded in the discernment of God and is concerned with "the human task," that it requires "eschatological reserve" and therefore humility in both its provisional conclusions and its messiness.[61] It is a Christian task which allows a "two-way street" between the Christian faith and the cultures within which it sits,[62] just as Walls has asserted in his pilgrim and indigenizing principles.

Before we leave Marsh, he adds a cautionary note[63] about the Tillichian perspective from Graham et al. They state[64] that it has a tendency in some forms to address "existential dilemmas rather than political concerns" and we noted this tension between Bevans and Schroeder's Type B and Type C theologies (and possibly also between the anthropological

58. Gorringe, *Furthering*, 4.

59. See also Marsh, *Cultural*, 50. For a review of the concept of flourishing life missiologically, see Niemandt, "*Missio Dei.*"

60. Marsh, *Cultural*, 45.

61. See also Marsh, *Cultural*, 50.

62. Marsh, *Cultural*, 51.

63. Marsh, *Cultural*, 53.

64. Graham et al., *Theological Reflection*, 168.

and praxis models in Bevans's description of them[65]) in chapter 3. Fortunately, Niven's book can help us with this re-balancing and it is to that work we turn next.

Our claim is that Kate Fox has discerned, without working within a Christian framework (which is not necessary, given the prior presence and activity of God in our understanding of the *missio Dei*) a *Gehalt* of Northernness (not the final definitive version by any means, but a start). In *Fuzzy Church* we folded lack of pretension into authenticity to give three, what we can now call northern theological trajectories in authenticity, community, and humor.[66] We now put these into further dialogue with the work of Niven, since he is concerned both with northern cultural artifacts and the North's socio-economics and politics.

The North will Rise Again: In Search of the Future in Northern Heartlands

It is hard to categorize Alex Niven's book which provides a further important interlocutor for us in this chapter. There is a strong element of autoethnography in the book, though Niven doesn't use that concept to describe the work he does on mining his and his parents' lives in relation to the North—we might say there is a sensitive and aware reflexivity about his work.[67] Both his parents died in fairly close succession when Niven was 21 years old and these painful events are part of the narrative. Born in 1984, Niven grows up in rural Northumberland West of Newcastle in a "lower middle-class" family and sinks deep roots in the North in his early life. Moving away for study and work to the South (his Oxford University PhD researched the northern poet Basil Bunting and is referenced several times in the book), he longs to return and eventually does so—he now lectures in English Literature at Newcastle University.

65. See Bevans, *Models*.

66. It is important to recognize that these aspects of the *Gehalt* of Northernness are not the exclusive claim of people in the North of England, and in reducing them to one word we have lost something of their particularity as Northern. For example, northern humor is connected in interesting ways to authenticity and certainly not the more southern preference for *double-entendre*, as we noted earlier in the chapter.

67. For instance, Niven, *North Will*, xiv: "Though I am not the main subject of this book, because it is a study of human emotion arising from attachment to specific places and communities it seemed important to make clear the links between my own life . . . and . . . the chapters that follow."

Beyond this personal thread the work ranges widely over history, literature, popular culture, especially music, socio-economics, and politics. Here is an important opening thesis to the book:

> this is a story about hope rising above despair. Amid the civic crisis and growing inequality that have dominated northern society . . . a strong tradition of northern modernism and revivalism has persisted . . . Driven by a belief that the North somehow holds the key to a freer, more progressive way of organizing and operating the country that has come to be called England, countless artists, writers, musicians, politicians, film-makers and ordinary citizens have used the North as both inspiration and ideal . . . Despite recent political setbacks, it is this tradition of passionate northern progressivism–based on the reasonable, righteous, even inevitable dream of northern renaissance that I think has something very important to say to us.[68]

Setting out further the task of the book, in the opening chapter Niven connects his project with the search for what we have called the *Gehalt* of Northernness:

> This story of the reclamation of the buried good things about modern northern life is central to this book, and it is one of the reasons why I do not want to lament how dark and depressing the North is. . . . everything I write here is to show how the North can and should be, and for me always has been, a place of *endless subtlety, exceptional generosity, fierce love and utopian possibility*.[69]

Throughout our engagement with a contextual theology of the North it has been hard to escape the accusation that we have reinforced the "grimness" of the North, despite our intention to do otherwise—and it is clear that Niven is concerned about this too. Earlier in this chapter we noted the other side of Niven's optimism and the need to lean into the "radically bleak psychic and actual landscape" of the North.[70] The reviews of both books we have written have stated that we seem to have failed to portray anything other than a grim North[71]—despite attempts in both of them to directly confront this question. Several possibilities present themselves. The reviewers may simply have not understood the

68. Niven, *North Will*, xiii-xiv.

69. Niven, *North Will*, 6, my emphasis.

70. Niven, *North Will*, 282.

71. See Bradley, *Modern Believing*, 207; and Billings, *Church Times*, 21.

argument fully, missing the relevant passages which present the counter-argument. Alternatively, "grim" is simply a deeply ingrained essentialist and even unchristian trope in England about its North which is hard to argue against. Finally, perhaps it is actually a both/and in that there is real grim darkness about the North alongside amazing possibility. We can certainly applaud Niven's attempts to *celebrate* the North despite its obvious challenges.

Moving on to reflect on the content of *The North will Rise Again,* in the first two parts of the book Niven describes the waxing and waning of the North, its economy, culture, and politics during the twentieth century, in the shadow of the Industrial Revolution and the rapid growth and expansion that flowed from that during the North's zenith in the nineteenth century. Personally, I think there is more to be taken account of before this period which shapes the North, but nevertheless the cataclysms it brought must be dealt with. Niven claims that the North "effectively *became* civilization—or at least the most vigorous, dynamic existing version of it."[72] Niven names the "sensibility" that describes this period as "modernity" and goes on to claim that the cities, towns, and "rural-industrial village-scapes" that then made up the North "were the real historic capitals of modernity."[73] A note of caution is required here as it is easy to be carried away by the force of what happened in the North, without relating it to the concomitant global expansion of the British colonial Empire at the same time. Much recent historical research has related this growth to the enslavement of Africans in the Caribbean and elsewhere, which enriched northern cities such as Liverpool. In a fascinating recent project, the origins of the *Guardian* newspaper in Manchester, and Manchester itself, have been connected with cotton slavery in the USA.[74]

With this caution it is possible to agree with Niven that there is in the North a "rebel commitment to modernism and progressive change."[75] What the North brings to the whole of England, then, is "the *idea of the future.*"[76] While this future orientation is often frustrated and unfulfilled, we can relate it, at least indirectly, to our theological concern about the coming kingdom of God which is always "now and not yet," since we

72. Niven, *North Will,* 8, his italics.

73. Niven, *North Will,* 9.

74. See Guardian, "Cotton Capital."

75. Niven, *North Will,* 10.

76. Niven, *North Will,* 10, his italics.

would not wish to equate progress with the kingdom *per se*. However, the provisionality of this perspective could help Niven when he laments that the North "is a place where a mostly forlorn desire for things that might be, rather than things that have been, is a sort of unshakeable collective inheritance."[77] What is clear is that it is a locus of *hope*.

In his introductory chapter Niven describes returning to the North in 2015, living there ever since and canvassing for the Labour Party in advance of the 2019 UK General Election. These experiences have given Niven the overall impression, that, despite significant moments of revival and hope in the twentieth century (which he will later rehearse), the overall feeling is one of severe "regression"[78] from its nineteenth-century zenith. Deindustrialization has taken its full course and is now "irreversibly complete."[79] Resentment and bitterness abound, finding an outlet in radically different voting patterns since the Brexit referendum of 2016. Despite some marginal and isolated new initiatives Niven concludes, "I'm not so sure how many of us in the bewildered, still marginalized, post-everything North have a really clear sense of what progress looks like any more."[80] Niven therefore asks what the response to all this should be, and he proposes looking into the recent past in order to find and then "endorse the cultural livelihood of the North, broadly defined."[81] In the delineation of this culture, he hopes to find the resources and motivation for a future. Again, we can say that he is searching for a future-oriented northern *Gehalt* when he states: "I am casting a net into the ocean of collective identity, and hoping that something solid and valuable might be dragged to the surface."[82] Niven's purpose then is stated clearly:

> As well as providing some sense of who we are and where we came from, the hope is that, maybe, at the end of this inquiry into the recent dream-life of northern faith and failure, we will get a very initial sense of where we are going, and of how Northerners might start to think about escaping from the endless loop of decline–followed by botched recovery–which has dominated their history for 50 years or more.[83]

77. Niven, *North Will*, 11.
78. Niven, *North Will*, 17.
79. Niven, *North Will*, 19.
80. Niven, *North Will*, 22.
81. Niven, *North Will*, 23.
82. Niven, *North Will*, 24.
83. Niven, *North Will*, 25.

Niven then goes on to review the influence of modernism and futurism in an appraisal of different cultural forms of the mid to late twentieth century in the North. There is a distinct uniqueness to this approach in the North[84] which he seeks to evidence from his experience and biography. As he later states from further evidence, the North seems to "exist above and outside of the mainstream of English culture."[85] From time to time this future oriented modernism asserts itself–exemplified by a story Niven tells about the northern poet Basil Bunting (the subject of his PhD) who had a revival in his career and popularity in the 1960s with his long poem *Briggflatts*.[86] Thus, Niven can assert that "at crucial moments in these years, a mood of modernist revival managed to win out against a more deep-seated feeling that deindustrialization marked the beginning of the end of northern society."[87] It was however inevitably short-lived and was subsumed by the neo-liberal government policies from the 1980s onwards which brought northern cultural artifacts in to the postmodern era.[88] This shift from the optimism of the 1960s and 1970s to the dark struggles of the 1980s and 1990s is summed up in Niven's phrase "failed dreams"; he tells several stories and elucidates how that phraseology works out in both film and popular music. Perhaps the nadir of this whole trajectory of deindustrialization is the description of the people of the North's relationship with alcohol, which is not a happy one[89] and which leaves many in a nihilistic fatalism fueled by dependence on alcohol. Niven puts the collective dependence on alcohol down to "learned helplessness" born of social decline in this period. Self-harm and fatalism are the result.[90] From this low point Niven concludes that any approach to the future must be "radical or nothing at all."[91] In passing, it may be worth pointing out that these deeply negative cultural aspects of the North are some of the elements of its culture that might be addressed in a countercultural manner in the "pilgrim" aspects of any northern contextualization of the gospel.

84. Niven, *North Will*, 40.
85. Niven, *North Will*, 95.
86. Niven, *North Will*, 50.
87. Niven, *North Will*, 53.
88. Niven, *North Will*, 110.
89. Niven, *North Will*, 131–45.
90. Niven, *North Will*, 146–47.
91. Niven, *North Will*, 147.

Niven relates two further brief, yet ultimately failing revivals: one in the northern 1990s music scene and the triumph of the Labour party in its northern heartlands from 1995 to 2010. Overall, he concludes that this period started out with great intention and potential, but ultimately turned into the "great betrayal" where the opportunity to create lasting structural reforms such as in transport and connectivity were missed.[92] Resentment created by this betrayal paves the way for the Brexit vote in 2016 and the swathe of Conservative Members of Parliament returned in the so-called "Red Wall" constituencies in the 2019 General Election. These changes in voter behavior were fed by the austerity placed upon the whole country, but unequally felt in North from 2010 onwards. Niven relates how his return to the North in 2015 was somewhat like Robin Hood (from his favorite film of his childhood years) returning home after the Crusade to find his home in ruin. I have written elsewhere of how the myth of Robin Hood operates to create a liminal imaginary between North and South throughout the various versions and mutations of it over the centuries.[93] Niven might make more of this than he does, given the question of radicalism and even revolution as responses to the dire situation in the North. In the myth., Robin Hood is never a revolutionary wanting to overturn the government of the day, but he does represent a deep heart-felt desire for justice via an alternative community where things don't have to be as they normally are—not unlike the kingdom of God, as I pointed out in *The Faith of the English*.[94]

Niven reviews two recent UK governmental initiatives for the North: the Northern Powerhouse[95] and levelling up.[96] He assesses the Northern Powerhouse as an abject failure in a period when the real power driving society was the removal of funding for public services under the "requirement" for austerity. This only exacerbated the underlying inequality in England between the North and the South-East. Levelling up offers a little more evidence for improvement but still the systemic drag factors which undermine such major infrastructure projects as the proposed HS2 high-speed rail network,[97] the second northern leg of which, at the

92. Niven, *North Will*, 195.

93. Rooms, *Faith*, 73–92.

94. Rooms, *Faith*, 92.

95. Niven, *North Will*, 222.

96. Niven, *North Will*, 227.

97. Niven, *North Will*, 230.

time of writing, has now been scrapped. It will now, bizarrely, only connect Birmingham to London.

This brings Niven's review of the recent cultural and political histories of the North right up to date and now he turns to proposals for the dilemmas they present. He is clear that first this is a question of addressing the imagination, that is, "attending to the traditions of imaginative escape and civic idealism" in the North.[98] We would agree that the strength and resilience of the North has to be in its culture and traditions and seeking a theology of them, and a trajectory for them is much of what this book is about. Second, by force of imagination a belief is required that could unite the region around its future—this would be a "mental leap of faith, far more than any ingenious political scheme, that will ultimately lead the way to northern revival."[99] However, concrete proposals are also required on a scale from the radical to the revolutionary.[100]

Niven looks at the possibility of Northern independence via a new political party founded in 2020 "to combat the growing injustice of the North/South divide."[101] While he concedes this is part of the kind of imagination that is required for northern people to rise up and act about their place in England, Niven notes that independence could easily lead to more inequality with the South freed from what might be perceived as the shackles of the North.[102] Independence would therefore be, in my view, a "flight" response to the threat from the South (to borrow from Family Systems Theory), whereas self-defining and staying in touch with the source of the threat is a more assertive and healthy position. We will need to return to this theme towards the end of the chapter.

Perhaps then some form of devolution is more desirable, and several alternatives, which remain much more radical than anything that has been or currently is on the table, are discussed.[103] Adjudicating these is beyond the scope of this book, but Niven's emphasis on addressing the needs of the whole region in "pan-northern co-operation"[104] is worth remarking on. Fascinatingly, Niven cites the two Provinces of the Church of England (York and Canterbury) as one model for how North

98. Niven, *North Will*, 232.

99. Niven, *North Will*, 232.

100. Niven, *North Will*, 233.

101. See https://www.freethenorth.co.uk/.

102. Niven, *North Will*, 237.

103. Niven, *North Will*, 239.

104. Niven, *North Will*, 240.

and South might relate,[105] although we might question how "separate and autonomous" the two provinces are in reality. I did very briefly address this question at the end of my essay about a bias to the North.[106] Since most of the power and the fiscal resource is found and directed from London-based Church institutions, the Northern Province lags far behind the Southern in most of the key metrics of the Church. Where I do agree with Niven is in his call for a UK-wide written constitution that could enshrine the kind of changes being called for here. There has been a long-standing campaign for this which is now championed by the organization *Unlock Democracy*.[107]

Niven's book ends rather curiously, even in an odd fashion. There is a final chapter and an "Epilogue," but I could not find where he summarizes what might be the "collective identity" of the people of the North—the project that he set out with at the start of the book. There are hints and clues however, which we will need to gather together.

The final chapter, "Acid Northumbria," utilizes a metaphor from psychedelic drug-taking culture to support a theme of the book which is that the battle for northern identity is ultimately one of imagination. Where is the resource to be found which might offer a different future for the North? Even in the drug-induced imaginative creativity of the 1960s northern poet Alan Hull, suggests Niven.[108] Yes, this is a form of escape from the subjectivity of northern life—the inability to be a citizen, "someone imprisoned inside certain dominant national, cultural and political structures."[109] On the other hand, it can also release a beatific vision of home in the North. Interestingly, the chapter ends with a description of the 2013 wedding of Niven's friend, the poet Tom Pickard, in a place evocative of the North as a whole. This occasions Niven's desire to move back to his spiritual home in the North.[110]

The theme of escape and potential return is dealt with in this final chapter too as Niven discusses the "northern stowaway tradition"[111] in film, literature, and popular music. That is portraying the desire for escape and its consequences in these different cultural forms. Often, escape

105. Niven, *North Will*, 242.
106. Wakefield and Rooms, *Northern Gospel*, 47.
107. Unlock Democracy, "About Unlock Democracy."
108. Niven, *North Will*, 248.
109. Niven, *North Will*, 249.
110. Niven, *North Will*, 269.
111. Niven, *North Will*, 250.

from the perceived limitations of a northern upbringing is "absurd, fantastic and forlorn," but he shows how it is possible, particularly through music to create an imagination about home which is both championing of it and critical of it at the same time.[112] Thus, via the imagination we can, "achieve forms of escape while staying at home, and that seeking exile from one's own family and friends in order to become a free and empowered citizen is neither inevitable or essential."[113] There are clear echoes here of Fox's affirmation and resistance that we noted earlier in this chapter.

However, I suggest that we should not underestimate the value of temporary exile. Niven's own biography demonstrates this: while he emphasizes his longing and return to the North, we do not hear very much of what his sojourn in the South offered him, both materially and imaginatively. I have never returned for more than a day or two to my home city of Hull since I left at 18 years old. Who knows whether I ever will go back to live there, yet some years ago, having learnt in Africa that home is defined largely by where one will be buried at the end of life, I bought my grave plot in a cemetery about 300 meters from the house where I was born. T. S. Eliot sums up the importance of crossing boundaries in exploration and return in this well-known short extract from the poem "Little Gidding" in *Four Quartets*:

> With the drawing of this Love and the voice of this Calling
> We shall not cease from exploration
> And the end of all our exploring
> Will be to arrive where we started
> And know the place for the first time.[114]

One of the more surprising, but clear, findings of our research in northern churches where "something was happening" was that a majority of their leaders had been away and returned.[115] The alternative horizon they had found in "exile" was brought to bear on their leadership back at home to good effect. My hunch is that it is more difficult (but not impossible, as Niven has shown) to gain a new imagination within the horizons of home than to move physically beyond one's immediate horizon before returning. As we pointed out in *Fuzzy Church*, this finding complexifies our

112. Niven, *North Will*, 255.

113. Niven, *North Will*, 255.

114. Elliot, *Four Quartets*, 43.

115. Rooms and Wort, *Fuzzy Church*, 103.

understanding and focus on so-called "indigenous" leadership.[116] Once again understanding this movement means that we cannot dismiss the South as irrelevant in the discussion of the North. Indeed some, perhaps many, are driven to escape and never return, but for those, like Niven who hear the deep call to return and make the longer journey that we also alluded to in the previous work[117] there is something fresh and new they bring from the horizon beyond home.

In the Epilogue to Niven's book (it is not clear why it is an Epilogue and not the final chapter) he discusses a tendency to Northern "messianism" exemplified by the footballer and then manager of Newcastle United Football Club in the 1990s, Kevin Keegan. This discussion is not really related to the hoped-for Jewish Messiah or the Christian understanding of Jesus as Messiah. Rather it is a metaphor for the projection of our unrealistic and ultimately failing dreams onto a hero figure. This is a clear theme of the whole book, which we referred to earlier and is worth repeating here:

> northern history is defined by a sort of endless back and forth: between surging, energetic bursts forward into a future way in advance of the conservative norms of English culture . . . and equally drastic recoilings into a radically bleak psychic and actual landscape which is the inevitable product of enduring marginality from an imperial civilization overwhelmingly centred on London.[118]

If the dreams of the rise of the North, along with any trust in false messiahs, are ultimately hopeless, what are the options, asks Niven. The first is to freeze and essentialize the North into a series of twee clichés such as the rugged, but beautiful.[119] The next, drawn from the poet Basil Bunting again, is to find a place of "contented humility"[120] which leads to a stance of resistance against the hegemonic South while at least accepting the North's subaltern reality. This is not enough for Niven, who on the penultimate page of the book makes the most surprising revelation:

> As a committed socialist—and indeed a practising Catholic—I do not think that life should be wasted in a condition of mere

116. Rooms and Wort, *Fuzzy Church*, 103.
117. Rooms and Wort, *Fuzzy Church*, 104.
118. Niven, *North Will*, 282.
119. Niven, *North Will*, 284.
120. Niven, *North Will*, 286.

> acceptance of the world as it is . . . we have to hope and strive for the fact that, on earth, there is always the possibility that life will one day be as it is in heaven. This determination to believe in spite of the empirical reality . . . is part of what I understand by northern identity.[121]

Here a religious and even theological commitment is made, by alluding to the Lord's Prayer (where Christians pray for the coming of the kingdom and God's will being done: "on earth as it is in heaven") to what we also have been naming as the kingdom of God. Niven remarkably equates this in part with northern identity. That is, in the North what is required is "prodigal hopefulness—or at least vaulting ambition."[122] I would suggest that the biblical notion of the kingdom is "revolutionary" in Niven's terms and we have discovered here a deep connection to it from within the history and the dreams of the North.

TOWARDS A NORTHERN *GEHALT* OR DEFINING NORTHERN CULTURAL CAPITAL

We are now in a position to bring the threads of this chapter together in what we are discerning about the North and its contextual theology from all the works we have interacted with so far.

We can confirm once again, with much certainty, the divide between the North and the South, and paradoxically their indivisibility, given how one is partly a function of the other. We began with the social geography of Danny Dorling which demonstrates a clear division in a diagonal line between the Bristol Channel and the Wash. We have noticed several potential responses to this reality. First is flight or escape to the South (denial is not really available given the clear division); this can bring some benefits, at least for the individual, if not the community. Fight or seeking some form of independence seems doomed given the unequal starting point. It is entirely possible for "self-defining and staying in touch" to be both an affirmation of the goodness of Northernness in its *Gehalt* and an assertive resistance to essentializing and colonizing approaches from the South. We have seen how both Kate Fox in her PhD thesis and Alex Niven have underlined this for us. The North and South in England are inextricably linked. Attending to their relationality from the perspective

121. Niven, *North Will*, 288.

122. Niven, *North Will*, 288.

of "prodigal hopefulness" in the North might even aim at some form of reconciliation as part of what it means for heaven to become a reality on this part of the earth. Eliot's "Love and Calling" might also be the ground on which such coming together could be founded.

Niven has offered a helpful political perspective on the recent history of the North. This has explained contemporary changes in electoral patterns arising from long-term resentment at the "boom-bust" cycle that characterized the North in much of the twentieth century. We remarked earlier in the chapter on the connection here with Karl Spracklen's emphasis on "sympathetic magic" in his explanation of the performance of Northernness, not unlike the inevitably of the pagan cycle of the seasons moving from the abundance of spring and summer to the death and destruction of autumn and winter. This approach, however, is rather a counsel of despair and while it might lead to some resistance it does not birth hope for radical change. In *Northern Gospel, Northern Church,* I made reference to Anthony Gormley's monumental sculpture, *The Angel of the North,* (it is 20m high with a 54m wingspan) placed strategically overlooking a valley by the main A1 motorway that leads through the North-east in south Tyneside and west of Sunderland (the Angel also forms the cover picture for this book). Gormley, speaking about his purpose in creating it, asks "Is it possible to make a work with purpose in a time that demands doubt? I wanted to make an object that would be a focus of hope at a painful time of transition for the people of the north-east, abandoned in the gap between the industrial and the information ages."[123]

From a theological standpoint what is coalescing here is an "eschatological reserve" within an understanding of the kingdom of God which is "now and not yet." Evidence for this is how the English legend of Robin Hood operates in the liminal "in-between" of North and South to create a social imaginary where oppression can be resisted and overcome. It echoes the way the Gospels describe the kingdom of God turning society and its relations upside-down. Niven has made the rather extraordinary claim that in fact one of the characteristics of northern identity is just this belief and the expectation that things don't have to be the way they are. He connects this with his own Christian faith, which is deeper and more life-giving than other, lesser responses to the dilemmas of being northern.

This is not to say that we can minimize the difficulty and darkness or what has been named as "grim" in the North. Niven has shown how

123. Wakefield and Rooms, *Northern Gospel,* 44.

this aspect of the North can and needs to be leant into and not minimized (despite his initial distancing from such lament). Our attempts in the past in writing books on the subject have not persuaded reviewers otherwise. The lesson here is that this is a reality, but it is not the whole story. There is an important countercultural element to contextualization here. In fact, it is of the essence of the gospel and the nature of discipleship that life comes not from denying or trying to cover over death with niceties, but by entering fully into it, by embracing it. We hinted at this theme in *Fuzzy Church*[124] and we will need to return to it in chapter 7. There is a cost to discipleship away from Bonhoeffer's "cheap grace" and we do no-one a favor by trying to avoid it.

There is a deep well of spiritual and imaginative or cultural capital that is available in the North; Niven has demonstrated this extremely well. And we are ready now to revisit Fox's delineation of the values that she discerned which make up northern cultural capital—or what we have theologically termed its *Gehalt*—in the light of Niven's work. We named these values as authenticity, community, and humor. I believe they are not quite sufficient now, having read Niven, and I want to qualify them with a paired word for each of them. The pairings are not designed to be paradoxical opposites creating a tension; rather, the second word qualifies and expands the meaning of the first, giving a more rounded sense of the whole. What is also intended in the addition of a further word is to move a little beyond simply "values" to include perhaps virtues as well as commitments, behaviors, and practices—all of which remind me of the anthropologist Kate Fox's[125] description of the "English cultural genome" which is based around three sets of "values, outlooks and reflexes."[126]

Authenticity—Realism

Readers may remember we combined authenticity with "lack of pretension" from Fox. Transparency, openness, and a lack of dissemination are important in the North. In addition, Niven has shown us that not pretending about the realities of the North is in itself a vital stance to take in being in and from the North. We termed this "leaning into" and

124. Rooms and Wort, *Fuzzy Church*, 109.

125. This is a different Kate Fox to the northern stand-up comic of the same name quoted in this chapter.

126. Fox, *Watching*, 570.

embracing the effects of the subaltern nature of the North, as well as its darker sides when it is not living up to being its best (for instance in the northern "chip on the shoulder").[127] This sensibility will also be the engine of resistance to any essentializing of the North—of saying that its grimness is not the last word by any means, for the actual reality is much bigger than that. Thus, flat caps, glottal stops, rugged landscapes, and many other essentialist tropes do not need to be what make up a social imaginary of the North. Realism will also lead us to the "reserve" in the needful eschatological reserve that the gospel brings us—the "not yet" in the "now and not yet" of the hope that we shall come to in a moment. And we'll therefore need to hold all these six elements of Northernness together as one.

Community—Home

Social cohesion, rootedness, and identity in community—even solidarity—are all available in the best of the North. We might just as easily have used the word "place" instead of "home," as the addition here, certainly this would connect with Jennings's emphasis on land, a particular geography. But "home" won out in my view as it is the humanizing name we give to our place, the place we are from and return to. It is at its best, also, in Jennings's terms a place of intimacy, as long as it remains open to the other across its boundary (as we shall see at the end of this chapter). While Niven doesn't use the word "community" very much, what is notable is that he often writes of communities of artists and poets that collaborate and support each other (for example, the poetry readings organized by a young Tom Pickard[128]). More than that though, Niven has shown us what the deep call (referencing Eliot again) of home to a place in the North looks like and which drives him back there, so full of beauty and meaning as it is for him. And we learn from him that the North stands or falls together as a region, as a whole, even a whole macro community—a key insight from his book.

127. We will return to this notion in chapter 7. At this stage we could describe it as projecting negative northern cultural capital in anger and even hatred against the (usually southern) other.

128. Niven, *North Will*, 50.

Humor—Hope

It is here I think that Fox's work can seriously complement Niven's in that he rarely, if ever, takes humor seriously in his review of northern cultural artifacts. As Fox points out, "too much autoethnography draws on serious and tragic modes" whereas she believes that stand-up comedians can be "militant utopians . . . creating critical and oppositional public spaces."[129] Northern humor can just as easily be essentialized as anything else northern,[130] but Fox demonstrates how it is a vehicle for affirmation and resistance and therefore offers a space which questions and even undermines the status quo. Thus, we can claim that humor is related to Niven's emphasis on "prodigal hope" and his sense that deep within Northernness are utopian dreams. What hope offers us is a horizon, an imaginative horizon that lifts us from myopic focus on only home and place. As someone once put it, we need "home *and* horizons of reach." How one engages people with their own home culture via an imaginative horizon which does not involve moving physically beyond it was the subject of my doctoral research and subsequent book.[131] Within northern culture itself, including within its particular humor, are the imaginative resources for finding hope and a future, despite the subaltern nature of the North. We also note Niven's assertion that the North offers England as a whole "the idea of a future," a theme we will return later in the book.

These six elements then form a trajectory for a northern *Gehalt*, embedded in affirmation and resistance and the eschatological reserve of the kingdom of God. We claim these are beyond essentialism and any nativism; this is the "depth-content" of northern spiritual and cultural capital and, as such, we take off our shoes before it, as it is holy ground.

Before concluding this chapter, let us attempt a kind of "back translation" of these six values into a contemporary cultural artifact, the film *The Old Oak* directed by Ken Loach and possibly his last film (released in 2023). As translators work with the translated text to turn it back to the original language to check its accuracy, can we find the northern *Gehalt* in a film set in the North? Loach has had a long career in the British film industry and is well known as a committed socialist for using his work

129. Fox, *Stand Up*, 51.

130. We note that we are talking about a particular northern humor here; see Fox, *Stand Up*, 58.

131. See Rooms, *Faith*.

to portray the reality of social conditions on the ground, especially in northern England. One of his renowned early films, *Kes* (1969), is set in Yorkshire. It developed Loach's use of first-time actors and locals as extras, as well as employing the local distinctive accents without change or apology. *The Old Oak* uses very much the same methods and political stance and is set firmly in the North in a post-industrial ex-mining "village" by the sea in County Durham. It is 2016 and a group of Syrian refugees is newly housed in the (very cheap) terraced homes in the village, causing disruption and upset in this impoverished community, all of which becomes focused on the local run-down public house (pub) of the film's name, run by its sympathetic publican "TJ." He quickly gets to know Yara, a photographer, the one refugee who speaks English, and she becomes a bridge person between the communities in her growing friendship with TJ. Both of these communities are deeply traumatized, the one by the displacement of war, and the other by the post-industrial demise of their lives and local economy. The question the film raises is how these two communities will deal with each other—by coming together, or by flying apart through misunderstanding, racism, and hatred. There is a memory of "strength, solidarity, and resistance" in the village from the Miners' Strike in the 1980s memorialized by photographs on the walls of a disused back room in the pub (the only public space left in the village). The memory, it seems of gaining strength through eating together in the strike when no-one was being paid has long faded and violence against each other is never far from the surface of life, epitomized by the nasty "attack" dogs that are owned by the local youth. Evil is very visible in this fraught portrayal of the post-industrial North. The plot develops around how the back room of the pub becomes a place of hope for the two communities to come and eat together and learn about each other's struggles—and the threats to it from those locals who wish their own place could be just for them. One of the most moving scenes is when, after a show of Yara's beautiful black and white photographs of both communities in the back room, the Syrians bring out a Miners' banner they have created which combines a picture of a tree (English Oak or Syrian Cedar?) with the words "Strength," "Solidarity" and "Resistance" in both English and Arabic—perhaps an inculturation of another kind. The banner is marched by both communities together in the annual Durham Miners' gala parade in the final scene.

So, is the *Gehalt* of Northernness discernible in the film?[132] I would argue very much so. Yes, there are political and social questions it clearly raises, but the depth is found in the six elements of the northern *Gehalt* which are evident throughout. The film is deeply authentic to Niven's description of northern "victimhood and hopeless dreaming" which is expertly portrayed; inevitably, just as something good and beautiful seems to be emerging it is dashed to the ground. Realism in the form of overt and visceral racism and hatred is on full display. (The local youth notice the help given to the Syrians and wonder why there is nothing for them, when they often go faintingly hungry.) And yet this is not the only possible response in the face of grief for what has and is being lost in both Syria and the village.

The strapline of the film, "It's not where you're from, it's what you bring" is authentic to the film and leads us into the questions the film raises about how community and home are formed from places of origin across cultural divides. For those with eyes to see and ears to hear, the arrival of the Syrians offers a far horizon on which to re-evaluate the life of an impoverished northern community and to re-imagine it in face-to-face relationship with these new others. That cultural capital can then turn into new kinds of community which are based in "strength, solidarity, and resistance." Here is the stuff of both the "now" of the kingdom—the trajectory of the value of community and home—and it's "not yet," since this new found community is fragile and constantly under threat.

At one point in the film TJ and Yara end up at Durham Cathedral, a symbol for TJ, not necessarily of God but of the workers who built such an amazing edifice. Yara tearfully listens to the beauty of the choir practicing, remembers home and then a discussion on hope ensues. She quotes a friend who thinks that hope is the worst kind of commodity since it always seems false and therefore kills. Yet that is not enough for her, and not in this place of all places—she sticks to what Niven has named as "prodigal hopefulness." Yara's photographs have encapsulated this hope as she mirrors back to both communities their strength and dignity—and along the way there is some humor in them which brings gentle smiles, hard won in the toughness of these lives but humor nevertheless. I also found myself laughing out loud at one point at the racism being spouted

132. I suppose similar films could be made in marginalized communities receiving refugees in many places around Western Europe. Yet this film, in its particularity, could only be made in the North of England; to think otherwise would be to universalize, unhelpfully, what it portrays about the North.

by certain characters; I recognized it in myself both, resistant and hopeful. *The Old Oak*, I would suggest, is a northern film shot through with Northernness.

In this and the previous two chapters we have set out an argument for a contemporary contextual theology in the North of England. There is more work to be done on it yet, but now it is time to turn to the empirical fieldwork we did in northern churches; it will ground our opening theological exploration in actual Christian communities where God was clearly at work.

5

The Field Research, its Methodology and Initial Findings

We turn in this chapter to the field research we undertook in local churches in the North of England. As in the previous chapter there will inevitably be some repetition of what we reported in the earlier book, *Fuzzy Church*. That book was what could be termed a "popular" introduction to the question of gospel and culture in the North of England. It was not without academic rigor, but it was written for an intended audience different from that of this book. Here in this chapter and the next we will go deeper both into the data itself and into how we collected it. We will place the original research under the critical spotlight of the work we have done in chapters 2 and 3.

In chapter 2 we recounted the desire, following Clemens Sedmak, to investigate a "regional theology" in the North of England utilizing field research. We have described this region in detail in the previous chapter and investigated the "depth content" of Northernness. In this chapter we will present the research question we began the project with, describe how we gathered data and undertook the fieldwork, and then analyzed the data which we had collected. We will rehearse some of the initial findings that were reported in *Fuzzy Church* which are relevant to this current work and then submit the whole methodology to critique, especially from Courtney Goto. In addition, we will note the clear limits of what we attempted, its imperfections and where it fell short of what might have been possible. It is worth noting that Elli Wort, my collaborator in the field research, is very present in this chapter, since as well as taking a full part in the research she also wrote the initial draft here. Thus, I will often use the first-person plural to describe what we did and found out.

THE INITIAL HYPOTHESIS AND RESEARCH QUESTION

Our research began, following on from the original work done in *Northern Gospel, Northern Church,* by aiming to establish the possible nature of the gospel in the North of England and identifying what a Northern gospel might look like. We set out on this journey because, as described in chapter 2, we knew there was some kind of relationship between culture/context and the gospel—if only from Vincent Donovan's experience with the Masai in Tanzania where he discovered the "gospel" that he had brought with him was perfectly useless. The initial hypothesis we brought to the research, from the funding proposal, was described as the possibility that there is such a thing as a "northern gospel," a particular good news which is at the heart of flourishing churches within their communities in the North. This led directly to the research question: *What Good News is at the heart of flourishing churches within their communities in the North of England?*

On reflection, the research question still stands up since it is an open-ended question that sets out to explore the initial hypothesis. That is, it does allow for a modification of the hypothesis from the research data when gathered and analyzed, which is what we discovered was required on the research journey. Indeed, we quickly realized there were two inherent flaws in such an approach, one major and one less so. First, the hypothesis assumes an overly essentialist, even nativist approach to Northernness and contextual theology—concepts we introduced in chapter 3. "We did not discover a northern gospel, partly because 'the North' is not one simple thing which can be equated in some kind of straight line with the gospel."[1] Thus, as we started to embark on our detailed field research and as we became aware of the nuanced nature of the northern contexts where our churches were situated, it became evident that we could not identify a simple, isolatable northern gospel. There are at least two reasons for this. The various northern communities in which our research churches were set were shown to be more varied and complex than we initially assumed in that they exist in a globalizing and post-industrial world and their communities are to some extent

1. Rooms and Wort, *Fuzzy Church,* 5.

post-Christian and certainly post-Christendom. They are not reducible to some universally northern "context" according to Goto's critique of that word. And inevitably we also came to see that the gospel in these places was deeper and more multifaceted than the phrase "northern gospel" would allow for, not least because the gospel is founded on the person of Christ, not just a set of static texts or ideas.

The second flaw in our starting point became obvious as we set out to identify some "flourishing churches" in the North that we could research. We worked with people with oversight in their Church bodies who knew their churches better than we ever could, and who could point us in their direction. This is how we remarked on what happened when we did this in *Fuzzy Church*:

> We'd used the word "flourishing" to indicate we were looking for churches where something interesting was going on, where God was at work, where growth might be happening, where people may be discovering the "gospel," however conceived for the first time. But the various Bishops, Missioners, Archdeacons and Communications Officers we spoke to struggled with our description: to them, "flourishing" meant "successful." And the churches they felt where something was happening, where good news was being expressed, were not always "successful." These were churches that could often be fragile, struggling, on the knife-edge between "success" and "failure."[2]

All data needs to be understood as good data in field research, and this informed much of the research from that point forwards. We will return to the detail of how we came to this conclusion below—that we were being invited now to work with the understanding that our research churches would be defined as where "something was happening." And, that was about as much as could be said about them at this early stage. The fundamental fragility of what was happening in them was a given.

There is a further assumption in the research question which we should also critically note at this point. We made a decision, in designing the research project, to limit our investigations to these so-called "flourishing" churches. Again, critically reflecting on that decision, I suppose we imagined that the gospel might be more transparent in such places. It was not that we didn't believe we could find research data in other churches, only that we felt it might be hidden behind more layers of practices and behaviors that could be obfuscating. We will return to the

2. Rooms and Wort, *Fuzzy Church*, 4.

question of how we understand "growing and flourishing" in the next chapter and we will need to revisit this research assumption at that point.

This was where we started our research, and we have to say it again, our initial research question came out of an essentialist imagination about the North. Nevertheless, we set out, rather naively it turned out, to look for Northern churches that were "flourishing" and to discover the gospel at the heart of these churches, the good news that was enabling these churches to "flourish."

It is worth noting here that there were particular parameters to our research that came from our funding, and which shaped our methodology. Our funding for the project was provided by a generous grant from the Susannah Wesley Foundation, based at Roehampton University in SW London. With that direct connection to the founders of Methodism, Methodist churches were obviously going to feature in the research. In addition to these churches, we chose to examine Anglican churches, as both researchers came from an Anglican background and this is where our previous work and research had focused; pragmatically speaking, we had the best networks with which to interest research subjects in the project. This is not to say that contextual theologies cannot be found in churches of other denominations, or independent churches; only that the limitations of time and funding meant that we concentrated on these two denominations. This raises the question of how representative the churches are and how much we might be able to extrapolate or transfer the results to other denominations and contexts. I suggest we can probably claim comparability across what we might call "mainstream" or broadly "Conciliar Protestant" denominations, not least because we deliberately sought out a wide range of types of these churches in varied contexts, as we will delineate in a moment. What we do not have is any comparison with say African, Black-led, Pentecostal or other diaspora-based churches. We recognize this as a limit and weakness of the research.

INITIAL DATA GATHERING

The first step to finding churches where we could engage in detailed field work was to gather a wide list of churches which might be "flourishing" in their Northern contexts. Although we both had churches we might nominate from years of working and living in the North, we did not want to rely solely on our own experiences, aware of the narrowness of vision that such an approach might bring.

We approached people with oversight of many churches across the North of England to ask for names and locations of churches which might be flourishing. In the Anglican church we approached Diocesan and Area Bishops, Directors of Mission and Ministry, and Communications Officers. In the Methodist Church, we approached Chairs of Districts and Circuit Superintendent Ministers; the Susannah Wesley Foundation also gave us some invaluable contacts.

From these conversations with people in positions of diocesan or district oversight, we gathered the names of forty-nine churches which were "flourishing" (or at least where "something was happening"). Some dioceses were more represented than others; in some places the people we asked for help did not reply to our queries. And here is another drawback of our initial approach: we relied on gatekeepers to provide us with information. Some people drew back their gates and provided us with plenty of detailed contacts; others did not. And of course, we were relying on these people's understandings of what a "flourishing" church looked like, and their own implicit ecclesiology. Here is how we discovered the problem with the word "flourishing" in more detail. In one conversation with an Area Bishop, Elli asked what they thought of a particular church she knew well and felt was flourishing in its context. The bishop replied that although that church did a lot of work with its community, including running a busy foodbank and substantial youth work, attendance at Sunday services was not stable. For that particular bishop, large and stable Sunday congregations were the measure of a flourishing church, not engagement with its community.[3] The maintenance of the institution of the Church is one of the many responsibilities of a bishop and it is therefore no surprise that they have an interest in large, stable, and indeed financially able congregations. Sam Ewell discusses at length the work of Ivan Illich with regard to the "institutional spectrum" and we are clearly in the polarity here between Illich's understanding of "process" and "product."[4] At this stage we simply note this tension, since we plan to revisit these questions in chapter 8. This research positions itself on

3. We recognize now that another way of approaching this research would have been to embark on an initial pilot project which would have worked at defining some criteria for "flourishing" and flushed out some of these potential misunderstandings about nomenclature.

4. Ewell, *Faith Seeking*, 151–52.

the edge of the institution rather than at its center and so here we both recognize our dependency on these gatekeepers of the research and we reserve the right to offer a critique of their approach.

This was the point at which we needed to revisit a wider assumption in our approach: the equating of "flourishing" with "success," where that success was limited to numbers and financial resources. We had chosen to use the word "flourishing" in the research question and had taken it to our conversations with senior stakeholders to convey a sense of something growing and starting to blossom. As a noteworthy aside there is a theme of cultivation metaphors throughout this research—partly because we both enjoy gardening, but also because we have come to understand that churches change and leadership has a place within that change. Human organizations such as churches can be likened to ecosystems in the natural world, so a "systems" approach to understanding them is very fruitful and can be integrated into a thoroughly practical ecclesiology. First, just like any living cell they need to have a porous, semi-permeable membrane or boundary to their context for continuing life (Open Systems Theory); second, they are not transformed in straight lines from one defined starting point to an envisioned endpoint—rather, small, subtle, and repeatable changes have to be introduced around which the whole system will adapt (Complex Adaptive Systems Theory). I have written more about this approach in a journal article,[5] and an introductory text to leadership which takes seriously the systems approach and utilizes a cultivation metaphor.[6] We believe that while this approach may not lead to massive growth it is "natural" and ingrained in the ecology of the human system, so it leads at the very least to sustainability. Chapter 6 will rehearse this emphasis on the "ecology of church growth" by the Anglican missiologist Stephen Spencer.

However, "flourishing" held different meanings for some of our gatekeepers, including the implication of being successful. This was illustrated in a conversation with a different Area Bishop, when talking about another church Elli felt was flourishing. The bishop was reluctant to suggest this church as a site to research: she felt that although they were doing amazing things, the situation at the church was too fragile to cope with a visit from a researcher and the concomitant scrutiny. Pastorally, the bishop did not want the fragile shoots of growth to be jeopardized by

5. See Rooms, "Understanding Local."

6. See Rooms and Keifert, *Spiritual Leadership.*

the work of "outsider" researchers. She did not see this church as "flourishing" (although she thought it was wonderful) as it was so fragile at that point.

In order to disrupt the association of "flourishing" with success, we instead started talking about churches where "something was happening" and we stuck to this definition for the rest of the project. This change in language allowed us to nuance what we were looking for: not churches that had to have large congregations and stable incomes, or churches where relationships were stable and growth was assured. Instead, this allowed us to make distinctions in different types of growth or blossoming and allowed us to introduce the idea that we were looking for churches where God might be "up to something." Of course, since this was research, we did not know fully what that "something" was—we left it open-ended and susceptible to *discernment,* another theme of this book. This reflection from the research occasions the writing of the next chapter in this book which will delve much more deeply into a typology of "growing and flourishing" in our research churches.

THE ONLINE SURVEY AND ITS RESULTS

Our next step was to invite our forty-nine identified churches to take part in an online survey. The aim of this survey was to get a "snapshot" of both quantitative and qualitative data on some questions, and to find churches which were willing to take part in deeper research via field visits. As well as ascertaining basic details such as their name and location, we asked all forty-nine churches the following questions[7] in several sections:

Leadership, on a four-point scale (Completely/Mostly/A bit/Not at all):

1. Taking the leadership of the church as a whole, how local are you?
2. Taking the leadership of the church as a whole, how regional are you?
3. Taking the leadership of the church as a whole, how northern are you?

7. At the time we set out on the research we were not aware of any similar projects. However, as someone interested in and actively accompanying churches in missional change, I was able to draw on some of that experience to design the survey questions. Two comparable studies now available from North America are: Lockhart, *West Coast Mission*; James, *Church Planting in Post-Christian Soil.*

Congregation, on a four-point scale (Completely/Mostly/A bit/Not at all):

4. Taking the congregation of the church as a whole, how local are you?
5. Taking the congregation of the church as a whole, how regional are you?
6. Taking the congregation of the church as a whole, how northern are you?
7. What is your church's mission statement, or vision statement?

People new to faith, on a four-point scale (Regularly/Occasionally/Very occasionally/Not at all)

8. Are people are coming to faith in your church?
9. Do these people "stick" in the church after professing faith?
10. Text Question: Have you any sense of what is enabling people to come to faith?

Church and Community

11. How do you perceive the relationship between your church and your wider local community? Register yourselves on a five-point scale from:
    - Completely cold/closed
    - Somewhat cold/closed
    - Somewhere in between
    - Somewhat warm/open
    - Completely warm/open
12. When doing things with the community, does the initiative come from:
    - Always the church
    - Mainly the church
    - Always the community
    - Mainly the community

- Always negotiating between church and community
- Mainly negotiating between church and community

13. Text Question: How do you think the people outside church and in the community would describe you as a church?
14. Thinking of how people in your church relate to Jesus what five words would you use to describe Jesus? Or, to put it another way, who is the Jesus people are worshipping at your church—what five words come to mind?

Questions 1 to 3 were designed to help us get an overview of these churches: were their leaders primarily local, northern people, or were they imports from the South? Questions 4 to 6 gave a similar overview of the congregations, allowing for the possibility that some of these churches had large student congregations who might be from different regions, or be "destination" churches where large proportions of the congregation came from further afield for a particular style of worship. Vision or Mission statements are important to capture for churches as they give a sense of the imagination and hope for the future which are available to the people in and around them. It was important to us to register that people were finding faith in these churches—that is, people were crossing the boundary and joining. In the other direction what was the relationship like between these churches and their wider community—was there a sense of porosity and how was it conceived? Finally, we wished to know, on the assumption that the gospel and the person of Jesus are connected, how these churches would describe him.

Of the forty-nine churches we approached, the answers to the above questions came from eighteen churches: a response rate of 37%. While this was not an exceptional response, it remained above one-third of the whole which is considered to be representative in this kind of "cold-calling" survey-based research. That is, we could only communicate (electronically) with the designated contact in the church via the address given to us by the Church body—in most cases this was the Minister or Vicar. These too were gatekeepers then, of the project and some were prepared to be open to us. We did suggest that, if possible, the survey was filled in as a group or leadership team exercise; however, no doubt because of time constraints, we discovered later that the vast majority had been filled in by one person, more often than not the leader with overall responsibility. Of these eighteen churches, sixteen said they would be willing for researchers to come for field visits.

Since this data has not changed since we published it in *Fuzzy Church,* I feel the best way of presenting it is to reproduce those initial findings here:

> Seventy-eight percent of our respondents said their church leadership was completely or mostly local, and 94% said their church leadership was completely or mostly northern or regional. All respondents said their church congregation was completely or mostly local and northern. The vision statements of our respondents' churches included "Nobody's Perfect—Anything's Possible," "To know Jesus and make Him known," and "I came that they may have life, and have it abundantly." Three churches mentioned the name of their parish or community in their statement, and three either didn't have a mission statement or were reviewing it.
>
> All our respondents said people were coming to faith in their churches: 44% saw people regularly coming to faith, and 56% saw people occasionally coming to faith. Forty-four percent of respondents said these new Christians were regularly sticking in their church after professing faith, and 50% said these people were occasionally staying in church after professing faith: 94% in total. When describing what was enabling people to come to faith, our participants described "strong sense of family, belonging and welcome," being an inclusive church, encouraging people to ask questions, and "fresh starts and a new hope." Three respondents mentioned the Alpha course, one mentioned Fresh Expressions of worship, and one mentioned funerals, weddings, and baptisms.
>
> Ninety-five percent of our respondents said that the relationship between their church and the community was somewhat or completely warm and open. When doing things with the community, 55% of our respondents said that the initiative came mainly from the church, and 44% said that the initiative came mainly from negotiating between church and community. When describing how the people outside the church might speak about the church, our participants mentioned being "friendly," "welcoming," "lively," "at the heart of the community," and a practical help to people: one participant said, "literally a quotation I hear from time to time [is], 'Yours is the Church that really helps people.'" When our participants shared the five words they used to describe Jesus, the most common one was

> "friend," with ten mentions. "Love" or "loving" came joint second with "saviour," at seven mentions each. "Lord" was used by five participants, and "teacher" by four.[8]

In summary, then, our online survey gave us a "snapshot" or overview of churches led by mostly Northern and local people, with congregations who were completely or mostly northern and local. This was important to us as this data embedded our research subjects firmly in the North. These churches were places where people were coming to faith—not always regularly, which was perhaps another indication of fragility or where growth was assured, but where "something was happening". So we knew we had a basis for investigating this phenomenon further by going and meeting these people and learning more about them. These were churches which had good relationships with their local community, there was porosity available (for further investigation) although events or projects were often (but not always) initiated by the church. And we had some clues about how they thought about Jesus and we will return to this data about Jesus later in the chapter.

It is worth noting here that we used the responses to the open-ended questions 7, 10, 13, and 14 in our field visits, especially in conversation with the churches' leadership teams, when we would ask the other leaders if they agreed with the person who filled in the survey. This was a way of checking the initial data with a wider set of people.

FIELDWORK

In order to identify the churches that we would like to research further, we entered the sixteen churches that were open to a visit into an informal grid. We knew we did not have the capacity to visit them all and we knew we needed a cross-section of the whole to represent as wide a constituency as possible. The grid consisted of criteria around denomination, church tradition (the spectrum of catholic-evangelical via the "central" category in Anglicanism, at least), context (urban, rural, suburban, coastal, etc.), geographical spread across the North (i.e. North-East, North-West, and more southerly locations), and socio-economics plus deprivation. We initially selected ten churches to approach, knowing some would probably change their minds about participating when they found out what was actually involved, as indeed turned out to be the case. Eight initially

8. Rooms and Wort, *Fuzzy Church*, 7–9.

agreed and then one dropped out nearer the time for the visit as other priorities had taken over. We were left with seven to research in greater depth which we felt was sufficient for a project of this size and scope—and as we'll see, these churches generated more than enough qualitative data to work with. We described these churches in *Fuzzy Church* with enough detail to demonstrate their variety, but no more since this would reduce their anonymity, which we had agreed with them:

We did some analysis of the relative poverty of our research parishes using the Church Urban Fund's database (https://cuf.org.uk/lookup-tool). The rankings offered here were observed before our research visits and have changed slightly since (and so cannot be used to identify the churches). There are 12,382 parishes in England and the lower the ranking the poorer is the parish out of all that number.

A—A Methodist church in Derbyshire. The church is in a town of *c.*11,000 people which had a history of mining. Rank: 1,567.

B—An Evangelical Anglican church in Lancashire. The church is in a town of *c.*15,000 people. The church was built in the Victorian era and was substantially reordered in the 1970s and 1980s. Rank: 5,663.

C—A new worshipping community in Yorkshire. Located in a town of 88,000 people, this church is made up of mainly homeless and vulnerable people. It meets in a Methodist church building, had an Anglican minister when we visited, and is supported by churches of all denominations. Rank: 1,186.

D—An Anglican church on a social-housing estate of a few thousand people in Lancashire. The church building closed in 2013/14, and the church now worships in a community centre. Rank: 297.

E—An Anglican church in Yorkshire. The church is located in a town of 138,000 people which had a history of mining. The church was built in the Victorian era, and was reordered and a community centre added recently. Rank: 2.

F—An Anglican benefice of five churches in rural Yorkshire. The five villages have a combined population of *c.*1,200. The data on these villages was too low to have a ranking in the look-up tool.

G—An Ecumenical Team Ministry of three churches in a town in the North-east. The town has a population of *c.*43,000 and a history of mining and shipbuilding. Of the three churches, one is a Victorian Anglican church, one is an Anglican/Methodist/URC church founded in the 1980s, and one is a Victorian Anglican church which has been converted recently into a chapel of ease. Rank: 1,423.[9]

So, these were the churches where "something was happening" that agreed to be research subjects. Elli and I did the first visit together (to C) in order to test out and agree on our joint approach and then to save time and some expense we divided the others up to be visited by one of us (Nigel visited A, B, and D; Elli visited E, F, and G). Overall, we felt that we had a good representation of the criteria we were looking for, not least because "Four of the churches were Anglican, one was Methodist and the two others[10] had some ecumenical connection between a mainly Anglican foundation and the Methodist and other Churches."[11] It was significant for the research that all of the churches were in the 50% poorest half of all the parishes in England as a whole.

Our field visits[12] contained four main elements: A tour of the area local to the church led by someone with intimate knowledge of it, attendance at a Sunday service, a focus group interview with the church's leaders, and a focus group interview with people who had recently come to faith through the church.

The tour of the area local to the church

This gave us an overall sense of the church's locale, and a picture of what was within the horizon of the church and its members, including the edges of its self-understanding of place. This allowed the guide (a church leader, a church member or in some cases someone from the community with an intimate knowledge of it) to describe their local community in the ways that were most important to them. This often included the history of the area, other churches that they did or did not work with,

9. Rooms and Wort, *Fuzzy Church*, 130–1.

10. On revisiting the data for the next chapter, it emerged that Church F also had some significant Ecumenical connections with the Methodist Church and Methodists were involved in the current arrangements.

11. Rooms and Wort, *Fuzzy Church*, 9.

12. Inevitably, and again with hindsight it would have been better to make several visits to these churches and their worship over an extended period, say a year. Unfortunately, the resources we had at our disposal as "loving semi-professional amateurs" did not stretch this far.

the type of work and housing available in the local area, and where their church members lived. It also allowed us to ask questions about places or people that the church or its members had a relationship with and about other places of local significance in their own right. We made mental and written notes of these visits as we went along.

Attendance at a Sunday service

We took detailed notes in these services in order to generate a "thick description" of the event and the performance of worship following Fiddes and Ward's ethnographic approach to a baptism service in Oxford.[13] We described the building, its physical structure, something of its history, and the kind of space it created; the start and finish times of the service, the welcome as we arrived, what happens before the service begins and after it ends, and the approximate number of people present. We noted both the events and some observations on them: when the congregation was engaged or disengaged, and the emotional feel of the worship and congregations as the service ebbed and flowed. We also noted details such as the use of technology, and microphones and who holds them. We described the liturgical stages or elements of the worship, and paid particular attention to the sermon and the prayers looking for "indigeneity" in voice, accent, and language. We also paid close attention to whether prayers and sermons mentioned the local community or national or international issues.

Focus group interview with the church's leaders

We allowed the church to define who they felt were the leaders of the church, but we suggested this should be a group of people and not just the incumbent or minister. Of forty-one respondents, group size varied from eight at one church down to four at two churches. In these group interviews, we revisited the church's initial responses to our online survey. We began by looking again at how local, regional or northern the leadership and congregation were, whether they felt it matters where the leadership comes from, and whether the localness of the church members affected how the church operated. We asked them to reflect more on their mission or vision statement, where it came from, and how it shaped what the

13. Fiddes and Ward, "Affirming Faith," 51–56.

church is doing. We revisited the questions about people finding Christian faith, whether they "stick" in the church, and what was enabling people to find faith, and we explored these answers in more depth. We asked them to reflect on the relationship between church and community, exploring what enabled people outside the church to be "warm" to them, and what might "put them off." We also revisited the church's five words to describe Jesus, asking the group if they agreed with what had been written in the survey, whether the congregation might agree with these words or whether they would give other words. We asked the group what Jesus might be like if he walked the streets of their community today (if that question was acceptable to the group).

Focus group interview with people new to faith

These people were identified and gathered by the local minster or leadership team, except in two cases (C and E) where it proved logistically impossible within the parameters of the twenty-four hour visit to gather a group (despite having given the leadership plenty of prior warning—perhaps another cultural/contextual issue). In one case (D) leaders were present in this meeting, since there was no available meeting place other than the Minister's home and so I suggested they participate as little as possible, in order not to skew the data collection too much. And in another church (F), none of the people who had recently come to faith could come to the organized interview, so the group was made up of more established church members. Once again this is evidence for the fragility of the "something" that was happening at these churches—the inability in some churches to gather new disciples into an open-ended discussion of their experiences.

In total twenty-eight people participated in these five focus groups, the most we had was seven people and the least five. This interview partly involved visual research methods (specifically photo elicitation) as participants were shown a range of seventeen photographs. This is how we described some of the pictures in *Fuzzy Church*:

> There was Holman Hunt's picture of Jesus as the light of the world, a Chinese depiction of Jesus among the little children, and a Native American picture of Jesus and the Sacred Heart. We included pictures of Jesus as a white-skinned man, and a picture of Jesus as a crucified woman, or Christa. We also included pictures which might have particularly northern resonance: a

> fisherman on a North Atlantic trawler, the Angel of the North, a picture of Jesus in the Blackpool illuminations, and a man dressed as Jesus in a football crowd, holding up a sign in support of the team's manager.[14]

We asked the respondents the following five questions:

- Please could you choose a picture which reminds you most of how you see Jesus?
- Why did you pick that one? Why not any of the others?
- When you started coming to church, were there any things you felt you had to give up, or stop doing?
- When you started coming to church, were there any things you felt you had to pick up, or start doing?
- If you were telling a friend about your experience of being a Christian, what would you say?

We chose to use photo elicitation for interviews with the new Christians for a few reasons: to put the participants at their ease at the start of the session, to empower them and enable them to be "experts" in their own faith, and to gain rich and deep data. At its simplest, photo elicitation is the process of inserting photographs into the interview process.[15] The practice of looking at photographs together can feel much less confrontational than asking questions, since it introduces another object of focus other than the interviewer. As we noted in *Fuzzy Church*,[16] an image utilizes parts of the brain that process visual rather than verbal information which opens up a bigger space for conversation, especially where religion and spirituality are concerned.

Most of the visits took twenty-four hours over two days, with the churches often kindly putting us up overnight and generously providing meals. This inevitably led to informal conversations about the churches which also informed our findings, as well as breaking down the inevitable barriers between researcher and some of the subjects.

In terms of research ethics, all of the churches participated entirely voluntarily and we made it clear that they could withdraw at any time, and indeed one did. All the participants in both Focus Groups were given

14. Rooms and Wort, *Fuzzy Church*, 10. Full description available from the author.
15. Harper, "Talking About," 13.
16. Rooms and Wort, *Fuzzy Church*, 11.

a paper sheet of information describing the research purpose and process, explaining the audio-recording and use of their data alongside their ultimate anonymity in any reporting of what they said. It was also made clear they were free not to answer any questions and withdraw from the questioning at any time. All gave their verbal assent to this before the audio recording began. Our presence as researchers was announced at each of the worship services. We "closed the research loop" by sending each participating church a copy of *Fuzzy Church* when it was published.

We carried out these four main research elements in slightly different ways from location to location as circumstances demanded. At location C, a church leader not only drove us around the town and pointed out areas where people who came to the church lived, and other churches they had relationships with, they also drove us to an escarpment over the town to get a bird's eye view of the bigger area. At church E, it was raining heavily on the day of the visit and the churchwarden also needed to let people into the building, so we used a map to prompt discussion on the area and the relationships between the church and the community. As many people in location C often had chaotic lifestyles that meant coming to a focus group might be difficult, we decided instead to join in with the after-worship food distribution and café time (an already established and regular practice) and ask people questions there. These are the nitty-gritty challenges of field work in real-world research situations and while they reduce the range of our data somewhat, we do not believe it is flawed in any serious way.

DATA ANALYSIS

After all field visits were completed, we could address the data we had collected. We wrote up field notes to five of the seven locations. This text amounted to around 17,000 words in total. We sent the recorded audio files to a professional transcriber which returned approximately 56,000 words for the leaders' Focus Groups and 31,000 words for the people new to faith. Given that this amounts to 104,000 words in total we felt we had more than enough data to work with and make some significant and robust conclusions.

We analyzed our data manually and by computer. First, we read over each other's notes from our field visits and compared our thoughts and memories. Following the close reading of our own and each other's transcripts, we grouped the themes that emerged into eleven categories (or codes as are they known in the technical language of qualitative data analysis).

After this initial process, we used NVivo (the popular qualitative data analysis software) to compare the findings generated here with our initial thoughts. We analyzed the frequency of words used in the four main research elements of our field visits and identified the themes which emerged. We discovered that the themes which emerged from our work with NVivo tallied closely with the themes we had found in our manual analysis: this was our first time working with NVivo, so we initially worried we had misunderstood its capabilities, or were using it wrongly. Elli discussed this issue with a colleague researcher at the Church Army Research Unit (Elli by this time had started working as a teacher and trainer with the Church Army), who uses NVivo frequently. She was reassured that these correlations were due to good initial analysis rather than any problems with our use of NVivo.

The eleven categories that emerged from our analysis, both from our own examination of the data and using NVivo word searches, were as follows:

1. Hospitality/Reality/Northernness/Authenticity
2. Porosity/Engagement/Community
3. Leader/Charismatic/Teaching/Intentionality
4. Family
5. Jesus/Friend
6. Fragility/Complexity
7. Class/Politics/Socialism
8. Facebook/International cultural influences
9. Freedom/Kingdom/Justice
10. Death/Life/Bereavement
11. Sacrament/Baptism/Eucharist

How these are related to the initial findings we will address below.

INITIAL FINDINGS

In this section we largely rehearse the reported findings of the research in *Fuzzy Church*, while relating them to the NVivo categories and the six elements of the *Gehalt* of Northernness from Fox and Niven. We called this section in the original book, "The gospel in a northern dialect" which was an effective way, in our view, of distancing ourselves from the notion of a direct relationship between gospel and culture. We took this idea from the Brazilian Bishop Pedro Casaldáliga who wrote that "the universal word speaks only dialect."[17] Dialects are subtle, even elusive, variations on language which are nevertheless discernible when listening deeply beneath the surface of speech.

We note initially that our first NVivo category, "Hospitality/Reality/Northernness/Authenticity," has significant overlap with "Authenticity–Realism" in the northern *Gehalt,* some examples we quote are from leaders at churches F and G.

> I think there's probably a distinctiveness about northern in that, it's like the sort of analogy of the Northerner on the tube [in London] smiling and talking to people. I think that's what, if you're going to use that analogy, that's what, what we've, what I feel we're here to do. To open conversation with people, to introduce, just all of that. I think there is, that's a northern thing, about people are much more open. I'm probably . . . probably a tad too open for them . . . well, I just can't help it, it's out and I think, "Well, no, it's about being honest." I've got a very, very dear friend who is very frightfully posh, [name], and she loves my family, she loves to come here because . . . she can be herself, she doesn't have to pretend.[18]

We note also the immediate connection between NVivo categories 1 and 2 since honesty and the authenticity that is based on it creates a hospitable space which allows for the formation of community across porous boundaries. This is how the notion of "fuzzy" in the book title *Fuzzy Church* arose from a participant in Church F when discussing how people were coming to faith in the church.

> I think there's a bit of fluffy edges though that when I say people are coming to faith, it's quite hard to know when that is because there is no point at which they sign on the dotted line. But, but

17. Casaldáliga, *Creio na,* 211.

18. Rooms and Wort, *Fuzzy Church,* 74–75.

> what we can see is people who didn't come to church, were not bothered about God, who now are and who will have conversations. So, I guess that's perhaps what we're talking about when we say coming to faith. There are not, not necessarily those overt signs but I, I, I think again it's a fuzzy edge about a few things, that it's about community and feeling part of something and belonging. And that's, it's a little bit to do with the village community but it's probably more to do with the church community.[19]

Thus the "Community–Home" elements of northern *Gehalt* are evident at this point, but this is not an insular privatized home, although we did have some concerns about the recurrence of family (NVivo category 4) in the data as it can lead to a closed system, yet this did not seem to be wholly the case in the research churches.[20] They were alive and "happening" because they had porous boundaries to their publics and were being changed by those who were joining them. There was a particular of example of this in church C where the leadership had intentionally engaged across class boundaries;[21] this connects with NVivo category 7, which perhaps should not have been a surprise given the nature of the communities we were researching. We discussed the demonstration of porosity in some detail[22] in relation to Open Systems Theory and the reversal of the traditional "flow" of the church to its community according to the work of Al Barrett.[23] The porosity of our research churches also extended on social media in several cases and internationally through the internet (NVivo category 8). For example, church D showed a video of a Christian stand-up comedian from the United States as a countdown to the start of the worship (there was an actual countdown clock on the screen, and we understood this happened most weeks as a way to encourage the worship to begin on time, in a community where this was not usual).

Intentional leadership (NVivo category 3) which creates the "holding space" for safe engagement across boundaries was also found to be beneficial and we noted this in church G:

> But it's that welcome isn't it, and that fellowship that people can feel like they are in a safe space, that they can come and be themselves and people will accept them for who they are.

19. Rooms and Wort, *Fuzzy Church,* ix.
20. Rooms and Wort, *Fuzzy Church,* 88.
21. Rooms and Wort, *Fuzzy Church,* 79.
22. Rooms and Wort, *Fuzzy Church,* 80–84.
23. See Barrett, *Interrupting.*

> I don't think that's a given in any place, I think that is because of our congregations and the way that they are. And I think it comes from the leadership as well that we are welcoming and inclusive.[24]

NVivo categories 6 and 9 were combined in a theme we discerned in the data of "fragility and freedom." Fragility, because what was happening in them was vulnerable and very new (and as we discovered almost all the churches were in the lower half of deprivation nationally and some were severely challenged there). In addition, the theme of death and new life was evident in the data (NVivo category 10). The majority of the research churches had faced some form of death as a result of their post-Christendom reality, but were finding new life and freedom beyond that dying. We noted that two of our seven churches had labelled themselves or a key community project with the word freedom. Two others either spoke eloquently about it or demonstrated it by placing a banner in their worship space proclaiming it. While the others may not have mentioned freedom *per se* it is clear the new Christians were finding freedom in their faith.

Church A made a direct link between a literal "free" event they were putting on, the kingdom and the community project named "Freedom" that arose from that first engagement:

> The very first thing that happened before it was Freedom, before it was a ministry, we had a week, and we had a marquee on a local community area, and the idea behind that was that the concept was that people always expected the church to be asking for money, asking for things. And we wanted this week to be where the church gave. So, everything, for the whole week, it was morning afternoon and evening, was free. So that's your "Free." And the fact at that time was that it was a church activity, so we were open that that would be a stepping stone into the king*dom*. So, it's "Free*dom*." Ok? [*Laughter.*][25]

We do not believe this use of freedom is directly related to a liberationist theological perspective, nevertheless it is a very suggestive aspect of the data, especially in its relation to kingdom theology and therefore, inevitably, hope—which we paired with humor in the third of our aspects of northern *Gehalt*, that is "Humor—Hope." We note the laughter in the

24. Rooms and Wort, *Fuzzy Church*, 83.

25. Rooms and Wort, *Fuzzy Church*, 78.

interview above and when we went looking further for laughter in the data the following remarks could be made:

> we can record that there are 73 occasions where the transcription of the focus groups notes that there was laughter and six occasions where laughing is referred to by a speaker. We know that there are many different types of laughter, including the nervous, anxious sort which might be expected in an interview. Without doing a further detailed study of how each occasion of laughter sounded we can still suggest that this number of occasions is remarkable evidence for the importance of humour where something is happening related to the gospel and the kingdom. Our respondents, it seems were having fun (perhaps even experiencing joy) participating in the life of God flowing among them.[26]

We also noted that fragility and freedom came together at church D with a profound understanding of the Eucharist (NVivo category 11) as radically open to anyone regardless of baptism or belief.

> No belief whatsoever is required for the reception of the consecrated elements (so it is not just baptism that is not required as in the open table stance)—in fact when I observed the worship it seemed there was an innate expectation that everyone, no matter who they were, would participate. In both focus groups this stance was affirmed first by someone who spoke about their experience of communion: "It's the closest you get to him [Jesus] because it's [the bread and wine] a part of him [Silence]."[27]

Finally, we come to findings about the person of Jesus (NVivo category 4) which was a major focus of the research because of the theological relationship between Jesus and the gospel. We collected data both in the initial survey and the focus groups. We reported the survey data where we had asked respondents to describe how they and their church understood Jesus in five words as follows:

> Out of the 84 responses the most frequent was friend (10) followed by variations on love (7) and savior (7). There were 5 mentions of Jesus as Lord and interestingly, given the discussion above, 5 who named Jesus as "accepting" of everyone and non-judgmental. Next were teacher (4), healer (3), kind (2), King (2), alive (2), challenging (2) and forgiving (2). Of the 33 single

26. Rooms and Wort, *Fuzzy Church*, 73.

27. Rooms and Wort, *Fuzzy Church*, 78.

> occurrences we think some the ones of note for our research are liberator, restorer, real, down-to-earth and joy-giving.[28]

Then in the focus groups with new Christians there were 278 places where Jesus was mentioned which resulted in four statements from the data about who Jesus is: someone we can have a relationship with; someone who changes us; Jesus is God; and Jesus is someone known in community.[29] We were then able to comment on this data as follows and offer several examples from the data:

> The main point that arises for us from this extensive data is that Jesus emerges as *both* a personal, private Jesus (friend, protector, lover) *and* a public Christ (saviour, Lord, God). In fact, we can note the progression from the private to the public Jesus Christ in the descriptions of Jesus derived from the focus group conversations.[30]

We were particularly drawn to the following quotation from church G when they were asked what Jesus would look like if he were to appear among them today:

> Somebody that you feel, you know, is just part of this community that you can just relate to. You would feel comfortable sitting next to him on a bus, just to chat and I think somebody, who is probably quite . . . they don't offer lots of words, but you can tell they're interested in you and maybe over listening conversations that imagine if you were sitting church, just taking it all it in and enjoying it.[31]

In conclusion of the presentation of the findings from the data we were able to say:

> We can describe our research churches as "Fuzzy Church"—they have learnt how to create a fuzzy boundary at their edge, to be changed by those who are joining them and to witness to a public, transformational Christ within the world around them. This is good news, gospel arising authentically from who they are and who they are becoming.[32]

28. Rooms and Wort, *Fuzzy Church*, 85.
29. Rooms and Wort, *Fuzzy Church*, 85–86
30. Rooms and Wort, *Fuzzy Church*, 86–87.
31. Rooms and Wort, *Fuzzy Church*, 87.
32. Rooms and Wort, *Fuzzy Church*, 88.

And in addition, here we have described how the analysis of the research data both manually and with the aid of computer software generated meaningful codes or themes which demonstrate the breadth and complexity of the gospel evident in these churches. At the same time there is a relationship between the "depth-content" of Northernness and these findings in northern churches where "something is happening." That relationship is an indirect, nuanced and complex one, but nevertheless it exists.

OUTPUTS FROM THE RESEARCH

Before moving on to offering a reflexive critique of the methodology we have described, it is worth sharing what "outputs" the research has generated. It goes without saying that the publication of *Fuzzy Church* was a major result of the project and at this point we should also remark on the existence of chapter 5 of *Fuzzy Church* since it is too long to be reproduced in this book. The chapter is an agglomerated and imagined "thick description" of the northern churches we visited based on our field notes and memories of the visits. We think it stands alone as both a tribute to our research subjects and a hopeful imaginary of what is possible in northern churches. Before the publication of the book, we wrote a short report for the funders at the Susanna Wesley Foundation.[33] The publication of the book in 2021 also occasioned some other events we were both or separately involved in. Without describing them exhaustively here there were research seminars at Roehampton University (courtesy of the funders) and the Queens Foundation for Ecumenical Theological Education in Birmingham (where Nigel is an honorary research fellow). A webinar discussed the research and our findings at York St. John University where happily Kate Fox, author of the important PhD research that informed ours was also able to participate. The event was provocatively titled, "Is God Northern?" and a recording was made, which at the time of writing is still available.[34] A brief radio interview on BBC Radio York also developed from this interaction. In addition, Nigel ran an impromptu workshop on Northernness at the Greenbelt Arts Festival in 2021, which was possible since it was a pared-down event due to the Covid-19 pandemic. The main feedback we received at these events was

33. See Susanna Wesley Foundation, "Northern Gospel."

34. See York St. John University, "Is God Northern?"

that participants, especially those from the North, felt "seen" and represented, some for the very first time. As Dr. Sharon Jagger from York St. John University noted during the webinar, "it's representation really."[35] This was confirmation of the importance of this theological work for a region that suffers coloniality. And finally, of course we note the production of this further book as the final output from the original research project. While we were able to secure some funding for the project, this was much more on a "stipend" basis and certainly hasn't matched the number of hours we both put into it.

REFLEXIVE CRITIQUE

In chapter 3 we engaged with Goto's critique of contemporary research methodologies in practical theology, of which this study is one example. She discussed the pitfalls of nativism, which we have engaged with seriously and noted our own shortcomings as we set out as researchers. At the end of her chapter 5[36] she asks nine critical questions which should be put to any research methodology. Having explained our methodology, we now address them here, and pair them up where necessary. Goto's questions are meant to be asked prospectively, which we were unable to, thus this reflection can only note where we fulfilled Goto's expectations for excellence in research and the limits of what we did when we fell short.

Who defined the research problem?

This has been, at heart, a personal labor of love (of home?) which begins in my own experience, gifting, and vocation. I discovered the notion of contextual theology as a new priest in Stoke-on-Trent in the early 1990s, given the particularity of that place in the North Midlands with its distinct and unique features, but which also resonated with my own origins in Hull, East Yorkshire. There is also a real sense that the international community of missiologists, such as Steve Bevans, Anthony Gittins, and Clemens Sedmak, who have worked on questions of faith and culture, at the very least have defined the parameters of the problem. What this research project did was to bring concepts regarding the relationship of faith and culture, born out of missiological experience globally (including

35. Jagger is quoted on the webpage referenced above.

36. Goto, *Taking on Practical Theology*, 161–62.

my own in Africa), into dialogue with the grounded reality of churches in the North of England. Thus, the research tests and challenges the starting concepts with actual field research while playing intentionally in the arena of contextual theology. I remember a conversation early on in the project with Steve Bevans where he noted a dearth of this kind of research which would complexify accepted approaches in the field. And this book, as opposed to *Fuzzy Church,* is where these emphases can be more fully developed as a contribution to contextualization in World Christianity from the particularity of the North of England.

Then I discovered an able and willing co-researcher in Elli who was willing to give her time and energy to the project and co-create it with me. It is worth noting that both of us are active Christian disciples and faith leaders (one ordained) who have a research interest in contextual theology. Goto discusses "training insiders" for research,[37] but our positioning would complexify the insider/outsider notion in this research. We are what she names as "faith community leaders" as well as researchers. Thus, we could argue that the locus of theology generated by this project is much more in the local church and the systems that support it (Church bodies and theological training institutions) than the "academy" as Goto presents it.

For whom is this study worthy and relevant? Who says so?

I think we'd like to argue that ultimately this work represents all people in the North of England, and by extension England as a whole. I think the way in which the work of people like Kate Fox and Alex Niven has informed it is testament to its regional and public significance. We are not naïve, however in thinking that a work of contextual theology is going to have an enormous reach. Nevertheless, the York St John webinar discussing whether God could be imagined as northern is evidence that we have something here which is highly worthy and relevant. Clearly the project also has relevance to local churches and church bodies in the North of England. We had five endorsements for *Fuzzy Church* (printed in the preliminary pages of the book) from English Anglican and Methodist Church leaders (one of the main intended audiences of that book)—alongside three international endorsements, which means the work has

37. Goto, *Taking on Practical Theology,* 163.

relevance beyond the UK as well, a dimension which we hope to enhance with the publication of this further book.

What knowledge will the community gain from this study?

There are various communities at play here. Northern churches, their leaders and people can learn through this project the strength and depth of their "indigenous" culture and how it connects, albeit in complex ways, to the good news of the kingdom of God. One would hope that they and the Church bodies that represent them can extend this learning into how to go about mission and evangelism that works with the grain of northern culture, in a post-colonial fashion, away from the insertion of a supra-cultural gospel into their culture. Church leaders training or moving to be ministers in the North, whether insiders or outsiders, should benefit from an understanding of the North that can form a foundation for their approach to their future ministry. The international research community in the field of contextual theology gains knowledge of how notions of faith and culture play out in a particular post-Christendom, northern European regional context.

What knowledge will the researcher gain from this study?

We both feel we gained a great deal from the study, as post-doctoral researchers. We know much more about research itself and the limitations of what we did. We noted above that we are "insiders" as well as "faith community leaders" and so the research has informed our understanding of the North and our practice in many and varied nuanced ways. In addition, we are now conscientized to simplistic correlations between gospel and culture, and the ways in which these tend to draw on essentialism and nativism.

What are the likely positive outcomes from this study?

We have already seen how people, especially Christians who consider themselves northern find themselves in this study and are pleased to be represented, perhaps for the first time. We believe there is a prophetic edge to this research for the Church in England to take seriously the gift of what we have learnt from these northern churches where something is happening. In *Fuzzy Church* we suggested that our research subject churches offer hope (and we could now add a "future," following Niven) for the post-Christendom (declining) English Church as a whole. We developed a series of *what if* questions:

> *What if* northern churches where something is happening are the clue to the future of the English, if not Western church? *What if* "fuzzy" church, discovered in the North, became the watchword for how church can be alive and flourishing? *What if* the decomposing northern church is the soil in which there is resurrection for Christians in a post-colonial world?[38]

We also hope that the study will contribute to a complexifying of the relationship of faith and culture in the international field of contextual theology and its concomitant literature.

What are some possible negative outcomes? How can the negative outcomes be eliminated?

The main critique of our methodology which we touched on in chapter 3 is how we utilized our research subjects. They were not co-creators of the final outputs, as in some versions of *Theological Action Research* or as explicated in Goto's "Critical Intersubjective Approach."[39] Rather, we are more clearly located in what Goto calls the "Critical Subjective Approach"[40] where she draws on Bevan's definition of contextual theology and this is a clear limit of our methodology. Nevertheless, there are some mitigations we can note here. We surveyed eighteen locations and entered seven of them as participant observers and researchers. Goto cautions that "the themes that emerge from one location are not necessarily transferable to any other,"[41] though through our agglomeration of the seven subject churches we have claimed some scalability of the research findings. Finally, while we missed the opportunity for intersubjective research with participants, the sites of ministry[42] at the boundaries of our research churches which we have described as "fuzzy" or porous are indeed well on the way to being intersubjective. Insiders to the church are

38. Rooms and Wort, *Fuzzy Church*, 112.
39. Goto, *Taking on Practical Theology*, 97.
40. Goto, *Taking on Practical Theology*, 95.
41. Goto, *Taking on Practical Theology*, 95.
42. Goto, *Taking on Practical Theology*, 233.

being changed by the outsiders, whether they are joiners or not. If there was an opportunity to re-run this research these spaces would be a great place to locate the researcher.

To whom is the researcher accountable?

Accountability also worked at several levels in this project. First there was clear accountability in the letter of agreement we signed with the funders at the Susanna Wesley Foundation in 2017. Then there was mutual accountability between the two co-researchers. Being sent out in pairs has a long pedigree in the Church starting with the Seventy in Luke 10 and followed by Paul and Barnabas in the book of Acts. Steve Bevans acted as a research consultant to both of us and we met and talked on at least two occasions. The eight readers of *Fuzzy Church* who were prepared to endorse the research count as a sounding board for what we did. The research subjects and others who told us that they recognized themselves in the outputs also demonstrate a vital locus of accountability. Finally, this book has also been peer reviewed by one (anonymous) person, and therefore we are accountable in that sense also.

In this chapter we have thoroughly rehearsed the field research we undertook in northern churches and subjected it to dialogue with and critique from the previous chapters in this book. We have been transparent about the shortcomings of the research and its methodology especially at the beginning of the project. Nevertheless, we believe we have sound data and findings to work with in the rest of the book as we build on the foundations we started in *Fuzzy Church*. We now turn to questions of "growing and flourishing" in understanding more deeply what was going on in our research churches.

6

Growing and Flourishing

INTRODUCTION

In this chapter we will place our research in dialogue with a comparative research project based in the local church, presented by Stephen Spencer and Mwita Akiri in *Growing and Flourishing: The Ecology of Church Growth,*[1] which crosses over with many of the themes and concepts contained in this book. Spencer is one of a handful of better-known missiologists in the UK as the author of a core text,[2] among his other contributions to the field. *Growing and Flourishing* arises from his experience as an Anglican priest and seminary teacher in a Yorkshire (northern) diocese which had a longstanding partnership with a Tanzanian diocese in the Mara region (northern Tanzania between the Serengeti National Park and Lake Victoria).[3] Such is the growth of the original Tanzanian diocese in contrast to decline in England, that it is now three dioceses whereas

1. Officially (and in my view unfortunately) only Spencer is named as the author of the book on the cover though Akiri is acknowledged in the Introduction. I will therefore refer to the book as Spencer, *Growing and Flourishing*, but have also named Akiri in the bibliography.

2. See Spencer, *SCM Study Guide*. He has recently added: *Types of Christian Mission: An Introduction*.

3. For several decades the Anglican Communion has used the umbrella body called Partnership for World Mission to create and sustain "Companion Links" between dioceses on different continents for their mutual enrichment and fellowship in the gospel. It is one of these Companion Links that Spencer is describing in the book.

as the original link English Diocese of Wakefield has been subsumed under the larger Diocese of Leeds. Mwita Akiri is the bishop of one of the three Tanzanian dioceses and contributes significant commentary and perspective on what Spencer writes and observes throughout the book.

Before we begin, it is worth asking why we are bringing Spencer's work into play here, especially when we are making a deliberate (if temporary) move away from a consideration of the northern context of our churches *per se*. First, I believe his is a unique book in its aim and scope. Spencer, through the Companion Link, is exposed to the remarkable growth of the Anglican Church in the Mara region where one diocese quickly becomes three—and (as was the case in my experience in the same country and Church), despite the new daughter dioceses being divided off in weakness, with very few resources they continue to grow and flourish.[4] Spencer is curious and decides to research what is going on in Tanzania, which is worthwhile in itself, but also with the aim of seeing if what is learnt there can be brought to bear on churches in his home diocese in the North of England. It seems to me this is a stance of humility in the spirit of the post-colonial approach of this book which believes that the African Church can teach present-day representatives from the national Church of the previously colonizing power. In the spirit of this approach Spencer recognizes he needs to write the book *with* Akiri as a critical friend to what he is discovering. In this sense the book brings a new dimension to the concept of the "blessed reflex," that intuition of the Victorian missionaries to Africa in the nineteenth century that their work would bear fruit for the sending church in good time. Harvey Kwiyani describes this phenomenon very well in his important book *Sent Forth*,[5] where Africans now come to the West as missionaries (with varying degrees of effectiveness, it must be said), but here is another version of the same effect. Mission is now polycentric, from everywhere to everywhere.

The region that Spencer finds himself linked with is, from some perspectives such as the economic, highly marginalized.[6] And yet it also has many gifts,[7] not least of which is the remarkable church growth which is taking place there. In this sense there is resonance with our research where we noticed that almost all our churches were among the lower half of English parishes when it came to deprivation indices, yet

4. Spencer, *Growing and Flourishing*, 3.

5. See Kwiyani, *Sent Forth.*

6. Spencer, *Growing and Flourishing*, 7.

7. Spencer, *Growing and Flourishing*, 8–11.

"something was happening" in them despite their marginality, some of which was new people finding faith. While Spencer does not use the language of inculturation or contextualization overtly, the questions we have raised in this book are very much to the fore in Spencer's work, perhaps in two ways. He notes at several points in the book the way in which the message of the gospel both connects with and critiques the prevailing culture in this part of Tanzania in what we have noted are Walls's pilgrim and indigenizing principles. And then there is the question of how much can be transferred from Tanzania to the English church while recognizing the enormous gaps between the two places from many perspectives, including the obvious cultural differences. We will need to return to these questions later in this chapter.

Next, Spencer also intentionally employs an organic metaphor for his critical study of church growth throughout the book when he speaks of its "ecology." He begins by taking the example of St. Paul in 1 Cor 3:6 about his planting, Apollos' watering and God giving growth[8] and then sets out the detail of the metaphor:

> The organic analogy provides some helpful orientation as we begin to identify stages of church growth. It points to the way growth in the natural world, such as with a tree, takes place through a number of stages not defined by fixed periods of time but by qualitative differences. A tree begins its life as a seed germinating in the ground. This may take only a few hours. It grows into a tender sapling, over the course of a few days or weeks and then after a year or two becomes a young tree. Finally in its own time it gradually stretches up and out to become a mature tree with a complex ecology, which can take decades.[9]

Church growth, Spencer continues, is therefore comparable in this metaphor; it does not take place in mechanistic, straight lines over repeatable fixed periods of time. We too in the previous chapter have noted the importance of understanding what happens in local churches through organic metaphors, and Spencer's work here, we believe, will add to our understanding of seeing churches in this way.

Finally, Spencer's research question is very similar to ours given that he wishes to understand church growth in a specific local region of Tanzania: "Beginning at the local level, then, with the experience of new Christians, the question would be this: what was drawing these people

8. Spencer, *Growing and Flourishing*, 49.

9. Spencer, *Growing and Flourishing*, 55.

into an active Christian faith?"[10] The research presented here does not seem to be quite as rigorous as ours in the collection and analysis of large amounts of qualitative data; nevertheless, Spencer draws on his participant observations of the diocese over many visits (during seven years) with a resonant description of life there.[11] He is able to report the voices of new Christians now training for Christian ministry themselves[12] (and, significant in itself, the newly converted are trained to spread their faith) alongside leaders both of local churches and in the wider diocese.[13]

Before moving on to describe the content of Spencer's approach we can now address a methodological question left over from the previous chapter when we said we would return to the question of how we understand "growing and flourishing" and why this became the starting point for the research.[14] Spencer points out that his concern is growth, because that is the concern of his national Church going back to the Archbishopric of Rowan Williams.[15] It is a question on which there is a significant literature and he wishes to engage with it beyond the question of simple numerical growth to include spiritual growth, and growth which connects with the wider community beyond the gathered church, as well as other aspects which emerge from the research. It seems to me that Spencer's internal "intuitive researcher" reaches for the answer to questions about growth to somewhere where it is actually happening, namely in Tanzania. This was our reflex too when asking ourselves where we look for manifestations of anything we could call a northern gospel—going to places where there was something positive happening. This approach can be traced back to the New Testament and especially the books of Luke-Acts as well as, perhaps finding its culmination in an understanding of the *missio Dei*. In Luke 10 when the seventy are sent out to announce the kingdom they are instructed to stay where they are welcome (where something, undefended hospitality, is happening) and to "wipe the dust

10. Spencer, *Growing and Flourishing*, 19.

11. Spencer, *Growing and Flourishing*, 16–19.

12. Spencer, *Growing and Flourishing*, 19–24.

13. Spencer, *Growing and Flourishing*, 24–37.

14. It is worth noting that since the beginning of this research "flourishing" has become a major subject of international research, both in society and at the local church level which has entailed being very clear about what constitutes human flourishing. See Human Flourishing Program, "Global Flourishing Study," and for flourishing applied to churches in Europe https://www.i-m-k.org/english/ressourcen/european-flourishing-and-the-church/.

15. Spencer, *Growing and Flourishing*, 1–2.

off their feet" if they are not welcome; that is, they are not to hang around hoping for a change of heart, but to move on. St. Paul on his missionary journeys reflects this practice in often starting at the place where Jews gather for worship, for instance at Philippi in Acts 16. The assumption is that God is at work as the God of mission, the *missio Dei,* in these places and it is an excellent place to start. So, we have a theological grounding for our motivation in researching churches where something is happening. And the ecological metaphor helps us here, more than I think Spencer realizes. Small trees and even saplings are extremely vulnerable. Tree planting in Africa is encouraged and widespread, often supported with development aid money, but my experience was that it wasn't a problem planting the trees, it was caring for and protecting them for the five to ten years it would take for them to become inedible by goats. Thus, we could understand now even better the reluctance of church leaders to allow us to research any church that might be "flourishing." We might also wonder whether Spencer missed asking a question about whether any of the attempts at planting churches in Tanzania that he described had not been effective in developing a sustainable local congregation.

In conclusion, Spencer investigates a church where remarkable recent growth has taken place, despite a significant lack of resources, drought, and other trying circumstances: "over 25 years Mara Diocese had grown by over a hundredfold."[16] This from just twelve churches (which are named as "parishes" in Tanzanian terms) in 1985 to more than 140 in 2010 when the diocese was divided up.[17] At that point four or five new churches were started each year and:

> this church growth has not just been about congregational enlargement: it has gone hand in hand with a range of development projects at parish and diocesan level, from weekday children's nurseries to digging wells for drinking water to pastoral and medical support for victims of HIV/AIDS. Church schools have been started and extended, agricultural development work has taken place and theological education extended.[18]

16. Spencer, *Growing and Flourishing,* 18.
17. Spencer, *Growing and Flourishing,* 15.
18. Spencer, *Growing and Flourishing,* 18.

FACTORS AFFECTING CHURCH GROWTH IN TANZANIA AND THE DIMENSIONS OF THAT GROWTH

From this point onwards for a while we will need to summarize the findings of Spencer's research, before we can move to placing them in dialogue with our own. I believe it is important to follow Spencer's argument here which I hope I can faithfully convey even if it is pared down somewhat from the original for the purposes of this book.

What Draws People to Christian Faith in Tanzania?

First, a gospel message about the kingdom of God in the face of the fragility of life—Spencer names this as security and safety.[19] We might say these new Christians are "held" in a fresh imaginative space which gives them "hope and assurance." Alongside this imagination come practical ways of being together in the Christian community which are noticed in the villages. Pastoral care and the offering of prayer, including prayer for healing (which is distinguished from a Pentecostal approach[20]), is an important part of this community life.[21] Jesus is at the heart of the kingdom and is understood as a savior who forgives sins (emphasized also by Akiri[22]), in which there is a clear element of new freedom. As one interviewee states, "you can live a life free of worldly burdens—conflict, adultery, witchcraft, gossip,"[23] which Spencer understands overall as discipleship. Next there is an attractive "liveliness of worship" in the churches which, Akiri states, is connected to the main tribal group in this diocese (the Kuria people) being a "partying society."[24] At this distance it is hard to assess the claim and any essentialism that might be behind it, so we will need to take it at face value, and we do note the connection being made here between culture and faith. Spencer names this as a "sacramental dimension to church life"[25] in what I think is an important move which he will return to. Such an embodied worship in music, singing, and dance is a sign of the grace at work in these new converts, which is also publicly visible and audible.

19. Spencer, *Growing and Flourishing*, 20.
20. Spencer, *Growing and Flourishing*, 23.
21. Spencer, *Growing and Flourishing*, 22.
22. Spencer, *Growing and Flourishing*, 23.
23. Spencer, *Growing and Flourishing*, 20.
24. Spencer, *Growing and Flourishing*, 21.
25. Spencer, *Growing and Flourishing*, 21.

Other interviewees mention the way in which social action projects create a plausibility structure for faith in the wider community. These relate to such things as farming methods, HIV/AIDS interventions, attention to sourcing safe drinking water, and even a goat lending scheme. Spencer notes importantly that this kind of social action is, "rendered for its own sake and not with any ulterior motive but it nevertheless contributes to the standing and the growth of the church community."[26] Spencer summarizes these findings into five elements: "effective communication of the gospel, mutual support in congregational life, powerful 'sacramental' expression of the faith, service of the wider community and meaningful discipleship."[27]

Spencer then thickens this description with the testimony of a parish priest who underlines some of these elements and adds some more. He has a practice of house-to-house evangelism[28] which is by invitation and the evangelists have to "come into the home of those they are talking to and depend on the welcome and hospitality of that home."[29] Here is a distinct echo again of the sending of the seventy in Luke 10. Spencer notes that these visits are done in an atmosphere of prayer and worship, which "brings a third party into the room, which is God's presence"[30] and adds to the sense of sacramentality he noted in the worship. A choice to be Christian is offered which is open-ended and seemingly without pressure—a refusal is certainly possible.[31] Challenges are made to tribal cultural practices such as Female Genital Mutilation (FGM), engaging Walls's pilgrim principle. Evangelism also takes place in public and it is clear that the Christian faith is understood and preached as a public gospel. It is, according to Akiri, "not a private commodity."[32] Spencer makes an important observation on the mission practices of the priest which he has revealed in the interview:

> [his] primary intention is not to increase the size of the church: our conversation has shown that his passion is to communicate the liberating gospel of Christ to the people of his community,

26. Spencer, *Growing and Flourishing*, 22.
27. Spencer, *Growing and Flourishing*, 24.
28. Spencer, *Growing and Flourishing*, 25.
29. Spencer, *Growing and Flourishing*, 25.
30. Spencer, *Growing and Flourishing*, 26.
31. Spencer, *Growing and Flourishing*, 27.
32. Spencer, *Growing and Flourishing*, 30.

> so that they may be freed from all that oppresses them and become joy-filled disciples of Christ.[33]

Spencer can conclude then that church growth is a "multi-dimensional phenomenon."[34] It is certainly not restricted in any way to numerical growth.

Next, Spencer introduces a wider systemic element to how church growth happens by engaging with the diocesan "Director of Evangelism," thereby bringing an "institutional dimension of church growth to the centre of attention."[35] This person takes a strategic overview to starting new churches, avoids places that already have churches, and includes other denominations in discussions about diocesan church planting initiatives. When starting something new, fairly new Christians from nearby places are sent for the initial meeting in the settlement. He takes the pilgrim principles of transforming culture and stands against practices such as FGM and bride price[36] and the method of public evangelism is tailored to the people[37] utilizing open-air preaching and showing a film of the life of Jesus.[38] Thus, Spencer notes there is strategy *and* spiritual discernment about what is required to be effective. Starting a new church can then take only a few weeks as the sacrament of baptism is administered, leadership is quickly handed over to local elders, confirmation and the Eucharist ensue and the evangelism team moves on elsewhere in a strong resonance with the approach recommended by Roland Allen more than a hundred years ago.[39]

This leads directly to some further elements of what makes church growth happen in this region. The new converts and embryonic church are afforded what we have named as theological agency: from the beginning of their life together, "they are being empowered with ownership of their own life as a body of believers."[40] In addition, sacramentality turns into the actual sacraments of baptism and Eucharist fairly rapidly and there is an immediate catholicity available to the new congregation as it connects to

33. Spencer, *Growing and Flourishing*, 29.
34. Spencer, *Growing and Flourishing*, 31.
35. Spencer, *Growing and Flourishing*, 31.
36. Spencer, *Growing and Flourishing*, 32.
37. Spencer, *Growing and Flourishing*, 33.
38. Spencer, *Growing and Flourishing*, 34.
39. See Allen, *Missionary Methods.*
40. Spencer, *Growing and Flourishing*, 35.

neighboring parishes and the whole diocese. Finally, Spencer extends this catholicity to the influence of the Companion Link itself, which has developed strong local partnerships between parishes in an English diocese and this region of Tanzania over thirty years. This post-colonial stance has "instilled a sense of confidence" in the Tanzanian parishes, such that Spencer can claim, "This is not a donor–recipient relationship but one where connection of friendship is primary and any practical support is a secondary by-product of that relationship."[41] A tangible sense of confidence and support through catholicity is available to the Tanzanians through these wider relationships even if they may not name it as such.

Describing the Dimensions of Church Growth: An Ecclesiological Approach

In his second chapter Spencer reviews the findings of his research and develops his initial hypothesis of five elements of church growth in Tanzania to six more generic "dimensions." He works with these in the rest of the book and names them together as a "complex ecology of growth."[42]

First is the "organizational growth" of the whole church which, he notes, is not about aiming at certain numbers of converts: "At no point did any of those who were interviewed indicate that the purpose of what they were doing was to increase the size of the institution. Instead, they made it clear that their aim was to evangelize on the basis of good relationships."[43] Spencer describes this as a qualitative respectful approach which is open-ended. We could add it also is unconsciously cognizant of a principle of the "Open Systems" understanding of organizations: they require a focus on the "primary task" or purpose[44] but they are tempted instead to seek after lesser alternatives. Here it seems the primary task is clearly stated and continuously enacted as evangelism on the basis of good relationships.

The importance of relationships is also emphasized in the second dimension[45]—that of congregational relationships. We noted how new congregations in Mara are quickly entrusted with their own leadership

41. Spencer, *Growing and Flourishing*, 37.
42. Spencer, *Growing and Flourishing*, 43.
43. Spencer, *Growing and Flourishing*, 40.
44. See Rooms, "Understanding Local."
45. Spencer, *Growing and Flourishing*, 40.

and encouraged to start new churches in neighboring villages. And there is a regional and international aspect to these relationships which develops over time, strengthening this aspect of their growth. Thus, the third dimension, "evangelistic communication," is an extension of the first two, with a "clear and definite message about the sovereignty of God in creation and the gospel of Christ"[46] alongside. This is a challenge to some aspects of people's traditional culture, while remaining sensitive to contextual factors in communicating all this. Next the importance of "sacramental expression" to the growth of the church is demonstrated, much of it related to aspects of the local culture in embodied worship within a "partying" culture and an emphasis on rites of passage for initiation and reconciliation which are picked up in the sacraments of baptism and Eucharist.[47] "Community service" interventions on many fronts are a fifth dimension surrounding all the others and preparing the people for further engagement; "they were regarded as part of the overall 'holistic' nature of Christian mission."[48] Finally, discipleship, often based in the home and for each new Christian, is a dimension of the Mara growth that cannot be overlooked. There is a freedom from alternative ways of life and clear pathways for spiritual growth as a Christian. Taking the six dimensions overall, Spencer comments:

> Each dimension has been seen to be integral to the whole, showing a rich interconnectedness to what was happening. In terms of the way growth actually unfolded in the villages, it can be summed up as growth that is rooted in community service, led by an interactive evangelism; this includes sacramental expression, with deeply respectful congregational relationships, and bearing fruit in discipleship and institutional enlargement.[49]

Spencer then takes these six dimensions of Tanzanian church growth and places them in dialogue with Avery Dulles's six "models of Church" in his classic text of that name.[50] It is worth noting that Bevans took his cue from Dulles when developing his models of contextual theology.[51] It is important for Spencer that Dulles treated each model as an aspect

46. Spencer, *Growing and Flourishing*, 41.
47. Spencer, *Growing and Flourishing*, 41.
48. Spencer, *Growing and Flourishing*, 42.
49. Spencer, *Growing and Flourishing*, 42–3.
50. See Dulles, *Models of the Church*.
51. Bevans, *Models of Contextual*, 28.

of "Church" as a whole;[52] what each model affirms could be helpfully incorporated into a holistic understanding of Church.[53] Spencer finds significant overlap between his six dimensions and the equal number of Dulles's models.[54]

The church as "institution" is clearly present in how the Mara diocese organizes itself for growth and is reflected in the model where the church is understood as

> as a corporate body existing through human history, with formal structures of membership, leadership, delivery and accountability. Like other institutions it is quantifiable and therefore its component parts can be counted, such as the number of congregations, of members and attendance at services.[55]

Dulles's second model, "mystical communion," is reflected in the strong communitarian aspects of Spencer's second dimension of congregational relationships where there is "a fusion of people in a divine common life,"[56] which, in contrast to the first dimension, is definitely not quantifiable in numbers.

The third model, Church as "sacrament," is also evident in the Mara research. Spencer comments that these Christians, "in preaching, singing and dancing, and the use of actual sacraments, do not just convey information about Christ but in tangible ways convey the gift of his presence into the lived experience of those who participate in them."[57] Thus, following Dulles's work and Catholic teaching in *Lumen Gentium*, the Church is "the Kingdom of heaven now present in mystery"[58] and there-

52. The question of the use of models in theology is dealt with by Bevans in *Models of Contextual*, 29–33. He distinguishes between exclusive models (more of a paradigm) and inclusive or complementary ones–which offer an aspect of the whole and with which he (and Dulles) are working. He notes, with Sallie McFague a caution about the relationship between models and the metaphorical nature of all language. Thus, the model, while it, "affirms something real it never really captures that reality." We must remember the "is" and "is not" tension in any kind of thinking about models.

53. Spencer, *Growing and Flourishing*, 43.

54. It is hard not to wonder whether Dulles's models were not in mind when Spencer developed his six dimensions, such is the almost complete overlap between them. On the other hand, this could be an argument for the veracity of Dulles's typology and Spencer's research in the one, holy, catholic, and apostolic Church. Spencer intimates as much on page 48.

55. Spencer, *Growing and Flourishing*, 44.

56. Spencer, *Growing and Flourishing*, 44.

57. Spencer, *Growing and Flourishing*, 45.

58. Spencer, *Growing and Flourishing*, 45.

fore has an eschatological dimension which is always pointing to a fuller consummation of the kingdom of God.

"Church as herald," the fourth model of Dulles, is obviously present in the preaching and evangelism observable in Mara Christianity, which nevertheless "is done both through public proclamation and also through interactive conversation in the intimacy of an enquirer's home. It again shows the communitarian bias of this whole approach."[59] But proclamation is additionally embedded in community service which relates to Dulles's fifth model of church as "servant," where the boundary between church and world is not solid, but permeable in both directions. Finally, church as a "community of disciples" is focused on, "growing to spiritual maturity as followers of Christ, both when they meet together and in their home and working lives."[60]

Having established correspondence between church growth in Mara and Dulles's models, Spencer then asks: "How can all these models or dimensions of growth be viewed as a whole?"[61] He seeks an analogy or metaphor that "captures their diversity in unity in a memorable image." We noted his choice of the organic metaphor of a tree in the introduction to this chapter and this works well, particularly in how a tree is a "living and breathing organism"[62] which only grows in interaction with its environment. This metaphor connects suggestively with Dulles's conflation of all his models:

> The Church's existence is a continual alternation between two phases. Like systole and diastole in the movement of the heart, like inhalation and exhalation in the process of breathing, assembly and mission succeed each other in the life of the Church. Discipleship would be stunted unless it included both the centripetal phase of worship and the centrifugal phase of mission.[63]

While this book's primary purpose is not an ecclesiological one, ecclesiology clearly bears on our research and subject matter. We discovered the concept of "fuzzy church" in the field research and rehearsed that again in the previous chapter. So, an ecclesiological tangent is worth explicating here. In an article describing the local church through the lens of

59. Spencer, *Growing and Flourishing*, 46.
60. Spencer, *Growing and Flourishing*, 48.
61. Spencer, *Growing and Flourishing*, 49.
62. Spencer, *Growing and Flourishing*, 50.
63. Quoted in Spencer, *Growing and Flourishing*, 50.

systems theory[64] I suggested that maybe Dulles's models were not sufficient to capture the breadth of understanding of church that is available to us through that lens. Having interacted with Dulles through Spencer's research, I would like now to make a tentative contribution to models of Church, from the perspective of this research. I am a little unclear as to whether my proposal is for another model or simply a connecting, including metaphor which crosses over and connects the existing models (others more qualified than I may be able to develop these ideas further).

I wish to develop the organic metaphor of the tree as a living and breathing entity deeply connected to its environment. My suggestion would be to describe the Church as a "*living organism*" based on both open systems and complex adaptive systems theories as I described in the article referred to above. For me this metaphor or model encapsulates the requirement for the Church to be a "thing" and have a boundary (as human institution, as system) as well as an internal life which enacts what it signifies in its purpose (or primary task), that is, worship and mission which begins and ends in God. It transforms those inside the boundary and reaches across its boundary to participate in God's prior work in the world. The boundary then becomes semi-permeable (fuzzy) to its surroundings, which are also transformed by this movement. The complexity of such a way of thinking about the Church speaks for itself and this is why I think it adds something to the whole, where some theologies tend to reduce church flourishing and growth to one or two of the models.

Spencer might agree and he summarizes the organic approach to church he is taking by saying, "It is, in other words, all about an increase in interaction with its surrounding community in which neither side loses itself but in which both build up purposeful and life-giving relationships."[65] The organic metaphor that Spencer develops allows him to move to the next step of the argument since all living things have "stages of growth" as they move to maturity.

Stages of Church Growth

Possibly for simplicity's sake, Spencer divides the journey from birth to maturity for each of the six dimensions of church growth into three. This is not without precedent in, say, the craft guilds of old with their

64. See Rooms, "Understanding Local."

65. Spencer, *Growing and Flourishing*, 51.

apprentices, journeymen, and masters (with apologies for the original gendered language) or in storytelling when there is always a beginning, middle, and end. There are some limits to how Spencer utilizes the metaphor. We have already noted he has not really allowed for failure of new churches especially in their vulnerable early stages (trees produce a lot of seeds, only a very few of which turn into trees)[66] and we might also wonder how both life and growth exist alongside decline and death. (We will develop theologically how decline and death are part of the life of the Church as the body of Christ in the next chapter.) The human body, for instance, regenerates its billions of cells over different time frames in different parts of the body. Thus, in healthy churches some initiatives are allowed to come to a natural end while others are growing fruitfully. Maturity also seems to be a sufficient endpoint in Spencer's schema (which, indeed, has a beginning, middle, and end[67]) whereas an eschatological perspective would understand that the Church is radically unfinished and is focused on meeting the coming kingdom from the future in its life together. These, therefore, are limits to the metaphor but, since we are exploring new growth and how Christian community is formed, it remains valid for this investigation.

The next chapter of *Growing and Flourishing* begins by telling the story of one of the oldest churches in the Mara diocese so as to illustrate the way in which growth can be understood by the "qualitative differences" in the three stages rather than a church's numerical size being "the barometer of its health and growth."[68] Each of the six dimensions is then treated in turn and evidence is offered from Mara churches to describe the quality of each of the three stages, which are then named or summed up in a single word or phrase. It is worth reproducing the resulting table here as we do not need to repeat the argument for the eighteen stages in full, but we will need to describe briefly the meaning and qualitative nature of each one, since we plan to use them to look further into the research data from our northern churches.

66. In my limited experience of church planting, new churches remain vulnerable for some considerable time, at least until the second or third leader after the founder or planter has left. For a contemporary example of this phenomenon see Sarah McDonald Haden, "On the Ground: Life, Death and Resurrection in Church Planting," in Bradbury et al., *Being the People*, 70–74.

67. Spencer, *Growing and Flourishing*, 56.

68. Spencer, *Growing and Flourishing*, 55.

Taking the six dimensions in turn we describe Spencer's understanding of each of their three stages of growth. Needless to say, there is inevitable variation and increasing complexity across the stages. They are not necessarily "one thing" alone, and we will try to nuance them somewhat in the description that follows. We also allow critiques of Spencer's approach from time to time, which may change the nomenclature we finally use in the table.

Institutional Growth

Here in this first dimension (and this one only) Spencer utilizes a typology he takes directly from Helen Cameron[69] that describes various kinds of churches from a small gathered group meeting on its own terms to a "voluntary association" which generally has a more structured life, with formal procedures and even a constitution and membership lists. Third is the "public utility," which is a description Cameron takes directly from the sociologist of religion in Europe Grace Davie, describing the typical historic English parish church which exists for the whole community.[70]

Table 1: Six dimensions and eighteen stages of church growth[71]

	Stage 1	Stage 2	Stage 3
Organizational growth	Friendship group	Voluntary association	Public utility
Congregational relationships	Donor-recipient	Partnership	Trinitarian
Evangelistic communication	Uni-vocal	Interactive	Three-way
Sacramental expression	Spontaneous	Intentional	Holistic
Community service	Occasional	Singular	Multiple
Discipleship	Enquiry	Apprenticeship	Friendship

There is an issue here in that both Stages 2 and 3 are described in the western world and then applied to the Tanzanian context. Voluntary association would seem to assume a decision on behalf of the individual

69. Cameron, *Resourcing Mission*, 24.

70. Cameron, *Resourcing Mission*, 25.

71. Taken from Spencer, *Growing and Flourishing*, 93.

to join as a recognized member of the church. This is a largely Protestant way of organizing the church, as Spencer himself admits, quoting the rise of Congregationalism.[72] It travelled to the USA with the Pilgrim Fathers and has since been spread throughout the world, as Duerksen and Dyrness show.[73] However, Duerksen and Dyrness also note places in the world where church has emerged as a minority faith within other major religions that cannot be described in this way because of the effect of a "reverse hermeneutic" from the prevailing culture that creates very different forms of church. Volunteering as a member is an individual decision based in a Protestant worldview which does not prevail everywhere. I'm not sure that Spencer recognizes enough, in his descriptor for his Stage 2, that Tanzanians may act more out of communitarian values than individual ones when they gather as an associated body. I suggest that the first stage of a "friendship group" is clearly a free association of people ("free" in the sense of free from formal organizational forms and structures) and the second stage might be better termed a "structured association." Spencer himself points out that Tanzanian churches, despite naming themselves as "parishes," do not operate like English parishes in the State Church[74] so I would additionally argue that "public utility" from Davie for Stage 3 is not really applicable either. I would suggest that the kinds of activities he describes mature churches undertaking across their boundary make this stage a move to being a "public actor"—that is, they have made a corporate decision to act together in public under the authority of their "structured association" that they gained in Stage 2. Renaming these second two stages is appropriate, I believe, not only in Tanzania but also in the post-Christendom English church where the church must take its place in public alongside many other actors rather than assume its importance, as it has done in the past under the aegis of Christendom.

Congregational Relationships

What Spencer is engaging with here is not the internal nature of the relationships within a congregation, but how it relates to those outside itself, both in the wider Church system (diocese) and its community.

72. Spencer, *Growing and Flourishing*, 58–59.

73. See Duerksen and Dyrness, *Seeking Church*.

74. Spencer, *Growing and Flourishing*, 60.

Spencer has discerned the stages from his research in Mara where new churches are started by teams of Christians going to a place without a church and creating the conditions for a new church to be born. This approach he describes as donor–recipient and he believes it has to be this way around, which is somewhat questionable since it does not fully recognize the agency of the recipient in the potential exchange that is expected. Nevertheless, there will always be some imbalance at the start of such an enterprise; naming and being aware of it is the most important thing. Actually, because of the emphasis on the speedy withdrawal of the planting team, the second stage can ensue rapidly when the local church becomes an equal partner within the diocese in contributing to it and sharing itself in other locations.

I am not at all convinced by Spencer's third stage in this dimension in which he believes a conscious realization of partnership with a third party, the Trinity becomes available to all the actors. Personally, I think there are ways of making this a present reality from the start—and while not everyone will be fully conscious of the presence and activity of God (within the *missio Dei*) at the beginning, the whole project will be stronger if it sets out on this footing. I believe this Trinitarian dimension is better expressed in the fourth dimension of sacramentality for which there is evidence for from the UK.[75] A better way of expressing Stage 3 would be to extend the notion of partnership (single) to multiple partnerships within the wider Church body and beyond it. There is good evidence from research in the USA that churches there only need three or four of these partnerships to remain sustainable and I would suggest this is transferable to other places beyond the USA.[76] Overall this dimension is an extension of the first where public acting in Stage 3 results in tangible "mission partnerships" (in the plural) which give life to the participating bodies.

Evangelistic Communication

The movement between stages in this dimension is clearer and more straightforward. In Tanzania what many people would call "verbal proclamation" in public is an entirely acceptable practice. Such a practice is by definition univocal or one-way, except, as Spencer points out, for the

75. Spencer, *Growing and Flourishing*, 68.

76. Benac, *Adaptive Church*, 119.

prior listening to local culture and idiom, which hopefully shapes the message.[77] For several decades this practice has been less and less acceptable in the West[78] much to the puzzlement of African diaspora churches that attempt to continue it. (For a good example of research on this, readers might consult the work of John Neate.[79]) Nevertheless, it cannot be entirely discounted as most preaching remains firmly in this mode. More fruitful is interactive or dialogue evangelism where there is a "two-way" discussion.[80] As Spencer points out,[81] this is by far the most preferred method in the UK, especially through what can be called "nurture courses" or in more general terms a renewed catechumenate. I would suggest there is much more possibility here of the "evangelist" being evangelized by the hearer in a "two-way street" as in the encounter between St. Peter and Cornelius in the book of Acts. Darrel Whiteman has a suggestive article on this encounter which underlines that effective evangelism goes both ways.[82] The third stage is an extension of the first two when the new believers become evangelists themselves and give away their new found faith to others. A virtuous circle results where growth becomes a normal way of life for a church in "donating" that life to others.

Sacramental Expression

Before we begin on this dimension it is worth picking up the argument about the Trinity again. Throughout this book we have understood the *missio Dei* as saying something about the Church's participation in the presence and activity God, which is always and everywhere in time and place. This leaves us with a sacramental world where we can "never be sure where Christ is not" and the task, as we remarked in chapter 4, is always one of discernment. And there are stages in the apprehension of this reality both within and outside the church. The first stage, "spontaneous" sacramentality, can therefore begin almost anywhere—Spencer refers to St. Augustine of Hippo, who "listed almost 300 things he

77. Spencer, *Growing and Flourishing*, 71.

78. Spencer, *Growing and Flourishing*, 74.

79. Neate, "Cultural Perceptions."

80. For a full explication of "conversational evangelism," see Butler, "Pedagogy."

81. Spencer, *Growing and Flourishing*, 74.

82. Whiteman, "Conversion."

regarded as sacraments."[83] In Tanzania, as we have seen above, it often begins in exuberant singing and dancing which connects us with Bevans and Schroeder's dance of God the Trinity.[84] The next stage is the introduction of the sacraments of the Church, namely baptism and Eucharist. Spencer notes a difference from the first stage, "not only because these are officially designated as sacraments of the church but because those administering and receiving them have an intentionality about them."[85] They are the "canonical" sacraments instituted and commanded by Jesus in the Gospels and enacted ever since by the Church.

A final stage in this dimension is related to the equivalent final stage in the first two dimensions outlined above. It is possible that such is the sacramental participation in the presence and activity of God in all that a local church is being and doing that this is noticed by those outside of it, in the wider community. That is, there is public recognition of what is happening through what God is up to in and from the church. Spencer describes this recognition, "when others see it [the whole life of a local church] as being genuinely Christ-like, a fruit of a sacrificial maturity."[86] He describes this stage therefore as the sacramental recognized in the totality of what happens between church and community—as a "holistic" stage, and we can heartily concur. The church then is truly the "hermeneutic of the gospel" in the classic phrase of Lesslie Newbigin.[87]

Community Service

When considering service in the community there is a specific gradation in this dimension of church growth. It begins in individual acts of kindness and care within and outside of the church. When the structure of the church is robust enough it can take on a particular and focused work in its community; Spencer gives the example in Tanzania of setting up a nursery school,[88] something which many UK churches also do. If this works well it can develop into the third stage where multiple interventions can be made across the boundary of the church. Two caveats

83. Spencer, *Growing and Flourishing*, 80.
84. Bevans and Schroeder, *Prophetic Dialogue*, 17–18.
85. Spencer, *Growing and Flourishing*, 77.
86. Spencer, *Growing and Flourishing*, 79.
87. Newbigin, *Gospel*, 227.
88. Spencer, *Growing and Flourishing*, 83.

apply here, especially in the UK context. Initially I suspect the first stage is characterized more by individuals deciding to act in a private capacity (rather than authorized by the governing body of the church). The next two stages are where public action takes place, authorized and resourced by the whole church. Then perhaps the three stages should be: occasional/private; singular/public; multiple/public.

Also, there is a question hidden within this dimension of growth about how the church engages with its community. Spencer rather falls into the "deficit model" of community development which identifies "needs" which are met by the intervention. This kind of approach tends to doing things *to and for* people which reduces their agency in whatever happens. Acting *with* those in the community on the basis of their inherent giftedness as in Asset Based Community Development is another way of approaching this issue of how to engage.[89] We will return to this theme in much more detail in chapter 8 when discussing the thought of Ivan Illich.

Discipleship

The final dimension of growth is fairly simple in its progression from an initial curious enquiry into the faith to a period of learning, or apprenticeship in Spencer's terms,[90] and after baptism and confirmation entry into the final stage which he calls "friendship" with Jesus. I think it is more accurate to employ other nomenclature which Spencer uses later for it, naming this stage "whole life" and, therefore, lifelong discipleship.[91] There is a clear overlap here with the Catholic Church's "Rite of Christian Initiation of Adults," which follows a similar three-stage process with the intermediate stage being that of the catechumenate, which I believe is a more accurate term than apprenticeship.

One further point of note is worth making on this table as a whole before we present our modified version of it. Spencer remarks at several points[92] on how maturity in new churches often refers back to Henry Venn's (1796–1873) notion of the "three-self" indigenous church from the missionary movement in the nineteenth century. Bevans and Schroeder

89. See McKnight and Block, *Abundant*.

90. Spencer, *Growing and Flourishing*, 88.

91. Spencer, *Growing and Flourishing*, 90.

92. For example, Spencer, *Growing and Flourishing*, 89.

describe this "formula" or "goal of mission" as establishing "churches that were self-supporting, self-governing and self-propagating."[93] Inevitably this simple formula begs lots of questions, not least in terms of catholicity. Venn was an English Anglican and General Secretary of the Church Missionary Society (as it was named then) and presumably still imagined diocesan structures around individual churches. And later in the twentieth century Paul Hiebert called for a fourth "self" to be added, that of "self-theologizing,"[94] which is a vital component in any local church—that its members have theological agency. We can see many dimensions of growth in the table as they move towards the three-self formula.

We are ready then to share a version of the church growth table that we believe is usable when looking further into the data from the seven northern research churches that we described overall as "fuzzy" in the earlier book.

Table 2: Six dimensions and eighteen stages of "fuzzy" church growth

	Stage 1	Stage 2	Stage 3
Organizational growth	Friendship group	Structured association	Public actor
Congregational relationships	Donor-recipient	Single partnership	Multiple partnerships
Evangelistic communication	Uni-vocal	Interactive	Three-way (giving away)
Sacramental expression	Spontaneous	Intentional	Holistic
Community service	Occasional/ private	Singular/public	Multiple/public
Discipleship	Enquiry	Catechumenate	Whole-life

The Ecology of Church Growth in the Research Churches

In order to place each of the seven churches on the table in the different categories, all the qualitative data was revisited, read through, and digested again. That is, the field visit reports alongside all the focus group interviews of leaders and new Christians were engaged with, at some distance from their original analysis. Inevitably there is a subjective dimension to placing each church on the grid in the six dimensions, however

93. Bevans and Schroeder, *Prophetic Dialogue*, 213.

94. See Hiebert, *Anthropological Insights*.

I will attempt to show some evidence from the data which backs up the decision-making in each dimension. This, reasonably, cannot be exhaustive, but I hope it will be illuminating for our research and demonstrate the usefulness of this approach to church growth that may be useful in other locations.

Before we begin, however, a word on what is missing here. What we didn't look at in much detail were two aspects of the first dimension—organizational growth. Five of the seven churches were still meeting in their historic building—though, as we noted in *Fuzzy Church,* all of them had been obliged to develop or change their buildings or structures of ministry in some way for the realities of the post-Christendom world they were now living in.[95] What we don't have data on is how structurally sound and financially stable these buildings were. We know this is a major concern for many historic churches, even when "something is happening." In addition, we didn't look at the financial arrangements and the consequent sustainability of ministry provision for our research churches. While this was beyond the scope of the study it would be relevant in any wider research on church growth.

Below we present the table with each church (or set of churches) given a letter as described in the previous chapter. All the stages are imagined as something of a continuum, so the gaps between the letters are deemed to be significant: the further to the right the letter, the more that church exhibits the stage of that dimension (except where there is no space between letters when there is little difference on the continuum in the order in which they are presented).

Overall Observations

The usefulness of this task is first found in taking a step back and looking the table as a whole. None of the research churches were in Stage 1 in any of the dimensions, which is to be expected and confirms that we had found research subjects where "something was happening"—and had been for some time. In two cases, we note clear evidence that they had begun in Stage 1 as their recent history was talked about in the interviews. The churches are then almost evenly distributed between Stages 2 and 3; twenty occurrences in Stage 2 and twenty-two in Stage 3. Only two churches occur in Stage 3 for Evangelistic Communication and

95. Rooms and Wort, *Fuzzy Church,* 55.

Sacramental Expression and perhaps this is evidence that these are challenging goals for churches in their context at the present time, an issue we will discuss in more detail below.

Church F is actually a collection of five rural churches and is the exception, both in the table (where it shows up on the left of all the other churches in every dimension) and among the other research subjects. It is fairly self-evident that the context of five sparsely populated villages (1,200 people in total) is vastly different from suburbs, towns, and cities with much denser populations and a higher concentration of public institutions. Thus, we may have found a limitation of this way of categorizing church growth for the UK context and we can return to this question below when we look at more evidence from church F.

Churches B and E demonstrate the most occurrences in Stage 3. Interestingly they have quite different theological traditions, but have a lot of the same strengths in their ecology. Let us then turn to examine each of the dimensions in some detail. In each dimension we will generally present evidence for the decision to place churches at each end of the continuum and in the middle.

Table 3: The research churches categorized along the six dimensions of church growth

	Stage 1	Stage 2	Stage 3
Organizational growth	Friendship group	Structured association **F DC**	Public actor **G ABE**
Congregational relationships	Donor-recipient **(C&D when begun)**	Single Partnership **F C D**	Multiple Partnerships **G ABE**
Evangelistic communication	Uni-vocal	Interactive **FC D G A**	Three-way (giving away) **BE**
Sacramental expression	Spontaneous	Intentional **F C A G D**	Holistic **BE**
Community service	Occasional - private	Singular - public **F**	Multiple – public **CD G ABE**
Discipleship	Enquiry	Catechumenate **F CD**	Whole-life **GE AB**

Organizational Growth

Church A is a clear "public actor," having had a long history in the town where it is based and in engagement with that place. Fairly recently a social entrepreneur initiated the "Freedom Community Project" which offers a range of services, both locally and even regionally. The project has an office space in the church building. What is important, I have realized in reading this data again that this project is not dependent upon the will and energy of the minister—that is, it would outlast whoever is the current leader of the congregation. This is not the case with the public action of, say, churches C and D where the leader (or the leader and their spouse in one case) was key in crossing the boundary of the church into public space which is why I have placed them in Stage 2 here. For instance, at church C, it was clear that it was the minister that had created and held the relationship with the local council authority, though the action the church took in the local community through its Food Bank and other activities would no doubt continue beyond the leader herself. This was less clear in church D. Church F is placed in "structured association" partly because of its rural context. Elli, my co-researcher, made this field note when attending a "Family Service" at one of the villages:

> The church's noticeboard is bare, with just the name of the church on it. There was nothing outside the church to indicate that any services took place, let alone the Family Service would be taking place: I suspect that given the rural setting, the advertising and news about the service seems to be mainly via word of mouth.[96]

One respondent in the lay focus group at this church noted how "coffee mornings" have been helpful, and had expanded recently in crossing over between church and village, while at the same time these churches were clearly able to create a "fuzzy" edge (since the original quotation that gave us that title for the book was made in this church). Perhaps "structured association." as long as it crosses the boundary of the church, is enough for an ecology of growth in a rural setting.

Congregational Relationships

The strongest example of a Stage 3 church in this dimension is our church B. It had the advantage of having a Church School in its parish,[97] though it was clear that there was a lively relationship between the two (church G also had relationships with schools). In addition, they had partnerships with the local Food Bank, a Debt Counselling Centre, and a mentoring project for young people called "Transforming Lives for Good." One of the people in the new Christians focus group had just returned from a partnership visit from the church to a project in Kenya.

Both churches C and D had started from nothing. C arose out of users at a Food Bank assuming they were a church and wondering why the leadership were reluctant to own this fact. In the Leaders' Focus Group, a respondent commented, "Yeah, [Minister] heard someone speaking on

96. Wort, unpublished field research notes.

97. In England the historical development of education was led by the Church of England and this means that many dioceses still offer education at both primary and secondary level. The nature of the structural relationship between the local church and any school does however vary.

their mobile phone quite early on saying, 'I can't talk I'm at church.' And we're like 'we're not a church.' But they, that's how they refer to us."[98]

Thus, the original and literal "Donor–recipient" relationship develops, although it is fair to say even several years later when we visited it was still partially predicated on this form of relationality, perhaps because of the fragile nature of the lives of its members.

Church D began, as we noted, some years after the original church on the social housing estate where it was located had closed. The Minister and spouse moved into the old Vicarage which the Diocese still owned and began by inviting their immediate neighbor to join them for worship on Sunday at 4.30pm. Three or so years later, the couple's model of incarnational ministry had borne fruit: when we visited, around 30 people worshipped at the same time on Sunday afternoon in a community center.

Evangelistic Communication

I placed churches B and E furthest along the stages in this dimension. Interestingly, they both regularly ran the Evangelical catechetical program called the Alpha Course, and it was also clear that those being evangelized were able to give this away to others. When we visited church E, an Iranian refugee and convert to Christianity was about to start an Alpha course in Farsi for his fellow Iranians. Listen to the new Christians at church B when asked how they would commend their experience of faith to others:

Respondent 1: Oh, I'd say imagine pleasure and times it by a thousand, thousand. [*Laughs.*]

Respondent 5: That's amazing. Can I steal that? I'll use that.

Respondent 2: My life is as hard as yours but at least I'm not on my own.

Respondent 3: I would say something along those lines, fear not, fear not.

Respondent 4: I think we need to have something up our sleeves for that moment. When that opportunity comes. Yeah, I think I'd say something along the lines of don't worry, you're never alone. When you have God, you've always got somebody to turn to.

98. Leader's Focus Group Church C.

Respondent 6: I think it's a sense and purpose that you've not had before, completely revolutionised what's life's about.

Respondent 5: I'd say quickly, come to church and find out. We'll show you.

Respondent 3: But there's no going back, is there. I've felt that, that now, I can't go back. I don't want to go back, but I can't. I'm caught.[99]

It is worth noting here that Respondent 5 seems less confident than others and it was noticeable that their instinct was to invite people to "come to church" which was a default position of several others in the research when asked this question. And indeed, this is a perfectly reasonably thing to do when one appreciates the church and its worship where one attends, but it is not quite the same as speaking from the heart of what faith means. There is a good example of this from a leader in the Focus Group at church F:

> I was having a chat with a young couple on Friday and they've got three young children, they love church. They really come as often as they, you know, they can. He works some shifts but generally, you know, they're there. And we were talking about things and I was saying how could we make things even better for the children and we were chatting a few ideas through. And he, he said, and I thought it was wonderful, he said "we get it, that we are the ones that have to invite our friends."[100]

Beyond these observations the data is somewhat limited here since we did not set out to research the evangelistic motivations and methods of our research churches; rather, they offered up this data incidentally as we explored the meaning of the gospel together.

Sacramental Expression

As we noted above, God's presence and activity are shot through all three stages of this dimension as we read in this response from a leader at church G:

> I always thank God for the people who do come through the door at St [X] and they start telling us their stories and things. Because

99. New Christians' Focus Group Church B.

100. Leader's Focus Group Church F.

> I think that is almost despite us, God is at work out in the world and then they come through and they'll share a bit. And you just think, "Well, thank God." God is still active because sometimes you don't see the fruit of what you're doing yourself.[101]

And we can note the spontaneous sacramentality of Stage 1 in the data, which may in fact be related to a method of evangelism before or even beyond a catechetical course in this interaction between the Minister and another leader at church D:

> Minister: Here we show "God love," we don't just preach it, we show "God love."" You know we feed the hungry and clothe the naked. We house the homeless and they don't have to believe in Jesus, we just show them what Jesus can do. And then obviously when they see the love of God, they can feel it as well, in here. [*Points to heart.*] So, they can feel it.
>
> Leader: Yeah, I was going to say that I think that the other side of that is the experience that they have, the encounter that they have with the living God. Which they can't always recognize when they come, they might just sit and often, just sit weeping if it's the first few weeks when they come in and it's that love of God that often is a physical feeling that they're having and an emotional encounter. So, I suppose it's that, you can't really deny it. And all that packaged together, that is Jesus.
>
> Minister: And they want to know why we do this work and why, why we love them and we just say, "because God loves you and you're worthy and you're worth it." And it like changes something inside of them and then God can do his work and then they come to church.[102]

Moving to Stage 2, there was no single mention of baptism or Eucharist in the data from churches A and F; clearly, they do practice these sacraments, but they were not doing so when we visited. Thus, the sacraments weren't immediately available in their imaginations as they talked about the gospel and its meaning for them. Churches C and D were interesting

101. Leader's Focus Group Church G

102. Leader's Focus Group Church D.

in this respect: the "newest" communities in the research, they had started from "nothing." Church C had majored on baptism since its inception; the leader told us they "inhabit" this sacrament and had performed at least 160 baptisms, mostly by full immersion in a pool which was physically present in the worship space. What they had struggled with was the introduction of Holy Communion and we witnessed an experiment with this on our visit. Conversely, at church D every Sunday worship service was eucharistic, albeit in a simplified but still reverent form. We noted in *Fuzzy Church* how they operated what we came to call an "open-open table" where everyone, regardless of their faith in God or baptismal status was expected to receive the bread and wine.[103] They had also performed some baptisms for those who had not been baptized previously and were new to faith.

Stage 3 of this dimension is where the presence and activity of God in the life of a local church is noticed by those outside of it in "holistic" fashion. While the data is obviously not gathered from people outside the church here is a leader at church B noting that they heard a local authority councillor saying, "the town would be in a mess if it wasn't for you Christians."[104]

And this quote from a leader at church E, where the Eucharist and baptism (especially of Iranian asylum seekers) feature strongly, is instructive: "when we did the big local service back in 2014, I think . . . when people were asked where is the heart of the community, they said . . . [the name of the church's community centre]."[105]

Community Service

This is the strongest of all the dimensions among the research churches with six of the seven being placed in Stage 3. Given the lack of possibilities in the rather wealthier villages of church F, perhaps that could be placed even further along the continuum. One example will suffice here, given that so many of the churches had initiatives and projects of their own (as opposed to partnerships, which we discussed under Congregational Relationships). I suspect this dimension is a strong indicator of where "something is happening."

103. Rooms and Wort, *Fuzzy Church*, 78.
104. Leader's Focus Group Church B.
105. Leader's Focus Group Church E.

Church E has a church-run community center physically connected to the church plant. It has its own center manager and the field notes reveal that it rivals any local authority community facilities in the area. There is clear cross-over between the community activities and the church. Our field notes list the following activities that happen at the community center:

- Family Fridays with a family worker—anyone can come in and bring their kids. They have been running a cooking course recently, funded by the local Environmental City.
- At Christmas, there was a nativity with a live donkey. The Big Local[106] gave funding for selection boxes. It was organized by the church, and they asked people from the community to get involved.
- There are tea-dances at the center for older people, run by someone who is not a church-goer.
- There is also Singing for the Brain, run by Alzheimers UK and hosted by the center. Someone else runs Sportivity for older people, which does not involve just physical exercise for he recently brought in old pictures of football teams to see who remembered the teams.
- They've recently been playing target Frisbee. There is also Youth and Children, which employs three family, children, and youth workers running after-school clubs, holiday clubs, and residentials.[107]

Discipleship

There are two helpful examples of Stage 3 whole-life discipleship from churches A and B. Part of this stage for me is where the boundaries between working life and faith become mixed up and also fuzzy. At church A we met, in the new Christians focus group, a respondent who admitted that between the ages of 10 and 70 she had not been to church, but then after retirement from being a primary school teacher found herself volunteering in the café at church A. Then she states that she met a met a man at church whose literacy group had stopped all of a sudden, and who really wanted to continue learning to read:

106. A local charitable enterprise.

107. Wort, Field Notes from visit to Church E.

> And I thought as I've been teaching folks reading all my life, and the joy of reading, because it's my, you know and everything, so I said, "Right I can do something about that." So, I went to [Freedom Community Project manager] and he said of course you can and that's how it started.[108]

At church B the new Christians were talking about the positive changes that had happened since they found faith and one respondent told this story:

> So, I . . . was working at the council and I was praying for a job. I didn't agree with things that were going on at the council and it was starting to depress me and I prayed for a change and anyway, just one day I'd had enough. Went to the toilets and prayed, like you do, and then just sent an email to the school, and just said, I'm thinking of becoming a teaching assistant, do you have a placement available and yes, they did. So, I managed to get a college course sorted, and then I wanted to be able to work, not just in any school, but in a faith school, because again, I want to be fed in a way, on the level of children. It's a simple way for me to learn more about God and get God deeper. So, now I'm in a Catholic primary school. I've completed my training course, so I'm in paid employment and tomorrow I'm doing my Lent display.[109]

Elsewhere there is similar, if less strong, evidence for discipleship development in the research respondents. We have also noted above the Alpha Course in two churches and how the sacramental also has a key part to play in spiritual growth.

FURTHER INTERACTION WITH GROWING AND FLOURISHING

Having placed our northern English research churches within Spencer's ecology of growth we can return to his book for some further reflection on how his Tanzanian research interacts with the British church before making some final conclusions about our learning from this chapter.

Spencer begins his fourth chapter by comparing and contrasting his approach to church growth with two other British examples—that of Church Planting initiatives and the Fresh Expressions movement. Two

108. New Christians' Focus Group Church A.

109. New Christians' Focus Group Church B.

of our research churches might fall into these categories—C and D, with some elements in F. There are many overlaps between Tanzanian growth and Spencer's main example of church planting in the Diocese of London, for which he cites extant research,[110] particularly in the "lively" worship, an emphasis on "gospel teaching" in an interactive style, and community service. The one important difference he discerns is the way in which the church planters in Tanzania quickly move on whereas in London they stay for the medium to long term. He concludes, "This contrast shows the church plant model underemphasizing the need for inherent community embeddedness compared to the Mara model."[111] We noted this issue in churches C and D, which did seem to be still fairly dependent on the founding leaders, further emphasizing the fragility of such work in the UK and the requirement for support and resourcing through several changes of leadership in the long term (even over 10–15 years).

Fresh Expressions have been researched and theologized about by Michael Moynagh in several books which Spencer then engages with. They much more clearly involve people the church has not traditionally reached (as is the case with primary evangelism in Mara Diocese) and so connect again with churches C and D, and we note the Iranian asylum seeker work in church E. Spencer notes how they take the local context and its people much more seriously and new congregations "are formed *by* and *for* the people who join them."[112] Spencer notes too the difference time makes in the different Tanzanian and British milieux. I have quoted elsewhere the research in the UK and USA which shows definitively that *on average* it takes four years to accompany an adult without Christian faith to a public identity in Christ.[113] This is vital data since the resourcing timelines that new initiatives such as these in the UK are often given shorter than this average! This is another reason why any kind of emphasis on sustainability and growth in church life has to be a *very long-term project*. Spencer agrees with this assessment.[114]

Spencer also discerns deficiencies in the approach of Fresh Expressions to his dimensions of Evangelistic Communication and Sacramental Expression.[115] Suggestively these were the least developed dimensions

110. Spencer, *Growing and Flourishing*, 96.

111. Spencer, *Growing and Flourishing*, 97.

112. Spencer, *Growing and Flourishing*, 99, his emphasis.

113. Rooms, *Missional Church*, 13.

114. Spencer, *Growing and Flourishing*, 106.

115. Spencer, *Growing and Flourishing*, 100–1.

along the stages in our research churches too, so perhaps this is a particular issue in the British church scene. There is a reluctance to engage in intentional evangelism and in some forms of new churches an avoidance of questions about the sacramental and the sacraments. Spencer is therefore able to conclude that the six dimensions do indeed describe a comprehensive ecology of growth. He then develops six concomitant "principles" for creating church growth in Britain which he describes and lists as a conclusion.[116]

In perhaps the weakest part of the book the penultimate chapter imagines these six principles applied to a single church that Spencer knows well in the North of England. He describes how the church focused in a fresh way on "outreach" first by setting up after-school clubs and then extending that to Messy Church and employing a Godly Play worker in the local schools. While these initiatives clearly fulfill some of the growth dimensions like Community Service what they consistently miss is a call to committed faith in Christ.[117] In my view this is largely because they focus entirely on children at the expense of their parents and the wider adult population of the parish. Our research churches give a much more rounded picture of what is possible as well as identifying the places where they are challenged most ecclesiologically.

CONCLUSIONS AT THIS STAGE

In this chapter we have tested and utilized Spencer's "ecology of church growth" in relation to our research churches. We believe it is a theologically sound ecology, given the way it was developed out of research in Tanzania and connected to Dulles's classic models of ecclesiology and other western sources. The six dimensions and their three stages are enormously helpful in dealing with the complexities of church growth in a holistic fashion. It employs an organic metaphor which is spacious enough for the intricacies of the question it addresses and moves us away from mechanical, technical, and modernist solutions to understanding the growth of the church. Other nuanced approaches to these questions are available.[118] What I like about it is how it engages with complexity and

116. Spencer, *Growing and Flourishing*, 110.

117. Spencer, *Growing and Flourishing*, 122.

118. For example, Ammerman, *Studying Congregations*. And more recently, Okesson, *Public Missiology*.

is able to include the sacramental. If it was to be used more widely it may need to include more practical questions of money, buildings, and ministry provision. It is worth emphasizing that this approach has come back to us from World Christianity, in particular in Mara Diocese, Tanzania, which has to be an occasion for joy.

Overall, the six dimensions, suitably modified after engaging with them and when utilized to categorize our seven research churches are very illuminating. We have identified a potential further metaphor or model for Church as a "living organism," the key to the future life of which is its interaction across its boundary to its immediate environment. We described this boundary crossing from our research data in the earlier book as the need for a "fuzzy" or porous church, where people and resources can move in both directions freely across its borders. From Spencer's six dimensions we can now describe (and even qualitatively assess) the content of this fuzziness, particularly since Stage 3 of every single dimension has an outward facing element beyond the boundary of the church. The six dimensions helpfully simplify the task of growing the church without making it simplistic (for example, by aiming to go from here to there in straight line as in other approaches to the question). We can see in the research churches that are in Stage 3 "what good looks like" which might be a real incentive to others to emulate these places where "something is happening."

In placing our churches on the grid, which was developed in Africa, some real challenges have been thrown up. We are challenged, as Spencer clearly was, to take intentional evangelism much more seriously across the various traditions. Enabling Christians, especially new Christians, to be confident enough to give their faith away to others, as opposed to simply inviting people into an experience of church has to be something that we focus on and learn to be better at. In addition, the importance of understanding church growth in a sacramental frame undergirded by the *missio Dei* is learning that I hope the reader can take away from this chapter, as I will. Our research churches grappled and struggled with this and it was a moment of joy when coming across those outside of the churches who recognize the presence and activity of God through them.

Revisiting the data in this chapter has underlined a conclusion we made in *Fuzzy Church* (see chapter 4) about the real fragility of the "something happening" in our research churches. We have noted that time in church growth operates differently between Tanzania and the west. What is required here in the western context is more long-term, slow, investment of people and resources so that sustainability over time might be possible. One of my dreams is that dioceses and even the Church of England (and other western church bodies) could take a twenty- to thirty-year strategic view beyond the lifetime of the current leadership (bishops and archbishops in my case). My experience is that every ten years or so (with the change of the most senior leader) new major initiatives are introduced, but they are not given the time to prove themselves fruitful. A good example would be the Fresh Expressions movement which was seriously resourced from 2004 to around 2014, when it was left to fend for itself; this was simply not long enough to assess its fruitfulness.

We are now ready to place the learning from this rather less-than-northern excursion into a comprehensive theological reflection for this project as a whole in the next chapter.

7

Post-colonial Theology and the Northern Research Subjects

A REQUIREMENT OF THIS chapter is to bring together the threads of this project and start to weave them into a whole. The end product may not be fully coherent, given the complexity of what we have attempted and our learning that this may not be a desirable outcome. What we hope to present here is a fuller, connective picture of the various arguments we have made across the preceding chapters (and, indeed, other works that are part of this enterprise).

A good place to start, perhaps, is in the initial essay which kick-started interest in the subject of the North and its gospel. In my chapter in *Northern Gospel, Northern Church*[1] I asked whether we should, as a church in England, be biased to the North:

> At the heart of the North–South divide is a mutual fear and suspicion encapsulated in the saying which presumably emanates from the South—"It's grim up North"—the other side of which is the Northern "chip on the shoulder." The sense of inferiority inherent in being from the North often provokes anger and dispute . . . To use the language and theory of Transactional Analysis, this could easily triangulate the Church as the "rescuer" between the persecuting South and victim of the North. A transformation of the drama triangle takes place where the victim takes up a proper vulnerability, the persecutor offers their power and resources to the whole, and the rescuer takes responsibility

1. Wakefield and Rooms, *Northern Gospel*, 45.

> for their own in-between position without attachment to either. The misplaced emotional energy of the chip on the shoulder can then be released to use the power and resources offered by those who have them to create something quite new and even beautiful. A robust gospel of reconciliation in the English Church will therefore be able to address the North–South divide . . . I believe it is proper then for the Church to call for a 'bias to the North' just as David Shepherd [the then Bishop of Liverpool] called for a bias to the poor in the 1980s.

Since that *cri de coeur* was made and the ensuing field research conducted, it has become clear that there can be no bias to the North without addressing the colonial conditions under which the North labors, we explored this especially in chapter 4. In this chapter then we will employ the categories of post-colonial theology from Robert Heaney[2] as, to use our metaphor of threads and weaving, a frame on which we can create a much-thickened approach to what it means to be biased to the North. Heaney's subtitle is *Finding God and Each Other amidst the Hate.* Perhaps it is only a small step from the anger noted in the quotation above to actual hatred and thus it is the search for God amidst that potential hate which we embark on here in developing a post-colonial northern contextual theology.

We began looking at our research findings through Heaney's post-colonial theology in *Fuzzy Church* alongside Barrett and Harley's approach to the mission of the local church, *Being Interrupted.*[3] Once again we will need to use that work in *Fuzzy Church* as a starting point for the deeper questions that we were unable to address in that book, but can engage with here.

Heaney defines "five main characteristics" of his approach to post-colonial theology, stating that it begins "in *particularity,* is the *agency* of marginalized voices, considers *coloniality,* as the best lens through which to view imperialist oppression, *practices* hybridization, and seeks to *resist* dominant forms of theology."[4] In *Fuzzy Church* we treated each of these characteristics in turn: particularity, agency, coloniality, hybridization, and resistance. It would seem sensible to do the same here as we embark on this chapter, and at the same time go deeper into their implications for the North.

2. See Heaney, *Post-Colonial.*
3. See Barrett and Harley, *Being Interrupted.*
4. Heaney, *Post-Colonial,* 1, his emphasis.

PARTICULARITY

Heaney's first characteristic, particularity, engenders an extensive reflection on his own locatedness as a white theologian with origins in Ireland, itself a place of colonization. This is necessary prior work before one can hear "the voice of others and the voice of God amidst the fear and hate."[5] We told the story of the origins of this research at the start of chapter 4, but should say more here about the particularity of the author/s. In the introduction to *Fuzzy Church,* we said: "We are both white, middle-class Anglican Christians, who have received high levels of education. Nigel is originally from the North but currently lives in the East Midlands; Elli is originally from the South but now lives in the North."[6]

I suggest a somewhat deeper work on reflexive locatedness is required here, if this study can make a claim to be post-colonial and we can hear the voices of our research respondents. I have reflected elsewhere and at some length in an autoethnographic fashion on my whiteness and concomitant privilege which goes right back to my birth and early life in a suburb of Hull in East Yorkshire.[7] As I pointed out in that article, and in a resonant connection with this study, there is no escape from "white-work" since faith and culture are "so deeply entwined."[8] I know that, for instance, my own "conversion" in my teenage years could be understood as a reaction against my middle-class (nice, safe, and yes deeply privileged) culture, even though that faith does seem to have stuck despite many ups and downs. "Leaning into my white fragility" in the article, I asked my privileged self several questions in relation to the "call of God to cross cultures, especially in Africa."[9] In working through my life story, I was able to relocate myself with an appropriate integration of my Tanzanian "self," thus owning more deeply my white privilege and power and resolving to foreground it in places like this.

In the autobiographical article I also attempted to answer the question, "Who am I?" using Reddie's exercise of five circles of importance.[10] Interestingly, my northern identity was placed in the third level, not at the center or indeed at the next level of importance. This still feels

5. Heaney, *Post-Colonial,* 11.
6. Rooms and Wort, *Fuzzy Church,* 3.
7. See Rooms, "God and my."
8. Rooms, "God and My Whiteness," 139.
9. Rooms, "God and My Whiteness," 139.
10. See Reddie, *Is God.*

about right; it is of significance to me and I cannot disown it, but it is not foremost. Nevertheless, as pointed out in chapter 4, some years ago, prompted by my African sisters and brothers for whom home is defined more from one's final resting place at death than any current location, I secured my grave plot in a cemetery a few hundred meters from where I was born and less than a mile from the font in which I was baptized. I could not think of anywhere else I would rather be buried, my resting place in the North, at "home." The point is worth making again as one of the threads of this study, which we also made in chapter 4 from Niven and the interview data on our church leaders that it is in the crossing of cultures that horizons are expanded and then the place of origin can be known "for the first time." In *Fuzzy Church* we concluded on the question of so-called leadership "indigeneity" that "where leaders have done personal inter-cultural work by changing their location they can be more effective at enabling a local church to be connected across its own boundaries with the community around it."[11]

Heaney too has crossed cultures, having lived and worked in Africa and the USA and taking this discussion further he notes the limits of location and particularity with respect to the post-colonial project:

> The determinative factor in defining a context and response as post-colonial relates to analyses and strategies around exercises of power. That does not mean that race, history, and geography are unimportant . . . [yet there is no] sense that particular races, particular histories, and particular places alone constitute the borders of what is post-colonial . . . Rather, a renewed post-colonialism will avoid essentialized nativism, naïve nationalism, and easy binaries of difference in favor of a more expansive inter-cultural post-colonialism. The particularities of place, race, class and time are not boundaries to be policed. They are boundaries that make us present to one another."[12]

A final personal reflection is therefore appropriate here. We have, I believe been alert to the pitfalls of essentialism and nativism in this regional (rather than overtly national) research, yet we also need to address the potential "easy binary" of the North–South divide. As we remarked in the quote at the start of the chapter, one of the effects of the cultural capital associated with Northernness is the development of what is known as the northern "chip on the shoulder." The origin of this idiom is in North

11. Rooms and Wort, *Fuzzy Church*, 104.

12. Heaney, *Post-Colonial*, 29.

America when a wronged person would place a literal chip of wood on their shoulder and challenge their opponent to knock it off. In its usage in this case, it becomes a permanent irremovable fixture which the owner would rather not have knocked off, since if it remains it is the excuse for ongoing fights. It becomes a permanent (and quite precious) resentment born of being from the "lesser" North. We made several references to this in *Fuzzy Church*[13] and I also recognize it in myself. This research has conscientized me to its presence on my shoulder and while it can reassert itself from time to time, I now know it is there and I also know there are better ways to live with it, as noted in *Fuzzy Church*.[14] Here the counter-cultural model of contextual theology is doing its work.

Having dealt with the personal particular we cannot leave this characteristic of the post-colonial world without addressing the more "public particular." Right at the start of chapter 2 we remarked on the "turn to the contextual" in missiology from the mid-twentieth century which coincided with the end of the Modern period which was characterized much more by a *universalism* which had tragic consequences over many centuries. This project is clearly in the flow of the turn to context as we engage with a region in northern England and yet the question of the universal has not gone away. We discussed the polarity between the particular and the universal at length in chapter 3 when we engaged with the work of Goto and Jennings. Goto herself found a limit to research if there is thought to be only the particular; this makes sense to me given the anthropological "cross-cultural universals" in human life of (at the very least) birth, sexual relations, and death. Jennings thought that the irresolvable polarity (or dialectic) of the particular and the universal was not the most important missiological question to be asked and this led to a discussion of Walter's theology of *promise* especially within "Act Four" of the drama of salvation, where the Church finds herself in our time. Before leaving the particular–universal polarity it is worth noting its relationship to another potential polarity in post-colonial relationships, that of reconciliation–reparation. I discussed this at the end of my autobiographical article[15] and it is relevant here, since the default of the powerful is to the universal/reconciliation rather than the nitty-gritty particulars of reparation. How this might work out practically between North and South within a bias to the North is the task for another book perhaps.

13. For example, see Rooms and Wort, *Fuzzy Church*, 49.

14. Rooms and Wort, *Fuzzy Church*, 52.

15. Rooms, "God and My Whiteness," 146.

On this side of chapters 5 and 6 however we have more data to address the issues raised by Jennings when he suggests that what is more important than translation is "an advent of a new form of communion with the possibility of a new kind of cultural intimacy between peoples that might yield a new cultural politic."[16] We have glimpses and hints of this new cultural politic, for instance, with regard to race at church E and class at church C, where those with power are prepared to be changed by the people meeting Jesus and joining them across their boundaries. The research data demonstrated that the Jesus they are meeting is both a personal *and* public Christ. The people finding faith have met with Jesus, the promise of God and embodiment of the gospel in the "scandal of the particular." Also, we have shown in the previous chapter how the presence and activity of the Spirit of Jesus in a Tanzanian diocese can be recognized by a priest from the "old country," the colonizer. Such recognition emerges out of a long-term relationship of friendship (even Jennings's intimacy) which no doubt was hard-won. I wonder therefore whether, it is not either translatability or communion/intimacy, but both. The two are actually related together in our research and one can easily lead towards the other in a virtuous circle.

AGENCY AND THEOLOGICAL AGENCY

Colonialism in the propagation of the Christian faith denies agency, especially theological agency, to the convert; the imperialist Christian defines the parameters of belief for those finding it for the first time. It is a "one-way street" where the evangelizer imagines they have the truth which is transferred to the evangelized in a transaction in which their only agency is to be grateful for what they have been given. Perhaps this is a rather crude way of describing how churches have operated in the past (we discussed this in chapter 2) and in the contemporary world, but it is one which can still be found in many places. As Heaney puts it, "Contextualization, therefore, cannot be seen as a one-way process of inculturating an imported gospel. Contextualization is contestation."[17] In chapter 3 we quoted Jennings, who is clear that "Centrally, translation should beget

16. Jennings, *Christian Imagination,* 265.

17. Heaney, *Post-Colonial,* 50.

Christian agency"[18] and Heaney takes this further in stating that "Every culture is needed for the fullest possible vision of God."[19]

In *Fuzzy Church* we observed that the privatization of religion in the Modern period has left Christians with a profound lack of agency especially in public, which is hardly surprising, even if slightly ironic given the universalizing tendencies of that era. In contrast:

> What is evident from this research is that the people we met, both leaders and new converts had a language and a set of behaviours that bucked this trend. They had, to employ Heaney's language, *theological agency*—permission to name what God was up to in their individual and collective lives. And to go further we noted the new Christians also had agency *per se* in their faith and action, they had a place and permission to be their best selves in the Christian community they were joining.[20]

Neither should we be naïve in believing that there was no evidence for "one-way street" Christian transmission in what was happening in the research churches, especially perhaps at B and C—another kind of contestation. We remarked that even Spencer allows for this kind of univocity in his stages of growth, and it is a moot point whether this is strictly necessary from the start of something new. Power is clearly at play here, and as Heaney suggested above it is at the heart of the post-colonial question. This is why Walter's theology of promise is so helpful at this point. If the promise is without closure or completion then we have "all the time in the world," since the time we find ourselves in is God's time. We have the time to generate agency for those exploring faith, so we do not need to use our power to anxiously impose upon them our "project timeframes," as we remarked at the end of the previous chapter. In addition, if the Spirit who is embodied by the faithful as witnesses is a weak power, "a power that is open to the other, welcomes the new, and does not attempt to preserve the present in the face of the past or the future,"[21] then power can be given away in the empowerment of the neophyte, allowing them to bring all they wish to the table. And speaking of tables, there is a Eucharistic thread from chapter 3 right through to the "sacramental expression" of Spencer's typology of church growth in chapter 6. We felt

18. Jennings, *Christian Imagination*, 155.

19. Heaney, *Post-Colonial*, 65.

20. Rooms and Wort, *Fuzzy Church*, 107.

21. Walter, *Being Promised*, 49.

this was at the heart of many of our research churches where one or both of the canonical sacraments were central to what was happening. I am reminded of a Lutheran church in Copenhagen I have visited and which participated in a theological action research project when large numbers of Iranian asylum seekers turned up looking to become Christian. It was related to me on visiting that the leadership were helped via theological reflection on hospitality to offer agency to these double seekers and some were given the task of offering the cup at the Eucharist. A white member of the congregation wrote a letter to the church council wondering if it was entirely correct that when one of these men offered her the cup, he accompanied the action of handing over the cup by the single word, "Jesus." The council replied that it was and thus the stranger was truly welcomed and handed their theological agency.

Ascribing agency, especially theological agency, to newcomers as in this story requires work—hard theological work. On reflection over the research data, such work is also evident in our church leaders—though we didn't necessarily go looking for it. I think of the minister at church A who had recently completed a Master's degree and, which clearly informed his practice. I also think of the wrestling with the meaning and practice of the Eucharist at church C and the theologically grounded acceptance of fuzziness at church F. Heaney[22] gives us some content for this work after an explication of the theology of John V. Taylor, who, he explains, reversed the trend of colonizing missionary work (in his case in Uganda) in the twentieth century, eventually becoming General Secretary of the Church Mission Society and then Bishop of Winchester. Working from Taylor's example, Heaney calls for "critical awareness, cultural humility, and inductive theologizing."[23] Critical awareness is "educating oneself about the history and theology of a particular context,"[24] which is exactly what we were attempting in chapter 4 and is a "reaching in." In contrast, cultural humility ("reaching out"[25]) is where, for instance, in Heaney's (and my) Anglican Communion is the possibility of learning and resourcing one another across the many different contexts, just as we endeavored to do in chapter 6 through an official partnership program. While I hesitate to compare myself to John V. Taylor, Heaney describes a

22. Heaney, *Post-Colonial*, 61–62.

23. Heaney, *Post-Colonial*, 63.

24. Heaney, *Post-Colonial*, 63.

25. Heaney, *Post-Colonial*, 64.

similar process of conversion from his western theological mindset[26] as I had which he then describes as Taylor doing "inductive theologizing" from experience:

> The example of Taylor suggests an inductive approach to theology. It was because of his experience in Uganda that he had a theological conversion. Luganda had an 'intractable concreteness' that took him back to the central Christian claim. By virtue of a theology of incarnation, the idea that the grace of God is translatable into a particular place, time, language, and social location is forever embedded in Christian theology . . . the mission of God is embodied in the life and work of a colonized Palestinian. In ascension (Acts 1:6–11), and through contextual contestation (Acts 15), this Jewish Messiah is recognized as Lord of the gentiles also.[27]

This is how agency is recovered in post-colonial theology, speaking to Jennings's critique of translatability that we have aired in this research—that it is tainted with supersessionism. There is a conversion to be experienced here for the sent one by the "other" to whom they are sent, whether in Uganda or on the streets of northern cities, towns, and villages. Here we connect with Barrett and Harley's call for working in a spiral of relocation, relinquishing, receptivity, and repentance.[28] We could imagine a "northerly biased" vocation arising from this research where Christian leaders were able to relinquish roles in the South for a call to relocate to the North, which would require receptivity to a new cultural reality and repentance from attitudes and beliefs about the North and its people.[29]

COLONIALITY

We come now to what I consider to be the "heart of the matter" in this study. Heaney defines coloniality as "a category that connects experiences of subjugation and resistance across a range of historical settings."[30] It is

26. Wider research evidence for this phenomenon is outlined in David Hollinger's book *Protestants Abroad: How Missionaries Tried to Change the World, but Changed America.*

27. Heaney, *Post-Colonial,* 64–65.

28. Heaney, *Post-Colonial,* 182.

29. And perhaps could include some significant cultural and contextual induction, training, and reflective practice with Northerners themselves.

30. Heaney, *Post-Colonial,* 69.

to be distinguished from formal colonialism, where the subjugation is much more all-encompassing at all levels of society and government. We have established at every stage of this project, and especially in chapter 4 in this book, the subaltern nature of the North of England in relation to the South. The North's coloniality begins in geography where the North contains the vast majority of English uplands. The Romans established the South of England before the rest of the country in their 400-year occupation which proceeded from the South to the North and which shaped forever the way transport and commerce are conducted. Thus, apart from a brief flowering in the industrial revolution, the socio-economics of the region have been dictated by the dominance of the South where the placement of the institutions of governmental and political power in London and its environs have reinforced the divide over many centuries. Culturally in language and dialect, beliefs and values, and in the arts and literature there is a significant gulf in how "cultural capital" operates between the two regions, with the more mainstream, acceptable and commercially viable culture operating in and from the South. The Church too is divided along the same lines, with two Provinces, one northern and one southern and it is clear which is the more powerful, better resourced and vocationally attractive.

Our project directly addresses such coloniality, first, by following Heaney's assertion that it is "the colonized Christ who makes the invisible visible."[31] The research and its outputs may be the first serious theological engagement with the North of England. It has been overlooked by theologians, who, if they have been concerned with context at all, have investigated the nation as a whole (dominated inevitably by the South). We now know that one of the outcomes from testing our outputs in various places was a recognizable representation of the North and its people, by Northerners themselves. In chapter 3 we foregrounded Goto's concerns about representation where any such representations could be "symbols that may point to reality with some accuracy but bear the imprint of their makers as all symbols do."[32] We will therefore need to "guard against privileging the researcher's assumptive world."[33] We accept that the representations we have made are ours and ours alone and can still remain biased to our concerns, yet we have tested them back in the "field," as it were (see chapter 5), and against a number of northern

31. Heaney, *Post-Colonial*, 84.

32. Goto, *Taking on Practical Theology*, 153.

33. Goto, *Taking on Practical Theology*, 161.

interlocutors such as Kate Fox and Alex Niven in chapter 4. We believe there is a robustness about them which is grounded in this critical work.

We can come, then, to the heart of this study. We have predicated this missiological research on the *missio Dei,* the idea that God is present and active within and far beyond the church, leaving local churches with the task of discerning and participating in that work. Heaney too has presented the task of post-colonial theology as "finding God and each other amidst the hate." In *Fuzzy Church* we located the question in this way: "We have been working on the assumption that God is at work in the North of England even where seemingly, the church-as-it-was is dying. Is it possible then to notice the activity of God in what has been happening in these last decades in the North?"[34] We continued to pose some possible, though tentative, answers to this question and did promise to return to them in this book.[35]

Our hypothesis goes like this. In chapter 3 and elsewhere we noted the "end of Christendom" in the west which has progressively occurred since the mid-twentieth century following on the end of the Modern period. David Bosch and others have named this phenomenon a paradigm shift that has deep and far-reaching consequences for belief, culture and behavior in western societies. We examined one missiological approach to this massive cultural change in Gert-Jan Roest's research in chapter 3, which remained largely untested in practice. The fragility and the possibility of death of the Church in the North of England which we discovered in our field research is but one small example of this wider transformation. That is, the word "flourishing" is disavowed by church leaders in favor of churches where "something is happening" and all of those we visited have faced up to and leant into the possibility, and in one case the reality, of actual death. Given that the Church in the North is starting from a more fragile and tenuous position because of its subaltern coloniality this is entirely to be expected, it is no surprise that local churches are more prone to failure and death in the North as Christendom comes to an end.

However, in leaning into death and discovering new life our churches have been living out authentic Christian discipleship, as we argued in this passage from *Fuzzy Church* utilizing the thought of an American theologian: Elaine Heath is a Methodist minister and scholar of mission

34. Rooms and Wort, *Fuzzy Church,* 108.

35. Rooms and Wort, *Fuzzy Church,* 109.

and evangelism based in the Eastern United States. Consistently over the last few years, starting with her important book on evangelism,[36] she has been calling the church to follow Jesus faithfully in discipleship. For Elaine this means embracing the same shape of life that Jesus did which is outlined by St. Paul in Philippians 2.5–11. In verse 5 the original Greek has the word *phronesis* which is often translated rather thinly as "mind." It describes a wisdom, a kind of knowing that arises from acting in our bodies and learning from that action—embodied knowing and practical wisdom.[37] In the following verses we have the whole movement of Christ from heaven to earth and back again which St. Paul is exhorting us to imitate in an embodied fashion. Elaine extrapolates a little between verses 8 and 9 from other places in the Bible and the creeds which describe what happens to Jesus between his death and resurrection—so she concludes that *the church has to follow Jesus to hell* (cf. 1 Pet 3.19).[38] When I first heard her say this there was a shocked silence in the room (and in myself, I must admit), but it seems some of the experiences we heard about on our travels were pretty "hellish." Others[39] speak of the importance of staying with the dead Christ on Holy Saturday as a way of learning relinquishment, powerlessness, and the chance to become compost.[40]

In the Christian faith death is the way to life, this emphasis was rather missing in Spencer's treatment of church growth in the previous chapter,[41] but we can easily recover it here. The hypothesis continues: if the Church in the subaltern North is the first to experience failure, then our research churches who have faced death and where new life is happening are at the *forefront of the future* of the whole Church in England and, if it is not too great a universalizing leap, perhaps also more broadly in the west.[42] Thus, another aspect of a bias to the North is the gift that the

36. See Heath, *Mystic*.

37. See Rooms, "Paul as Practical."

38. The reader can watch Elaine Heath speak about this at Work of the People, "Go to Hell," though there is a donation wall part way through.

39. For example, Barrett and Harley, *Being Interrupted*, 191, 200.

40. Rooms and Wort, *Fuzzy Church*, 108–9.

41. Perhaps adding a fourth stage of maturity might develop the grid in this direction where aspects of the six dimensions can be allowed to flourish, mature, wither, and die even while other aspects of those dimensions are beginning to grow and take their place.

42. This is not to assert that life will *always* emerge from death in some magical way. Church D may have stayed dead if a new initiative had not taken place, yet on the admission of the new priest what did emerge could not have happened without the prior

North brings to the Church in England and perhaps even further afield. Niven, as presented in chapter 4, would agree that the North offers "the idea of the future" to England as a whole. If these northern churches can find life, however fragile, after Christendom and in a subaltern region, then, as the foundations of Christendom continue to crumble in the South and elsewhere, there is hope from the North for the future. If we are correct here and we stay with this hypothesis then there is a further claim to be made: that a post-colonial contextual theology only emerges in the conditions of post-Christendom. Until the blinkers that Modernity allied with Christendom can be removed it is very hard to address the conditions of coloniality and seek ways beyond it.

It is not too great a claim from the data we have presented that our churches have been participating in the *missio Dei*, the work of God. One further potential discernment can be made—that the dying of Christendom is the work and will of God. Again, in *Fuzzy Church* we posited this:

> If this [Philippians 2] is the shape of discipleship that God in Christ himself has chosen then might we not be able to discern God's activity in the death of Christendom? Perhaps we might even say tentatively that God wills it, just as it seems the Israelites were taken into exile within the purposes of God, as described in the Hebrew bible. It is perhaps too easily done, but it is popular to speak of how the church in this country is constantly "rearranging the deckchairs on the *Titanic*" as a metaphor for the almost permanent reorganisation of parish, circuit and regional church boundaries that goes on as a response to the slow decline of the church, especially the numbers of available clergy. In this metaphor then we are hypothesising that God might be the iceberg, or at the very least wills it to be there for the church to founder on. Another shocking thought, perhaps.[43]

I have sat with this unsettling hypothesis for some years now and it has not gone away or been undermined, rather if anything it has been reinforced from several directions. I recently did some work on the themes we are airing here with senior leaders from the English regions of the Salvation Army. At the end of the time, the most senior person present blessed each participant with a few words and he named me, among

---

death. We know there are many places around the Mediterranean Sea where the church flourished and where it now, no longer exists, in the same form at least. What matters is how the liminal movement through death to life is held and handled. See Carson et al., *Crossing Thresholds*, 103, and the reference later in this chapter.

43. Rooms and Wort, *Fuzzy Church*, 109.

other things as a prophet. I had never thought of myself in these terms until that moment, but there it was spoken with authority over me. The hypothesis that the end of Christendom is the work, even the judgment of God over a deeply problematic (yet incredibly "successful" in some sense) period of the Church's life, is a prophetic stance that I can hold to.

What other responses to the decline of the Church in the west are available to inform the discussion here? I mention two at this point, which are by no means exhaustive, but do rather confirm what I am claiming here from very different standpoints.

Alison Milbank writes a passionate, even angry book in defense of the parish in the Church of England.[44] Milbank is clear and authoritative in her ecclesiology,[45] arguing for the Church's ongoing participation in God and an Anglican version of Dulles's model of mystical communion (without referring to the models specifically). What she is angry about is the Church of England's various responses to its decline over the past twenty years. I have a lot of sympathy with her critiques, especially of managerialism and the skewing of how resources are spent in the wrong places. Yet the book turns into an intra-Anglican argument which is rather myopic and locally focused. For instance, she is unaware of the work of Spencer[46] or that of Stefan Paas[47] when she discusses church planting. Her intent is to support an Anglican movement called "Save the Parish," which resists the current responses to decline.[48] Relevant for our purposes is her chapter 8, "Kill the Parish?," where she asks whether decline is inevitable and states: "The scale of recent decline is to a degree self-inflicted."[49] She claims that the decline neither of the parish nor of Christianity as a whole is inevitable. It is unclear how the Christianity she refers to is related to Christendom as there is no reference to that in the book. However, for such a theologically grounded book it is hard to understand why the possibility of the death of one way of being church (under the conditions of Christendom) might not be a possibility, given the shape of Christian discipleship in following Christ and carrying the cross, the symbol of death. Decline in the churches of the west is a statistical and factual reality which has to be dealt with in some fashion. Clearly

44. See Milbank, *Once and Future Parish.*

45. Milbank, *Once and Future Parish,* 4.

46. See Spencer, *Growing and Flourishing.*

47. See Paas, *Church Planting.*

48. See https://www.savetheparish.com/.

49. Milbank, *Once and Future Parish,* 126.

there are better and worse approaches to decline, but asking what God is doing in the midst of it is a much more fruitful question for me. Our research churches were all locally led, "parish" based responses to their contexts, but as we have demonstrated had also leant into the dying of what was, in order that something new could emerge. We will return to some of the institutional questions Milbank raises in our final chapter.

Michael Plekon is a priest of the Orthodox Church in America, having previously served in other western Churches in that country and worked ecumenically across denominational boundaries. His book is as astutely ecclesiologically grounded as Milbank's, and it is also parish based,[50] yet it is fully able to embrace the movement from death to resurrection as a response to the decline of the Church.[51] As a sociologist of religion, Plekon positions the church within the frame of community formation (hence his book title). He states categorically that for the USA (as in the UK) "the situation of most parishes remains tentative, fragile."[52] The paradigm shift we referred to at the start of this reflection is front and center in his book: "One of the aims of the present volume is to come to terms with profound and irrevocable change."[53] The types of response that Milbank explored are also critiqued: "Death and resurrection are part of the regular, ordinary lives of congregations."[54] The future is experimental, not everything works, but the shape of transition as a response to profound change is always through death and resurrection.[55] The body of the book is example after example of churches across the USA (with some in the UK) who have reinvented, repurposed, and restructured themselves—sometimes even relocating (which is less of an option in the UK). He has a whole chapter dedicated to the resurrection of the "small church,"[56] which gives a sense of where his commitments lie. While Plekon does not present exhaustive research, neither is his evidence anecdotal in any way; the examples he gives are ample support for his thesis. He is able to conclude, of these "death to resurrection" churches:

50. Plekon, *Community*, 5–10.
51. Plekon, *Community*, 52.
52. Plekon, *Community*, 14.
53. Plekon, *Community*, 58.
54. Plekon, *Community*, 60.
55. Plekon, *Community*, 61.
56. Plekon, *Community*, 151–91.

> Equally impressive are the creative, sometimes ingenious ways they found to redefine or reinvent themselves. Buildings were repurposed. New ties to the neighbourhood around the parish were investigated and pursued. Coalitions with other congregations, with not-for-profit agencies, were established. In many cases, while there were real breaks with the past, even then it was possible to see the continuity in praising God, being a community in faith, and love and serving God's people in that particular place.[57]

Plekon goes on to emphasize the importance of "ties to the neighborhood," following Loren Mead's and others' call for the church to "live for others" beyond itself, just as we have noted the fuzzy porosity at the boundary of our research churches. Plekon's work is important for us as it resonates deeply with the hypothesis we have set out drawn from the field research, and therefore confirms that the conclusions we present here may have a life and relevance beyond their origin in northern England.

Before we leave this section on coloniality we can weave in one or two more threads from earlier parts of the book and make some further observations. In chapter 3, when studying the contributions of Goto and Jennings, we came to a conclusion that humility was required in mission after Christendom to which an "eschatological reserve" should also be added from Roest's work. Not very much of the "something happening" in churches that we researched could be called very strong, permanent or stable; rather it was characterized by fragility and vulnerability.[58] And as Plekon notes too[59] in all his examples, whatever was happening in the churches he showcases was in *process*—a snapshot in a moment of time; there is little finality about it. And this is all good, since it leads to humility and the possibility of Barrett and Harley's composting of the old life to the new. Perhaps an example from chapter 6 might also illustrate this point. We made what could be thought of as a small shift in Stage 3 of organizational growth in Spencer's table of the ecology of church growth. We named it "public actor" rather than "public utility." Here is the post-colonial shift again. Rather than the Church being a "utility" like

57. Plekon, *Community*, 61.

58. We might add here that the work of Charles Taylor draws this conclusion in his classic work on the conditions for religion in the west since the dawn of the Enlightenment, *A Secular Age*. That belief (or indeed unbelief) will remain fragile *and* possible despite the forces of secularity in our contemporary western world that are ranged against it.

59. Plekon, *Community*, 14.

the essential water and electricity that are fed to our homes, the Church is not part of a societal package any more, but rather she can act in public across her boundary alongside many other actors for the good of all.

We have learnt here the importance of leaning into decline, demise, and even death as resurrection ensues. This stance helps with a dilemma we were left with from chapter 4 and which we aired at the start of this one about the "grim" North. We can now reinforce the idea we had in chapter 4 that we should indeed embrace this reality and not run from it. There is even a liberation available from the grimness itself, since it is definitely not the end of the story about the North; rather, it leads us to the gift that a bias to the North can bring. Our costly discipleship of dying to live can encompass such a reality and overcome it, which takes us back to good news, gospel.

Finally, it is hard not to escape the liminal nature of the movement we have described here in the dying and rising of local churches in the UK and USA—and that we hinted at from Elaine Heath. Liminality as a hermeneutical lens has been an interest of mine for many years and I have published, with others, a book on the subject which sought to bring the original anthropological concept within a practical theological and missiological frame.[60] In that work we offered a modified version of Otto Scharmer's "Theory U" of how a person or a system can move through a liminal change process.[61] For our purposes here what is suggestive about this model is the importance of "regression to dependence" (towards the Other, who is God) on the left leg of the U downwards to desolation and even death. This movement is described almost exactly by the "Paschal Mystery" of the Christ-hymn in Philippians 2:5–11 where Christ descends to the nadir of the cross and is raised and returns, ascending to heaven. There is resistance on the left leg of the U, but if it can be leant into (as for Christ in Gethsemane) and discerned as God's work, then dying and rising become possible (but again never inevitable). It is on this downward journey towards the *limen*, the threshold, that Heaney's (and now our) contestation of contextualization takes place. Victor Turner's word for what happens at the threshold was *communitas*,[62] the breaking and remaking of strongly bonded relationships across structures and hierarchies. *Communitas* is not without some disturbance, chaos, and awe on the way to the forming of new community. Our research churches

60. See Carson et. al., *Crossing Thresholds*.

61. Carson et al., *Crossing Thresholds*, 55.

62. Carson et al., *Crossing Thresholds*, 16–21.

were on this journey and, more often than not, different parts of them were in different places on the "U" simultaneously. Liminality is a "cross-cultural universal," given the nature of human birth, growth, and death. Utilizing liminality as a hermeneutical lens for our work is another confirmation of what we have discovered in the research and how it can be relevant beyond its beginnings in the North of England.

In the midst of coloniality, in this section I believe we have found God amidst the anger and even the hate. We have, as we set out to do, thickened a bias to the North in the visibility we have offered to its churches and people alongside the gift the North offers from its subaltern reality to the whole English Church and beyond.

HYBRIDIZATION AND MIMICRY

There is a sense in which hybridization is another way of describing the contestation between colonizer and colonized. Heaney states that it is a "strategy employed toward decolonization"[63] with a variety of methods and a broad reach, but which can be encapsulated in moves to break down unhelpful binaries such as civilized/uncivilized, developed/underdeveloped, and heathen/believer. Hybridization, therefore, "is not a *direct* move to overthrow a domineering colonialist culture. This may be because of a rejection of binaries of opposition or because power differentials would make it virtually impossible for the 'local' to compete with the 'imperialist.'"[64] I would like to illustrate this breaking down of binaries with the opening conversation between four leaders in their focus group at church D. They are the clergy person (CP) and their spouse (CS, who also has an official role in the church), a lay leader (LL) and a Ministry Experience student on placement at the church for a year (MS, who is from the South of England). Remember they are all ministering on a social housing estate with a poor reputation in a larger northern town which we'll call X.

INTWR: So, I wondered erm, do you think it matters where the leadership comes from in this kind of place?

CP: I don't know, it's quite funny, I think of myself as being from the North of England even

63. Heaney, *Post-Colonial*, 5.

64. Heaney, *Post-Colonial*, 5, his emphasis.

	through I'm not. I also think of myself as being from X even through I'm not but it just feels like my home town. Erm . . .
CS:	There's something and this is nothing against MS [laughter] obviously but there's something about . . .
CP:	Southerner.
CS:	There's something about credibility in the North. Erm, so there's something about if you're a Northerner you get it, you understand it. If you're not from the North you won't understand us, which is not true but it's, but it is.
LL:	It's not even if you're not from the north, if you don't sound like you're from the North. So, when Y [a previous student] was on placement she sounds dead posh but she, she's obviously from X.
CS:	She's from X, yeah . . .
LL:	But, it, they, it's all what, it's joking and stuff, but it was more that "you're a southerner" even though she is not and because she has got a posh accent . . .
CS:	Yeah, I think there's an additional barrier to break down, erm, if you're not from this area. Erm, I mean you even get that on estates, we've had to break down barriers on this estate because we, we're not *from* this estate, we're from X, that gives us some cred yeah, yeah. [*Laughter.*]
CP:	I feel like I'm from X, yeah.
CS:	Yeah, but you know I'm a X lad, LL is a X girl. So, you know we, they kind of, you've got that credibility of being a XXian, you know that's what they're called.
INTWR:	XXian?
CS:	XXians that's a X person.
LL:	You have to have been born in X and live in X your whole life [to be called XXian].
CS:	Erm, and I think CP's probably unique in the fact that she's from [another nation in UK] so they have their own kind of personality, acceptance everywhere. There is something about that, there is. There's something about the [other nation's] charm that gets accepted

everywhere. So, I don't know. What do you think MS?

MS: Erm, I think the person who makes jokes about you being Southern is you CS, but that's fine. [*Laughter.*] And so, I don't know if that's a big like, people in church, I don't know if they care that much. In church there's quite a lot of people, like N is from Suffolk and M is from London. Like people have moved around a bit.

CP: P's from Wales.

MS: Yeah, so there's like a mixture of people at church.

CS: There's a banter. There's a banter about North, South. Erm, how deep that goes . . . I don't . . .

MS: I don't think it massively affects how I interact with people in church.

LL: I think because you live in the community you're accepted in the community.

CP: Yeah, that's it we live on the estate. I don't think it matters too much where you come from it's the fact that we actually live on the estate. I think it makes a massive difference because there's so many organizations that drive onto the estate, do their work and drive home again to their nice comfortable leafy house in the suburbs. There's so many organizations do that whereas we actually live here and I know I live in the biggest house on the estate, I get that, but people just know this is a church house, this is used for ministry, so there's never an issue with that and it's not one we've come across.[65]

So here is a fascinating discussion, prompted only by an open-ended question at the start. There is a reversal of the usual North–South power dynamics because MS is alone as a southerner among people who are (or who identify as) northern. Yet MS is part of (I think) a national Ministry Experience Scheme, with a view to possible ordination down the line. Class and the accent that goes with it complexifies the discussion (and in fact the group went on to note this in more detail next). Yet what seems to be occurring here is both the revealing of the northern chip on CS's shoulder (they are the only one who calls out MS's southern identity and

65. Leader's Focus Group Church D.

needs to make jokes about it) and an amelioration of it via the way they, as leaders are incarnate in the community and are forming community and therefore accepting of MS's identity—"I think because you live in the community you're accepted in the community." The North–South binary is hybridized in several helpful ways in this conversation between two local (but not hyper-local on the estate) people, one who feels local and one southern outsider. This was a unique situation among the various research focus groups, yet it does demonstrate what is possible if the binary can be openly discussed and addressed within the frame of community formation.

In *Fuzzy Church* we remarked on how the worship practices we observed on our research visits were a hybrid of "traditional (Christendom) denominational practices" and a whole range of other practices borrowed from many different places.

> So, what's different about worship in these places that makes it "hybrid"? First it doesn't just happen on a Sunday, or even in some places ever on a Sunday! In fact, it is more a demonstration that Christian life and worship can be enacted anytime and anywhere throughout the week. Communion can be "tacked on" to a lunch club, but changes the whole nature of the hospitality that happens there. Traditional, what might be thought of as "Catholic" practices such as the lighting of candles are available alongside (almost everywhere) a version of Pentecostal "testimony" which sometimes gets mixed up in the Notices. Prayer for healing in various guises is possible. There are connections made between the local and the global, in the use of different languages and in the borrowing of Christian comedy culture from the United States in one place.[66]

While this isn't strictly hybridization between North and South, it is occurring between the previous dominant Christendom culture of worship and what is now possible in a globalizing world. It often seemed to us a rather pragmatic searching for what "works," that is, seeking forms Christian community in the margins of these (in themselves marginal) churches. It is perhaps therefore another aspect of the liminal nature of the fuzzy edges of our research subjects. A strong conclusion we made in the book *Crossing Thresholds* is that God seems particularly available to us in the margins, in liminal space and time. In the final chapter I wrote this:

66. Rooms and Wort, *Fuzzy Church*, 110.

> We know there are "thin places" where God seems more available but this means all the more that any place has the potential to be 'Beth-el, the house of God and gate of heaven' if and when God turns up, even in a dream (Genesis 28:17). Readers will be familiar with the credo of the liberation theology movement—that God has a "*bias to the poor*." Such a bias does not exclude anyone from knowing God or give the privileged non-poor a right to do things *for* the marginalized. Yet God in Christ identifies in true solidarity with people on the margins of society—the equivalent of the compromised and unclean (the filthy scum we might say), the "tax collectors and sinners" in the Gospels (e.g., Matthew 9:11).[67]

We have felt and touched this liminal reality in our research; we have found God on the contested and fuzzy edges of churches in a subaltern region of northern England. God therefore has a bias to the North.

Mimicry is related to the fuzziness of hybridization in that it is "being like, but ultimately unlike, the colonizer."[68] Sometimes it is impossible to avoid a version of acculturation "where the subject takes on the ways of the imported culture and/or religion." At other times it can be "directly subversive." In *Fuzzy Church* we commented that:

> There is no doubt that some of the churches we researched were most likely still complicit in many kinds of colonialism. Yet they were often, at the same time doing a subversive thing, subverting the "givenness" of secularisation and the death of the church in their communities and subverting traditional ways of being the church by becoming fuzzy on the inside and the outside.[69]

In chapter 3 we touched on Goto's treatment of mimicry in relation to field research and we should return briefly to that discussion here. Goto defines mimicry in a very similar way to Heaney in that it "refers to the way in which colonized people internalize colonial expectations, approximate the behaviour and values of those in power, yet paradoxically manage not to copy the colonizers perfectly."[70] People and churches in the North of England cannot *not* be in some sense national and therefore southern, but we have seen that their very marginality in the North is what can subvert them being lumped together with their more powerful

67. Carson et al., *Crossing Thresholds*, 222.
68. Heaney, *Post-Colonial*, 4.
69. Rooms and Wort, *Fuzzy Church*, 111.
70. Goto, *Taking on Practical Theology*, 182.

and better resourced neighbors. The existence of churches in the North where "something is happening," if it can be made visible as we have attempted in this research, upsets the assumption that the answers to the future of the Church in England will come from London and the South. Which takes us directly to the final section of this chapter.

RESISTANCE

The work we did on mining the *Gehalt* of the North in *Fuzzy Church* and then in chapters 4 and 5 in this book requires rehearsing here as we turn to the final aspect of Heaney's post-colonial theology: resistance. This is because we believe the seeds of resistance to the coloniality the North experiences are found *within itself.* We might understand this as an extension and interpretation of words attributed to Jesus in the Gospel of Luke that, "The kingdom of God is within you" (Lk 20.21), to use the translation in the King James Version. We could expand the idea here from other translations to the kingdom being "in the midst" or "among you." Whatever the translation, the saying confirms a key concept in the theology of contextualization that culture contains, already the seeds of the gospel (as another facet of the *missio Dei*), not that they are planted there by some external actor. We have confirmed this in this study and can set out the reasons for this stance here and how that contributes to northern post-colonial resistance.

The reader may remember that in chapter 4 we described northern *Gehalt* in three pairs of values, Authenticity–Realism, Community–Home and Humor–Hope. We tested this against our research data in chapter 5 and concluded there that there is a relationship between the depth-content of Northernness and these findings in northern churches where "something is happening." That relationship is an indirect, nuanced, and complex one but nevertheless it exists. There is no straight-line, direct relationship between gospel and culture. The work of contextualization as we have been attempting it here requires careful discernment away from quick and easy correlations—it is *contested* in the post-colonial world. We can however demonstrate how northern *Gehalt* provides resistance.

Authenticity–Realism

As we have seen in this chapter the first step on the way to addressing the northern "chip on the shoulder" is to acknowledge its actual presence. We cannot shy away from aspects of the "grim" in the North, its "boom-bust" cycle according to Niven and the essentialism with which it is often portrayed in tropes that do not do justice to the whole of its reality. We have seen how these aspects of the North's existence have to be leant into, not denied, ignored or glossed over. What the North requires therefore is *more* authenticity and realism which can set it on the downward journey of "regression to dependence" on the left leg of the "U" movement in liminality where the whole sense of what is the North can be made visible ("seeing from the whole" is Scharmer's name for this leg of the U). "The only way up is down," and the research churches demonstrated an ability to access this aspect of Northernness in how they were facing up to decline and even death in different ways. At the bottom of the U there is the possibility of vulnerability and humility which would seem to flow from a truly authentic and realistic stance about the way things are. This is costly, yet true and authentic discipleship is dependent on God, not only on external resources (however helpful or otherwise they may be). Vulnerability and humility are essential elements of a post-colonial theology, as we have demonstrated from Jennings, Plekon, and others.

I have often reflected on the different journeys of Christian and then his wife, Christiana portrayed by John Bunyan (1628–88) in the two parts of the classic work, *The Pilgrim's Progress* (1678). When Christian enters the Valley of Humiliation it is a very dark and difficult place which threatens him and his onward journey deeply. In contrast, Christiana finds it a beautiful valley with rolling hills; it gives her life and energy for continuing her journey. One definition of humility is living as close to reality as humanly possible (since it is probably impossible for humans to do so all of the time). Laying aside Bunyan's suggestive gendered differences in how humility meets us, we can affirm here how northern realism takes us to humility and vulnerability as well as that "eschatological reserve" we discovered was also necessary in our contemporary missiology. Perhaps, though, Bunyan does raise another question for us, one that probably requires further research. What is it in a person, and more importantly a whole church, that gets us started on this journey of ultimately, humility, vulnerability, and fragility? We researched seven churches out of thousands across the North. How many of these will still exist in thirty or fifty years' time is a moot point. I would like to think that some of the work we have done in this project might allow a few more of them to still be there where "something is happening."

Community–Home

It goes without saying that any group, organization, or region is stronger, more resilient and able to assert itself if it is a community, rather than a set of individuals. This is the principle behind any kind of community organizing or development, where the gifts and assets of the individuals are harnessed and power is foregrounded, distributed and exercised in getting things done for the good of the whole. A reflex, a tendency to community, is present in the *Gehalt* of the North and it requires more of it. For example, we could think of Niven's point that the North stands or falls in the future as a whole, and if some of the deep internal divisions could be laid aside it would be much the better for that.

When we add in the idea of home as well as community, there occurs a grounding or rooting of both people and community in land and history (following Jennings's call to take these things utterly seriously). Foundations are laid which provide a solid place in which to live, explore horizons, and return. When authenticity and realism are connected with home, a security of self-definition is possible out of which public love might emerge. Engagement with a whole host of "others" is then possible from the security of groundedness.

> This is not in any sense romantic love, but a public loving which builds on respect and esteem, wills the best for the other despite their potential and sometimes very real antagonism. Perhaps it is indeed love that knocks the chip from our northern shoulders that we might engage out of our commitment to community, hospitality and friendship.[71]

We gave a distinct example of this in the Leaders' conversation we rehearsed above, where the southern placement student was able to be assertive and was accepted in the community, despite the presence of northern "chippiness," and that loving inclusion was reciprocated by the estate community in responding to the presence of the church among them once again. Here is the resistant presence and activity of God amidst, if not full-blown hate, at least suspicion, fear, and mistrust.

71. Rooms and Wort, *Fuzzy Church*, 52.

Humor–Hope

I'm not sure I would have put humor and hope together before writing this reflection, but the research has taught me how they are intimately connected. I suspect it is very hard to tell a joke, even a "gallows humor" kind of joke, in a situation of profound and utter hopelessness. Humor and hope, I would suggest, are connected by narrative, the telling of stories. The "prodigal hopefulness" Niven found in the stories he told of the North provides a deep source for the kingdom of God to be revealed and realized at the fuzzy edges of northern churches, whose stories we have told. As we pointed out in *Fuzzy Church*,[72] it is easy to tell a tragic story about the "grim" North or essentialize it in another way in some twee romantic tale. There are two other types of story, according the scholars of literature[73] which are the ironic and the comic and so we were able to propose that:

> While bigger than just humour since comic stories turn out well and integrate difference and ironic stories deny the possibility of heroes and deal with the dreadful realities of life (perhaps pointing once again to authenticity), nevertheless we would be foolish to miss the connections here to the possibilities of "telling the North" in such a way as to resist othering.[74]

We have indeed told the stories of the seven research churches in this book and they have provided some real humor, irony, and hope. We returned to the question of narrative and resistance in *Fuzzy Church*[75] in relation to the only other research we have come across in northern churches, from Paul Bickley,[76] though his was a more practical reporting of what works in terms of "community resilience" than a theological treatise. He makes a distinction between "if only" stories (the tragic narrative) and "what if" stories which connects with the suggestion we made above about how to place our research churches at the forefront of the future given what we have discovered about them:

> *What if* northern churches where something is happening are the clue to the future of the English, if not Western church?

72. Rooms and Wort, *Fuzzy Church*, 52.
73. See Hopewell, *Congregation*.
74. Rooms and Wort, *Fuzzy Church*, 52.
75. Rooms and Wort, *Fuzzy Church*, 112.
76. See Bickley, *People, Place*.

> *What if* "fuzzy" church, discovered in the North, became the watchword for how church can be alive and flourishing? *What if* the decomposing northern church is the soil in which there is resurrection for Christians in a post-colonial world?[77]

Bickley goes on to suggest that narrating "what if" stories grows spiritual capital or, put another way, spiritual capital is a "stockpile of hope, activism and purpose,"[78] which prompted the further observation:

> This could be a description of our research churches. They had stockpiles of hope, activism and purpose and the combination of all three means, we think that they are less likely to burn-out. Without purpose and hope, activism becomes disparate, dissipated and de-energising. Without hope and activism, purpose is just a bunch of nice-to-have goals. Without activism and purpose, hope turns easily into pie-in-the-sky.[79]

We have attempted to demonstrate in this section the resources for resistance to the coloniality the North is subject to are already available in its *Gehalt,* where that deep culture is taken seriously and worked with in travelling down the U, in celebrating community, finding home, and reaching beyond horizons—in the prodigal hopefulness of telling different stories about the North. It is a call to the North to be more of its best self through which the kingdom of God might be revealed.

SUMMARY

In setting out on this chapter we wanted to weave together the threads of the project so far on the "frame" of Heaney's five characteristics of post-colonial theology and thicken our call for a bias to the North. This has been a fruitful exercise, and while the picture that has emerged might not be straightforward (an abstract patterned cloth rather than a simple checked pattern for instance) the whole does seem to be largely consistent within itself despite internal tensions. We have named this book "contested contextualization," also following Heaney's lead, and that is what I believe has been presented. The contestation which we have uncovered in the North where "something is happening" is more often than not to be celebrated and encouraged—at the fuzzy margins of churches, in the

77. Rooms and Wort, *Fuzzy Church,* 112.

78. Bickley, *People, Place,* 90

79. Rooms and Wort, *Fuzzy Church,* 112.

crossing of boundaries in intimacy and communion, in travelling down the U, in hybrid worship, in fragility and vulnerability, in re-narrating the North and what it can offer far beyond itself. This is the fuller content of a bias to the North.

All that is left now is to put the finishing touches to our weave which we will do by placing our work in a particular light from a final interlocutor in the next chapter.

8

Towards a Regional, Critical, and Post-Colonial Contextual Theology

THROUGHOUT THIS BOOK WE have engaged with a range of authors and their works in order to set this study in a wider theological, inter-disciplinary, and geographical frame beyond contextual theology and simply the North of England itself. These interactions have shaped the study in very significant ways. In the previous chapter we deliberately wove together the threads of thought and research that we have presented in the book under the heading of post-colonial theology. We now introduce a final book with which we shall engage as we conclude our reflections. Sam Ewell's *Seeking Conviviality* involves two interlocutors, not just one, since its subtitle is *Reflections on Ivan Illich, Christian Mission and the Promise of Life Together*. We briefly referred to it in an earlier chapter, but here we will delve much more deeply into it to affirm and critique the work we have been doing thus far, and by way of a conclusion[1] to it. If the previous chapters were a weaving together of the threads of the study into a complex, possibly somewhat abstract, but meaningful whole, then here we use Ewell to shine a light on that whole, just as a piece of art may be illuminated in a gallery. Such lighting may show up both the beauty and the flaws in the finished piece.

1. I realize when using the word conclusion that I don't really like it. It suggests an ending, as if there were one to a work of contextual and practical theology. The notion of "towards" in the title of this last chapter of the book suggests not an ending or a conclusion, but a way of noticing where we have arrived at the end of the study, which can only be a stepping off point for further work.

But why is Ewell's book specifically relevant for this task of illumination, the reader may ask? First, Ewell is engaging missiologically with the world as he experiences it. Ewell explains that he grew up and studied for Christian ministry in the USA, where he met his wife who was originally from Brazil. They travelled together, sponsored by a US church to be missionaries in Brazil, but a "conversion" experience there occurred for Ewell which came from those he was working alongside and offered him a deep critique of the motivation and purpose he had originally set out with. A key part of this experience was his introduction by a Brazilian colleague to the life and work of the Roman Catholic priest, thinker, and theologian Ivan Illich (1926–2002). He then seeks a "reverse mission" journey to the UK where he studies for a PhD in Birmingham which gives him the opportunity to research Illich's writing in depth, work out a renewed missiological practice for life in that city and write the book as a consequence of that journey of reflective practice. There are many resonances, overlaps, and touching places here with my own journey and the overall task of this work of contextual theology. Second, Ewell's book has a preface from Willie James Jennings, whom we have interacted seriously with, where he emphasizes the importance of "consistent presence" in friendship, particularity, and discernment, "To be formed to discern divine presence would also move us toward leading lives of consistent presence as we follow Jesus into the places and to the people that are sites of divine love and desire."[2] This is our project too, to discern God in the North of England and its people. Finally, there are many points in the book where there are direct connections with the work we have done, and since I only came across it while writing chapter 5 it can stand as both confirmation and critique of our research journey so far. For instance, Ewell sets his work within the task of addressing the "colonial wound"[3] and utilizes Sam Wells's five-act play as a framework for Christian history,[4] as we have also done. In fact, it has been a joy to come across such a work while writing and to be able to reflect further on what we have researched with Ewell's practical theological wisdom, supported by Illich's thought. In interacting with the book, we will proceed slightly differently in attempting to integrate its insights with this research as we unfold Ewell's argument alongside Illich's work. If it can be a light with which to notice what we have been weaving together then from time to

2. Ewell, *Seeking Conviviality*, xix–xx.

3. Ewell, *Seeking Conviviality*, 184–86.

4. Ewell, *Seeking Conviviality*, 64.

time we can stop and make a "noticing," remarking on what we see in the whole. In this way we can set a direction of travel "towards" a regional, critical, post-colonial theology from the North.

Ewell's introductory chapter is wide-ranging in its scope and sets his project firmly in a practical theology frame[5] which is a way of distancing it from the specialisms of professionalized theologians. He follows Terry Veling's introduction and understanding of the discipline,[6] not as a further specialization but as an integration of theology into everyday life. This allows Ewell to understand himself as an "amateur theologian," following Wendell Berry's distinction between the professional, paid "expert" and the amateur non-specialist—one who "acts and thinks out of love."[7] Straightaway here there is a reflection and connection with the work we have been doing. Steve Bevans begins his classic book on contextual theology with the immortal line, "There is no such thing as 'theology'; there is only *contextual* theology."[8] And while contextual theology and practical theology are not exactly the same thing they are deeply connected in their hermeneutics and method.[9] To combine Bevans's and Veling's insights, there is only contextual, practical theology. We saw in chapter 3 how Courtney Goto developed a critique of how *professional* practical theologians in the academy utilize context to the detriment of the very people they are attempting to study. In chapter 5 we addressed this critique in relation to our research. We can therefore understand the researchers in this project as, at the very most, "semi-professional" (some money changed hands to allow the research to happen and some expertise was required), yet because of our connections to the North, our desire to discover more about it and, yes, our love for it, there is much more of the amateur in what we have been doing. This approach has freed us to develop the critical contextual theology from the North in our book title. If contextual/practical theology is a way of life that is grounded in theology then the classic Modernist split of the subject/object (especially prevalent in professionalized theology) can also be overcome and theology, according to Ewell becomes a form of "witness," Ewell expands on this idea:

5. Ewell, *Seeking Conviviality,* 1.
6. See Veling, *Practical Theology.*
7. Ewell, *Seeking Conviviality,* 2.
8. Bevans, *Models of Contextual,* 3, his emphasis.
9. See Rooms and Ross, "Practical Theology."

> I am not investigating a topic "out there" divorced from my relationship with it; nor is it a private affair of introspective navel-gazing and trying to sort things out for my own sake. Rather, doing theology is an ongoing process of discovery that moves from personal experience to a new sense of awareness to sharing knowledge with others by taking a stand . . . in other words . . . being a witness.[10]

Ewell is located in multiple places—the USA, Brazil, and now the UK[11]—and he brings to the this lived experience and the questions it raises, not least the post-colonial question of interculturality. Following Nancy Bradford, Ewell articulates that such existence enables and even requires the ability to "speak of God from more than one place."[12] My own experience, as I have explained in several places in this book, is not dissimilar. It is the "rupture and renewal"[13] of the migrant when reflected upon theologically that allows another possibility beyond the old colonial one-way flow from the "west to the rest." And this is where Illich can appear in the narrative. Ewell tells how, when in Brazil as a "missionary," he meets a Brazilian colleague who becomes "my closest friend in Brazil but also an older brother figure"[14] and who introduces him to Illich's 1968 address to Catholic American short-term missionaries to Latin America, called *To Hell with Good Intentions*. Illich rails against the neo-colonial methods being employed by both his own Catholic Church in sending religious workers south in the context of the American State doing a very similar thing through the newly formed Peace Corps. He understood these movements as a thinly veiled attempt to export the American way of life (just as "civilization" went along with colonial missionary endeavours). Ewell quotes a key passage: "I am here to entreat you to use your money, your status, and your education to travel in Latin America. Come to look, come to climb our mountains, to enjoy our flowers. Come to study. But *do not come to help*."[15] This brings Ewell up short in the rupture of realizing that he may have set out to be with the Brazilian people, but that stance had become "hijacked by good intentions."[16] Thus, Illich is able to

10. Ewell, *Seeking Conviviality*, 13.
11. Ewell, *Seeking Conviviality*, 8.
12. Ewell, *Seeking Conviviality*, 9.
13. Ewell, *Seeking Conviviality*, 10.
14. Ewell, *Seeking Conviviality*, 14.
15. Ewell, *Seeking Conviviality*, 16, his emphasis.
16. Ewell, *Seeking Conviviality*, 17.

press Ewell "to question the certainties and assumptions that shape the way Christians imagine their place and role in relation to God's good intentions for the whole world."[17] This prompts Ewell into two further moves. First, to begin the practical theological task (following Rowan Williams and Dietrich Bonhoeffer) "in the middle of things," that is, in the midst of real life. Starting there it follows, secondly, that an ethnographic method is appropriate as a process to uncover emergent truth in the midst of life.[18]

Here is both confirmation and some critique of our research and reflection. We have attempted to make the reflection in this book multi-locational, especially in chapters 2 and 6 where we interacted with African inculturation and church growth respectively. My own epistemological "rupture" in Tanzania has also played a significant part in the approach to context we have trialled here. We have done our theology "in the midst" of the life in our research subject congregations using an ethnographic field research method which we know only presented a snapshot of them in a moment in time. We have placed this data in dialogue with a cultural and historical exploration of the North and another location in Africa within an "eschatological reserve" (from Roest), knowing that inculturation is always in process. Yet we might also be cautioned by Ewell and Illich since some of the crossing of the boundaries at the churches we visited could be construed as being based on "neediness" and good intentions. It will be helpful to return to this question as we proceed in this final chapter.

NOTICING ONE

Critical contextual theology emerges as witness from the "middle of life" via ethnography in any specific time and place (such as in the region which is the North of England), and is at the same time radically unfinished, this is part of its necessary contestation. The project presented here was created by loving semi-professional amateurs from more than one place, who had experienced rupture in how the colonial church operates in one direction only, leading to further contestation.

17. Ewell, *Seeking Conviviality*, 17.

18. Ewell, *Seeking Conviviality*, 19.

Ewell's two research questions are framed within colonial and neo-colonial missionary expansion (cf. our chapter 2). In the post-colonial world Ewell is interested in researching, "on what *basis* do we go on fulfilling the 'Great Commission' (Matt 28:16–20) as Christ's disciples?' And, "what makes it possible to embody a distinctive Christian presence that is *missionary* without being *manipulative*?"[19] In answering these questions Ewell turns to Illich's social commentary and his "understanding of the incarnation as the basis of mission" which creates an "incarnational pattern for mission and the cultivation of life together as responses to wider social concerns, such as economic and ecological crises."[20] Thus, the keywords and concepts for his work are incarnation and mission[21] which leads him via Illich to *conviviality*, which is employed to "delink mission from the lure of techniques in order to receive and share the peace of Christ relationally."[22] Conviviality is defined as "individual freedom realized in personal interdependence";[23] it seeks to manage the individual–community polarity which for so long has leant to the individual in the west.

Several initial chapters of Ewell's book are devoted to a brief biography of Illich and explaining his contribution (rather forgotten now) to twentieth-century intellectual, social, and theological thought with particular emphasis on his notion of "prolonging the incarnation," which provides "the basis for a shift from mission as expansion to mission as encounter."[24] Ewell shows how Illich's thought was subversive enough of the western *status quo* that the American secret service, the CIA, wrote an investigative report on him and his activities.[25] Illich's life is one of constant "pilgrimage," beginning as he did before World War II in Eastern Europe (Dalmatia), travelling as a half-Jewish refugee in Europe, thence to the US, and from there to Latin America. The lack of "home" in Illich's biography is significant, Ewell thinks that "what undergirds and permeates Illich's activity as a Christian intellectual, then, is this sense of Abrahamic dispossession."[26] Perhaps, as a ruptured outsider, he is

19. Ewell, *Seeking Conviviality,* 20, his emphasis.

20. Ewell, *Seeking Conviviality,* 20.

21. Ewell, *Seeking Conviviality,* 22–23.

22. Ewell, *Seeking Conviviality,* 25.

23. Ewell, *Seeking Conviviality,* 25.

24. Ewell, *Seeking Conviviality,* 37.

25. Ewell, *Seeking Conviviality,* 36.

26. Ewell, *Seeking Conviviality,* 42.

uniquely placed to disrupt the way things are; in his social vision he is able to question the expected assimilation to American ways via their new found power on the world stage in the Cold War during the 1960s and 1970s. And along with addressing assimilation, he critiques the western liberal projects of progress and development that were prevalent in the period (and often remain unchallenged even today). Ewell claims that these stances were deeply rooted Illich's theology of the incarnation, or "following the naked Christ"[27] as he puts it, which is connected with the pilgrimage theme in Illich's biography. "Illich's life is expressed apophatically to the extent that it enacts an Abrahamic dispossession—a quality of creaturely freedom, a self-transcendence that is not self-referential but rather 'ec-centric'—established in relation in the Incarnation as its 'center.'"[28]

Thus, all places in Illich's pilgrimage are relativized in relation to Christ, who nevertheless calls constantly towards fullness of life within each of them, while denying the possibility of "misplaced concreteness."

It is then a short step to connect with Sam Wells's Christian theo-drama of the five-act play, since, as we noted in chapters 2 and 3, Jesus and his incarnation is at the center of it all in Act Three. Illich interprets the parable of the Good Samaritan (Luke 10:29–37) in relation to the "surprise and newness that the incarnation makes possible."[29] The incarnation breaks through the traditional boundary drawn around an ethnic "we" exemplified by the way the Samaritan crosses the accepted cultural and political boundaries of the day to tend another wounded human being. Despite being born into a particular time and place, "the Incarnate Savior transgressed the boundaries of the ethnic 'we'"[30] and this movement occurs throughout the Gospels and continues in the book of Acts. Now it can be stated that:

> The Jewish-Gentile difference, the threshold that distinguished the people of God from 'the nations,' can be crossed in faith. This threshold has not been destroyed but has become porous through the opening of incarnational difference . . . The new 'we' is established solely in relation to a person, the Incarnate Savior.[31]

27. Ewell, *Seeking Conviviality*, 58.
28. Ewell, *Seeking Conviviality*, 64.
29. Ewell, *Seeking Conviviality*, 65.
30. Ewell, *Seeking Conviviality*, 66.
31. Ewell, *Seeking Conviviality*, 66.

Such a relationship has implications too for the formation of community. "The incarnation makes possible an alternative social space, a new 'inside' that we inhabit as co-breathing . . . a conspiracy, a deliberate, mutual, somatic, and gratuitous gift to one another."[32] This kind of space is also the basis for the, "missionary activity of the church" which, "entails the vocation toward 'risky presence to the Other, together with the openness to an absent loved third, no matter how fleeting.'"[33] This brings to mind the respondent at church G who, when asked what it would be like if Jesus were around today responded, in a suggestive mixture of the Other in the community and Christ:

> Somebody that you feel, you know, is just part of this community that you can just relate to. You would feel comfortable sitting next to him on a bus, just to chat and I think somebody, who is probably quite . . . they don't offer lots of words, but you can tell they're interested in you.[34]

We can remark here that Illich's approach to the incarnation resonates very much with the discussion we had in chapter 3 around Jennings's critique of Sanneh and Walls with regard to the questions of inculturation, translation, and supersessionism. Ewell is clear that the incarnation is "the basis for inculturation."[35] Illich was well-placed as a "half-Jew" to embody the "scandal of particularity," as Jennings put it, in recognizing that the new "we" created by Christ does not destroy the boundary between peoples in some universalist project that denies agency to those same peoples, but that it becomes porous to difference which is based on the incarnation of the Jewish savior, Christ. Once again, we find ourselves in the territory of porous boundaries and note this was a major finding of the research that northern churches where "something was happening" had the same porosity at their edges. We therefore return to the importance of attending to the edges in missiology and contextual theology—the subject of liminality that we touched on in the previous chapter and about which I have written in the book *Crossing Thresholds*. It is worth sharing here another parable reproduced from the chapter on liminality in missiology in that book:

The Parable of the Australian Livestock Ranch

32. Ewell, *Seeking Conviviality*, 76, quoting Illich directly.
33. Ewell, *Seeking Conviviality*, 78, quoting Illich.
34. Rooms and Wort, *Fuzzy Church*, 87.
35. Ewell, *Seeking Conviviality*, 79.

> Once upon a time a man discovered he had a long-lost cousin in Australia and decided, since he had never been there, to visit him. It turned out his cousin owned a ranch way out in the deep outback which could only be reached by a small plane. As our friend was flying in, the pilot pointed out when the plane was first over the ranch in question. Cattle and sheep were scattered far and wide in countless numbers.
>
> When the plane came in to land the two cousins embraced each other and then the burning question was asked:
>
> "Listen, as we flew over your land, I was amazed at the numbers of animals you have spread far and wide. What was even more amazing was that I never saw any fences. Which leaves me with a big question—how on earth do you keep them all in?"
>
> To which came the swift reply:
>
> "Aw, that's easy mate, we just dig wells."[36]

In our search for a regional contextual theology in the North of England we have considered from time to time its borders, both geographically and culturally especially in relation to the South of England. In doing so we have avoided the "misplaced concreteness" that could lead variously to its essentializing by insiders (developing the northern "chip on the shoulder") and outsiders (in unhelpful general attributed tropes), or its isolation as a hopeless site of pagan cycles.[37] The incarnation releases, even liberates, the North to be itself with its gifting of a unique *Gehalt* while remaining open in relationality across its boundaries.

There is a further scandal of the incarnation, according to Ewell following Illich, which delves deeper into the interpretation of the parable of the Good Samaritan. Illich noted the "slippage" that occurs in his time towards the meaning of the parable as "the normative obligation or duty to love anyone who is needy" rather than the "freedom and permission to embrace and be embraced by the other who is encountered."[38] Meeting needs is not the first thing that the parable might or even should bring to mind. This slippage is the introduction of a "codified norm" from which it is a short step to policing the boundary rather than allowing it to be truly porous. Staying with the radical new "we" against any attempt to control what happens in relationality across the border is defined as the act of "prolonging the incarnation," because again it, "liberates from the

36. Carson et al., *Crossing Thresholds*, 113

37. See Spracklen, "Theorizing Northernness," and to some extent Niven, *North Will*.

38. Ewell, *Seeking Conviviality*, 67.

ethnic boundary without destroying it."[39] Here then is the basis of Goto's two-way intersubjective or intercultural street, which we found elements and hints of in our research churches and which is confirmed by Gittins's distinction between the terms multicultural and intercultural,[40] since some versions of the multicultural do not take seriously enough the porous boundary.

NOTICING TWO

The incarnation of Christ and its prolongation is the basis and ongoing motivation of critical regional contextual theology (inculturation) which allows the possibility of life-giving porous boundaries against misplaced concreteness at the micro (local church) and macro (regional levels). There are many contesting forces ranged against this possibility, not least the Church herself, along with concomitant theological misconceptions which emphasize meeting the needs of others over unregulated encounter.

We have already observed Illich's critique of western assimilation, progress and development which is based on his theological stance of "prolonging the incarnation." It is now time to look into this more deeply so that we can follow the argument of Ewell and Illich towards the importance of conviviality. The incarnation stands against relying *solely* on technology and technical control over issues such as poverty, healthcare, energy use, food production, and creation care. If God is with us in Christ, then embodied presence has to take precedence over "technical control" in society as well as, by extension in Christian mission. There are "two ways of approaching mission: either as a technical problem to be controlled, or a relational possibility to be shared."[41]

Let us return for a moment to societal issues. The total reliance on a technological stance towards an unequal world in late modernity produces institutions which perpetuate the myth that this is the way to "salvation" for humanity. Allied with capitalism this produces a consumerist culture which permeates every corner of society. Perhaps Illich's best-known work is *Deschooling Society*, which utilizes the school as a case study in the consumerist nature of the western world. It is a complex

39. Ewell, *Seeking Conviviality*, 79, direct quote from Illich.

40. Gittins, *Living Mission*, 18–24.

41. Ewell, *Seeking Conviviality*, 131.

argument since Illich is not against the school *per se,* but rather wishes to reimagine its purpose as "to recover knowledge as interpersonal *process* that is not reducible to an institutional *product.*"[42] The common good "cannot be institutionalized and consumed."[43] In *Deschooling Society* Illich employs Greek mythology to buttress his argument. Prometheus and his brother Epimetheus represent for Illich the hubris of technology over against human relationality in his contemporary world. Again, the argument is sophisticated and we do not need to go into too much detail here. Prometheus, we could say is "hoisted with his own petard," just as our current climate crisis emerges from two centuries of fossil-fuel based industrial "development." Epimetheus, however, by marrying Pandora rather than being threatened by her, "lives by embracing the hope that comes through another."[44] There is therefore a distinction to be made between the expectation of technology and institutions and true (Epimethean) hope. Thus, we can now have the ability "to discriminate between authentic human flourishing and its institutionalized counterfeits."[45] Illich is not simply against the technological paradigm, he accepts that it is a current reality and can be usefully employed in very many ways, it is simply that it should not be the ruling or dominant paradigm at the expense of the relational. The argument here resonates very much with that of the polymath Iain McGilchrist in his important book *The Master and His Emissary* where he describes the disastrous takeover over of the western mind by the utilitarian biased left hemisphere of the brain—when the inherent relational epistemology of the right hemisphere would be a much better starting and end-point which could then simply incorporate the necessary gifts of the left brain.

We might at this point be able to put the hope we discerned in the northern *Gehalt* in a slightly different light. For via Ewell and Illich we can see that hope is a function of relationality—of "embodied presence" to and with each other, part of the prolongation of the incarnation. In our schema in chapter 4 we placed hope with humor, but perhaps now it could be just as easily be paired with community, that sense of togetherness that is deeply embedded in northern values. We know that our research churches were places of hope since their very porosity or fuzziness gave them a larger horizon in which to discern the *missio Dei.*

42. Ewell, *Seeking Conviviality*, 137, his emphasis.

43. Ewell, *Seeking Conviviality*, 137, his emphasis.

44. Ewell, *Seeking Conviviality*, 144.

45. Ewell, *Seeking Conviviality*, 145.

We can now make the final step in Illich's argument since *conviviality* is his antidote to the technological paradigm or "industrial productivity." Ewell quotes directly from Illich to fully define conviviality as

> . . . autonomous and creative intercourse among persons, and the intercourse of persons with their environment; and this in contrast with the conditioned response of persons to the demands made upon them by others, and by a man-made environment. I consider conviviality to be individual freedom realized in personal interdependence and, as such, an intrinsic ethical value.[46]

Illich's approach here takes us directly to an assessment of institutions[47] which lie on a spectrum (he is not against institutions in themselves) from those wedded to the capitalist, technological paradigm focused on a *product* for consumption to convivial institutions (like a public library) which are informal, voluntary, and focused on "people doing things, such as learning, moving and caring for themselves and others."[48] This latter mode of production is a *process* that people do based on action.

We can now take Illich's convivial insight back to our data. For example, at our visit to church D in the field notes we recorded the activities advertised on the church notices during the Sunday worship as follows:

Mon.	1–2.30pm Social Seniors (craft-based in the Community Centre where the Church meets) 7.30–9.30pm Choir (unclear whether this is an open or church-based choir, or both)
Tues.	10am Coffee Morning—Toby Carvery (a local public house—a "third space")
Weds.	9.15–11am Start Course (Catechetical course for enquirers to faith) 6–8pm Shed Men (Men's woodworking/craft group)
Thurs.	7–8.30pm Capacity (Leadership development for church members) 7.30–9pm Generation (Church young people's group)
Sun.	1.30pm Freewheelers cycling group

There are eight separate activities here and at least four (50%) of them (depending on the where the choir is focused) could be construed as

46. Ewell, *Seeking Conviviality*, 151.

47. Ewell, *Seeking Conviviality*, 151–52.

48. Ewell, *Seeking Conviviality*, 152.

"convivial," as ends in themselves not engaged specifically with church, or "institutional" business which require the free but interdependent association of their participants. And I suspect the others that are church focused are imbued with the convivial values that are created by the existence of the other events. Church D was not the only one with such an impressive list. For instance in chapter 6, when exploring the growth criterion of *Community Service,* we mentioned the long list of activities in the Community Centre based at Church E. These northern churches had learnt and demonstrated the importance of conviviality.

Further, in chapter 5 we discussed how we found our research churches via hierarchical figures in the institution, and how they were concerned that we were looking for "flourishing" churches, which in their terms would be places with larger numbers and stable finances. What we were pointed towards was something more fragile where "something was happening." We know that we were researching at the edge of the institution and a question worth returning to is: Where does the institutional church sit on the industrial–convivial spectrum? There is no doubt that the Church has been coercive towards an end product—the expansion of the institution globally, especially in the colonial period. A post-colonial regional theology must therefore take account of this reality and seek, with Ewell and Illich, to make the "convivial turn."

NOTICING THREE

A regional contextual theology arising from Churches in the North of England where "something is happening" demonstrates the hope embedded in their community and communities as they engage in conviviality at their fuzzy edges. The fragility and freedom we noticed in the data now takes on a further dimension, since their freedom could also be freedom from the deep need of industrial societies for growth at all costs and their fragility a necessary state of being that comes with freedom in community (or "freedom realized in personal interdependence"). We need more conviviality.

Ewell is not yet finished with problematizing the Church from Illich's thought. We have clarified the relationship in Illich's mind between prolonging the incarnation and the institutionalization of the Church. Illich understood the incarnation as "the decisive anthropological *horizon* by which to orient our perception of humanity's capacity for the 'fulness of life' (John 10:10)."[49] It is possible therefore to expose "incarnational counterfeits" or in other words the corruption of Christianity. As an example of this, Illich traces the origin of the Christian hospital from the parable of the Good Samaritan (one of his key biblical sources), via the establishment of Christendom, "how the incarnational threshold [in the parable] mutated into the institutionalization of hospitality [in the Church's hospital]."[50] The institution then services societies' needs in "impersonal, planned and expected" ways in contrast to the Samaritan's actions which are "personal, gratuitous and surprising."[51] Ewell summarizes powerfully the argument:

> In the light of the revelation of God in Christ, one may perceive that the freedom that comes from Christ's call to 'go and do likewise' (Luke 10:37) has become transmogrified into what Illich sees as the anti-Christic responsibility of trying to save or change or reform the world by attempting to manage the gospel.[52]

The gospel here has been co-opted within the Church, corrupted as she is by the institutionalization that occurred during Christendom. What started as the free crossing of a road to meet a very particular (and quite threatening) stranger has turned into the planned obligation to serve the "needy" masses. What is exciting, however, is that we are presented with a whole new set of opportunities for recovering and prolonging the incarnation after Christendom in the contemporary Church, since she now takes up a wholly changed position in western society. An example of this from the research could be church C, which we also referred to in chapter 6 since it was the "needy service-users" at a Food Bank that asked to be a church. Here is a fuller account from the Leaders' focus group transcript of what happened:

> Resp 1: Yeah, and in fact I'd go further than that because it's, I mean the original vision we had then sat down and we were serving them, weren't we? The food. And then I mean I remember the discussion we had in [Y City on a reflective away-day] that was the whole point we were

49. Ewell, *Seeking Conviviality,* 172, his emphasis.

50. Ewell, *Seeking Conviviality,* 172.

51. Ewell, *Seeking Conviviality,* 172.

52. Ewell, *Seeking Conviviality,* 173.

treating them as family as, as, yeah not as guest in that sense. Because we had a big discussion about what we call them to start with didn't we? Because we weren't, at the start we weren't comfortable deciding we were church and the folk decided we were church in the end.

Resp 2: Yeah, we were saying "we're not a church" to everyone "we are not a church."

Intvwr: So, they told you that . . .

Resp 3: That we were a church.

Intvwr: They told you that you were a church.

Resp 4: Yeah, [church leader] heard someone speaking on their mobile phone quite early on saying "I can't talk I'm at church." And we're like "we're not a church." But they, that's how they refer to us.

Resp 2: That's how they saw us and we had yeah, yeah, we had to come a long way to, to accept that.

Intvwr: What changed in you do you think for that to happen?

Resp 2: Well, it was, it was partly them going on about it and asking for sacramental ministry in the sense of wanting to be baptised.

Intvwr: They were asking for that?

Resp 2: They were asking for that, they wouldn't have used that language but they, the baptism stuff, yes, they were asking for.

Intvwr: How do you think they knew that that was what was required of them?

Resp 2: Well, it wasn't, because we didn't require it.

Intvwr: Yeah, so where did it come from? is my question.

Resp 2: I think it, I suspect it came, it came from the kids.

Resp 5: They'd seen something, they'd seen something we've watched.

Resp 4: It was the Jesus DVDs. it was when we were doing, when we doing those and Jesus was baptized in the river and John called on people to be baptized. And that somehow connected into we want to; well shouldn't we be baptized? And that was where that all kind of triggered off from.[53]

53. Leader's Focus Group Church C.

The project begins, in Illich's terms, in institutional mode—serving food to the poor of the town, with a disturbing problem of how to name these humans who were coming to "have their needs met." The church as institution can initiate a Food Bank, but it cannot call the event that results "church." Yet the people coming experience it as such and ask to be baptized. Somewhere along the way they have been shown a film of the life of Jesus where Jesus is baptized by John the Baptist. Theologically speaking, Jesus' baptism is often understood as an expression of his total acceptance of his full humanity, that is the incarnation of the Son of God (John is right that Jesus doesn't "need" to be baptized, but the text states that this is to "fulfil all righteousness"[54]). Here among these "needy" human beings the incarnation is prolonged in "personal, gratuitous and surprising ways."

Ewell discusses the implications of moving away from a "needs-based" approach to human development for theological anthropology. Again, the incarnation is the key to understanding the human since Christ is the, "One who is 'truly human' for our sake."[55] When theological anthropology is removed from this center in Christ then it simply becomes self-referential, and because of basic inequalities between human beings, human society is assessed on the basis of what we do not have, our needs. Human beings then become "individual units" with "input *requirements*."[56] Humans as autonomous beings are dependent then on anything other than the Godself—something which the Food Bank users seemed to know unconsciously. Ewell sums up:

> For Illich, the Christian life is the embrace of life in which we are not the measure of all things. This "not," however, does not mean lack, or *nihil,* but hope in the promise of a gift that we were created to receive and share . . . [Here is] an understanding of being human in which humanity is not its own measure, but rather is iconic, looking beyond itself to see itself fully, receiving the fullness of its being from a source that has the power to indwell it.[57]

Thus, we are returned to another theme of this book, the importance of the theological promise, following the work of Gregory Walter in *Being*

54. Matt 3:15, RSV

55. Ewell, *Seeking Conviviality,* 181, quoting Bonhoeffer.

56. Ewell, *Seeking Conviviality,* 182, his emphasis quoting Illich.

57. Ewell, *Seeking Conviviality,* 183.

Promised which we referred to in chapters 3 and 7. Placing the incarnate Christ at the center of how we understand humanity allows a re-imagining of what happens at the boundaries of churches as their people engage with neighbors, less on the basis of needs and more on everyone's enormous potential as fulfillers of the promise of fullness of life.

NOTICING FOUR

Contextualization requires contestation when it departs from prolonging the incarnation within the promise of God and the fullness of life in Christ. Contestation is particularly necessary when the institution of the church commodifies the very people it is intending to reach in coloniality. Freedom for the individual and the community is an outcome of contesting contextualization.

Ewell completes his book by cashing out what conviviality in mission looks like, with some concrete examples starting from his experience in Brazil with friends and colleagues. This takes him to land, place, and even soil, then the cycle of food production along with the composting of waste to, return full circle to the land—in all of which people, with names, come first and foremost. It is a localized "parish" vision for what is possible within the promise. Parish for Ewell is translated as being the place "around the home."[58] This approach "names an attempt to regenerate the conditions for convivial interdependence, an alternative 'security system' (for example, Mark 10:29–31) to the illusion of independence, or the threat of alienating dependencies, in a global economy."[59] It is in Wells's terms "faithful improvisation" in Act Four of the drama of salvation within the contemporary postmodern and globalizing context of the world.

Ewell has a similar issue with conclusions as we do: "Conclusion does not mean a 'pull-off-the-shelf' model to be applied. It is more of a narration of a discovery that might serve as (co)inspiration for others on a similar journey."[60] Which raises the question we do need to address of what *catholicity* or universalizability there may be in this study. We believe we have revealed, in this regional study in the North of England,

58. Ewell, *Seeking Conviviality*, 247.
59. Ewell, *Seeking Conviviality*, 247.
60. Ewell, *Seeking Conviviality*, 265.

how contextualization of the gospel is and needs to be contested—and this perhaps away from a specific approach of definitive models. (Not that they are not useful as far they go—we used them extensively in chapter 6.) Interestingly Ewell borrows, not one of Bevans's models of contextual theology, but an image of his of "entering into someone else's garden"[61] for a response to the original research question about how to go about mission in non-manipulative ways in the post-colony. This brings together a set of ecological images around gardening and food which resonate strongly with where we were in chapter 6 with a further model or connecting metaphor for the church as a "living organism." Perhaps, this could just as easily be a controlling "image" for churches struggling with finding their place in late modern western society.

We enter other's gardens in crossing the boundary of the church in mission, because this is exactly what our incarnate Lord did. It is our response of faith to Christ's prior action.[62] Ewell describes how this has worked out in his current practice in Birmingham, UK. "What if we imagined the work of entering into another 'garden' not by planting another church (as in Brazil) but by *cultivating abundant community from the ground up*?"[63] This works out in living out three core commitments of a) discipleship (as apprentices of Jesus' way), b) friendship (as *companions,* people who break bread together) and c) hospitality (both as guests and hosts).[64] Ewell is therefore able with these commitments to answer the question, "What do you do in someone else's garden?"[65] It is no surprise that Ewell connects with the Asset-Based Community Development approach[66] of McKnight and Block which we touched on in chapter 6 as a practical antidote to the needs-based or deficit model that is so prevalent in community development. The ecological imagery employed by Ewell takes him to what we have named in chapters 5 and 6 as a systems approach to congregational life: "gardening is the art of creating and facilitating beneficial interactions in an ecology of relationships . . . the same could be said about intercultural mission."[67] He pays attention too within this metaphor to the importance of what happens at the

61. Ewell, *Seeking Conviviality,* 266.
62. Ewell, *Seeking Conviviality,* 267.
63. Ewell, *Seeking Conviviality,* 274, his emphasis.
64. Ewell, *Seeking Conviviality,* 275.
65. Ewell, *Seeking Conviviality,* 275.
66. Ewell, *Seeking Conviviality,* 279.
67. Ewell, *Seeking Conviviality,* 281.

(ecological) edges since these are spaces of creativity and flourishing and lead him habitually to asking the question, "What is beneficial (or not) about the relationship between what we do in our own garden (as Christian community) and what we do when we find ourselves in someone else's garden?"[68] Here is further affirmation of the importance of paying attention to the fuzzy or porous edges of church life, and how people cross over that space and inhabit it. We can agree with Ewell wholeheartedly when he states:

> Without a two-way flow between the institutional church and neighborhood, institutional forms of church can become counterproductively preoccupied with maintenance of institutional forms and techniques for getting people to become consumers of institutional programs and services.[69]

At the end of his book Ewell summarizes his work with a final reference to Illich:

> "Faith seeking conviviality" expresses a concern for the "dignity of each [person] and each human relationship" as well as the integrity of our ecological relationships as members of "the community of creation," but is not reducible to mere humanism of ecological concern. Rather, as an expression of practical theology [from Veling], it offers "a *response* to the call of God in which we come to realize that our purpose for "being in the world" is to respond to the "purposes of God."[70]

NOTICING FIVE

We have described the contours of a "regional, critical, and post-colonial contextual theology" in this book. It is not one thing, nor does it have an ending; rather, it is a complex and contested human–divine space grounded in a particular place. It requires at all times discernment. *We have demonstrated by field work in churches in the North of England that a useful, fruitful, and potentially inspiring ecological approach to participating in the* missio Dei *is possible in the post-colonial world.*

68. Ewell, *Seeking Conviviality,* 282.
69. Ewell, *Seeking Conviviality,* 283
70. Ewell, *Seeking Conviviality,* 285, quoting Illich and Veling.

Bibliography

Allen, Roland. *Missionary Methods: St. Paul's or Ours?* Reprinted American Edition of 1962. Grand Rapids, MI: Eerdmans, 1999 [1912].

Ammerman, Nancy, ed. *Studying Congregations: A New Handbook.* Nashville: Abingdon, 1998.

Arbuckle, Gerald A. *Culture, Inculturation and Theologians: A Postmodern Critique.* Collegeville, MI: Liturgical Press, 2010.

Barrett, Al. *Interrupting the Church's Flow: A Radically Receptive Political Theology in the Urban Margins.* London: SCM, 2020.

Barrett, Al, and Ruth Harley. *Being Interrupted: Reimagining the Church's Mission from the Outside, In.* London: SCM, 2020.

Benac, Dustin D. *Adaptive Church: Collaboration and Community in a Changing World.* Waco, TX: Baylor University Press, 2022.

Bevans, Stephen B. ed. *Mission and Culture: The Louis J. Luzbetak Lectures.* Maryknoll, NY: Orbis, 2012.

———. *Models of Contextual Theology,* Revised and expanded edition. Maryknoll, NY: Orbis, 2004.

Bevans, Stephen B., and Roger P. Schroeder. *Constants in Context: A Theology of Mission for Today.* Maryknoll, NY: Orbis, 2004.

Bickley, Paul. *People, Place and Purpose: Churches and Neighbourhood Resilience in the North East.* London: Theos, 2018.

Billings, Alan. Review of *Fuzzy Church: Gospel and Culture in the North of England* by Nigel Rooms and Elli Wort. *Church Times,* 13.08.21, 21.

Bookfish. "Boeken van Gert-Jan Roest." https://bookfish.nl/auteur/gert-jan-roest/.

Bosch, David J. *Transforming Mission: Paradigm Shifts in the Theology of Mission.* Maryknoll, NY: Orbis, 1991.

Boucher Chisale, Claude. *The Gospel Seed: Culture and Faith in Malawi as Expressed in the Missio Banner.* Mtakataka, Malawi: KuNgoni Art Craft Centre, 2002.

Bowen, John P. "'What Happened Next?' Vincent Donovan Thirty-five Years On." *International Bulletin of Missionary Research* 33.2 (2009) 79–82.

Bradbury, Paul et al. *Being the People of God: Missional Ecclesiology for Uncertain Times.* London: SCM, 2025.

Bradley, Ian. Review of *Northern Gospel, Northern Church* by Nigel Rooms and Gavin Wakefield eds. *Modern Believing* 58.2 (2017) 207–8.

Butler, James. "The Pedagogy of Evangelism: Moving from a Didactic to a Conversational Model of Evangelism." *Mission Studies* 39.1 (2022) 95–116.

Campbell, Ted A. *The Gospel in Christian Traditions.* Oxford: Oxford University Press, 2009.

Cameron, Helen. *Resourcing Mission: Practical Theology for Changing Churches.* London: SCM, 2010.

Carson, Timothy, et al. *Crossing Thresholds: A Practical Theology of Liminality.* Cambridge: Lutterworth, 2021.

Casaldáliga, D. Pedro. *Creio na Justiça e na Esperença.* Rio de Janeiro: Civilição Brasiliera, 1978.

Cone, James H. *The Cross and the Lynching Tree.* Maryknoll, NY: Orbis, 2011.

Davison, Andrew. *Participation in God: A Study in Christian Doctrine and Metaphysics.* Cambridge: Cambridge University Press, 2019.

Donovan, Vincent J. *Christianity Rediscovered: An Epistle from the Masai.* London: SCM, 1982.

Dorling, Danny. *The Population of the UK,* 2nd ed. London: Sage, 2013.

Duerksen, Darren T., and William A. Dyrness. *Seeking Church: Emerging Witnesses to the Kingdom.* Downers Grove, IL: IVP, 2019.

Dulles, Avery. *Models of the Church.* Expanded ed. New York: Image, Doubleday, 2002 [1978].

Eliot, T. S. *Four Quartets.* London: Faber & Faber, 2001 [1944].

Ewell, Samuel E. III. *Faith Seeking Conviviality: Reflections on Ivan Illich, Christian Mission, and the Promise of Life Together.* Eugene, OR: Cascade, 2020.

Fiddes, Paul S., and Pete Ward. "Affirming Faith at a Service of Baptism in St. Aldates Church, Oxford." In *Explorations in Ecclesiology and Ethnography,* edited by Christian B. Scharen, 51–70. Grand Rapids, MI: Eerdmans, 2012.

Flett, John G. *The Witness of God: The Trinity,* Missio Dei, *Karl Barth, and the Nature of Christian Community.* Grand Rapids, MI: Eerdmans, 2010.

Fox, Kate. *Watching the English.* Second edition. London: Hodder and Stoughton, 2014.

Fox, Kathryn, E. "Stand Up and Be (En)Countered: Resistance in Solo Stand-up Performance by Northern English Women, Marginalised on the Basis of Gender, Class and Regional Identity." PhD Diss., University of Leeds, 2017.

Gadamer, Hans-Georg. *Truth and Method.* 2nd rev. ed. Translated by Joel Weinsheimer, Joel and Donald G. Marshall. 1975. London: Sheed and Ward, 1989.

Gittins, Anthony. *Living Mission Interculturally: Faith, Culture and the Renewal of Praxis.* Collegeville, MI: Liturgical Press, 2015.

Gorringe, Timothy. *Furthering Humanity: A Theology of Culture.* Aldershot: Ashgate, 2004.

Goto, Courtney. *Taking on Practical Theology: The Idolization of Context and the Hope of Community.* Leiden: Brill, 2018.

Graham, Elaine, et al. *Theological Reflection: Methods.* London: SCM, 2005.

———. *Theological Reflection: Sources.* London: SCM, 2007.

Goheen, Michael W. "The Future of Mission in the World Council of Churches: The Dialogue between Lesslie Newbigin and Konrad Raiser." *Mission Studies* 21.1 (2004) 97–111.

The Guardian. "Cotton Capital." 2023. https://www.theguardian.com/news/series/cotton-capital.

Harper, Douglas. "Talking about Pictures: A Case for Photo Elicitation." *Visual Studies* 17.1 (2002) 13–26.

Heaney, Robert. *Post-Colonial Theology: Finding God and Each Other Amidst the Hate.* Eugene, OR: Cascade, 2019.

Heath, Elaine. *The Mystic Way of Evangelism: A Contemplative Vision for Christian Outreach.* 2nd ed. Grand Rapids, MI: Baker Academic, 2017.

Hiebert, Paul G. *Anthropological Insights for Missionaries.* Grand Rapids, MI: Baker Academic, 1985.

Hodgson, Dorothy L. *Church of Women: Gendered Encounters between Maasai and Missionaries.* Bloomington, IN: Indiana University Press, 2005.

Hollinger, David. *Protestants Abroad: How Missionaries Tried to Change the World, but Changed America.* Oxford: Princeton University Press, 2017.

Hopewell, James. *Congregation: Stories and Structures.* London: SCM, 1988.

Hull, John. *Towards the Prophetic Church: A Study of Christian Mission.* London: SCM, 2014.

The Human Flourishing Program. "Global Flourishing Study." April 30, 2025. https://hfh.fas.harvard.edu/.

Hunt, Robert A. *The Gospel among the Nations: A Documentary History of Inculturation.* Maryknoll, NY: Orbis, 2010.

Illich, Ivan. *Deschooling Society.* London: Marion Boyars, 1971.

James, Christopher B. *Church Planting in Post-Christian Soil: Theology and Practice.* New York: Oxford University Press, 2018.

Jennings, Willie James. *The Christian Imagination: Theology and the Origins of Race,* New Haven, CT: Yale University Press, 2010.

Keifert, Patrick. *Welcoming the Stranger: A Public Theology of Worship and Evangelism.* Minneapolis, MN: Augsburg Fortress, 1992.

Keifert, Patrick, and Nigel Rooms. *Forming the Missional Church: Creating Deep Cultural Change in Congregations.* Cambridge: Grove, 2014.

Kraft, Charles H. *Christianity in Culture: A Study in Dynamic Biblical Theologizing in Cross-Cultural Perspective.* Maryknoll, NY: Orbis, 1979.

Kwiyani, Harvey. *Multicultural Kingdom: Ethnic Diversity, Mission and the Church.* London: SCM, 2020.

———. *Sent Forth: African Missionary Work in the West.* Maryknoll, NY: Orbis, 2014.

Leopando, Irwin. *A Pedagogy of Faith: The Theological Vision of Paul Freire.* London: Bloomsbury Academic, 2017.

Loach, Ken, dir. *The Old Oak.* Production by StudioCanal UK, Sixteen Films. Why Not Productions, 2023.

Lockhart, Ross A. *West Coast Mission: The Changing Nature of Christianity in Vancouver.* Montreal: McGill-Queen's University Press, 2024.

Luzbetak, Louis. *The Church and Cultures: An Applied Anthropology for the Religion Worker.* Pasadena, CA: William Carey Library, 1976.

Maconie, Stuart. *Pies and Prejudice: In Search of the North.* London: Random House, 2007.

Magesa, Laurenti. *Anatomy of Inculturation: Transforming the Church in Africa.* Maryknoll, NY: Orbis, 2004.

Marsh, Clive. *A Cultural Theology of Salvation.* Oxford: Oxford University Press, 2018.

McGilchrist, Iain. *The Master and His Emissary: The Divided Brain and the Making of the Western World.* New expanded ed. New Haven, CT: Yale University Press, 2018 [2009].

McKnight, John, and Peter Block. *The Abundant Community: Awakening the Power of Families and Neighbourhoods.* San Francisco: Berrett-Koehler, 2010.

Meyer, Eric Daryl. "The Ineradicable Supersessionism of the Christian Imagination." https://itself.blog/2015/02/08/the-ineradicable-supersessionism-of-the-christian-imagination/.

Milbank, Alison. *The Once and Future Parish.* London: SCM Press, 2023.

Moon, W. Jay. *Intercultural Discipleship: Learning from Global Approaches to Spiritual Formation.* Grand Rapids, MI: Baker Academic, 2017.

Muck, Terry C. Review of *Intercultural Hermeneutics: Vol. 1 Intercultural Theology* by Henning Wrogemann. *International Bulletin of Mission Research* 41.3 (2017) 194–202.

Neate, John. "Cultural Perceptions: A Barrier to the Role of Cross-Cultural Friendships in Mission?" *Ecclesial Futures* 3.2 (2022) 31–49.

Newbigin, Lesslie. *The Gospel in a Pluralist Society.* Grand Rapids, MI: Eerdmans, 1989.

Nida, Eugene A. *Customs and Cultures: Anthropology for Christian Missions.* New York: Harper & Row, 1954.

Niemandt, Nelus. "The *Missio Dei* as Flourishing Life." *Ecclesial Futures* 1.1 (2020) 11–30.

Niven, Alex. *The North Will Rise Again: In Search of the Future in Northern Heartlands.* London: Bloomsbury, 2023.

Okesson, Gregg. *A Public Missiology: How Local Churches Witness to a Complex World.* Grand Rapids: Baker Academic, 2020.

Paas, Stefan. *Church Planting in the Secular West: Learning from the European Experience.* Grand Rapids, MI: Eerdmans, 2016.

Plekon, Michael. *Community as Church, Church as Community.* Eugene, OR: Wipf & Stock, 2021.

PRES BITS. "BBC One Ident 2004 to 2006—Masaai." YouTube video, Oct. 6, 2011. https://www.youtube.com/watch?v=yJNftztVQAs.

The Queen's Foundation. "Prof. Robert Beckford." https://www.queens.ac.uk/people/consultants/robert-beckford.

Reddie, Anthony. *Is God Colour-blind? Insights from Black Theology for Christian Faith and Ministry.* New edition with an afterword on why Black Lives Matter. London: SPCK, 2020.

Reddie, Anthony G., and Carol Troupe. *Deconstructing Whiteness, Empire and Mission.* London: SCM, 2023.

Roest, Gert-Jan. *The Gospel in the Western Context: A Missiological Reading of Christology in Dialogue with Hendrikus Berkhof and Colin Gunton.* Studies in Reformed Theology 37. Leiden: Brill, 2019.

Rooms, Nigel. *The Faith of the English: Integrating Christ and Culture.* London: SPCK, 2011.

———. "God and My Whiteness: A Personal Theo-biography." *Practical Theology* 15.1–2 (2022) 137–47.

———. *Missional Church: What does Good Look Like?* Cambridge: Grove, 2019.

———. "Participation, *Missio Dei* and Contemporary Ecclesiological Controversies: A Missiologist Dialogues with Andrew Davison's *Participation in God*." In *Participation and Church Planting: Perspectives from Scripture, Tradition and Practice,* edited by Joshua Cockayne, 162–75. London: SCM, 2026.

———. "Paul as Practical Theologian: *Phronesis* in Philippians." *Practical Theology* 5.1 (2012) 81–94.

———. *Towards a Pedagogy for Inculturation: Adult Theological Education and the Interaction of Christian Faith and Culture.* ThD diss., Birmingham University, 2008.

———. "Understanding Local Church as Porous Living Systems: Insights from the Tavistock Tradition." *Ecclesial Practices* 6.2 (2019) 182–97.

Rooms, Nigel, and Patrick Keifert. *Spiritual Leadership in the Missional Church: A Systems Approach to Leadership as Cultivation.* Cambridge: Grove, 2019.

Rooms, Nigel, and Cathy Ross. "Practical Theology and Missiology—Can They Live Together?" *Practical Theology* 7.2 (2014) 144–47.

Rooms, Nigel, and Elli Wort. *Fuzzy Church: Gospel and Culture in the North of England.* Durham, UK: Sacristy Press, 2021.

Russell, Dave. *Looking North: Northern England and the National Imagination.* Manchester: Manchester University Press, 2004.

Sanneh, Lamin. *Translating the Message: The Missionary Impact on Culture.* Maryknoll, NY: Orbis, 1989.

Schreiter, Robert, ed. *Faces of Jesus in Africa.* London: SCM, 1992.

———. "Missiology's Future at the Intersection of the Intercultural and the Interreligious." In *Mission and Culture: The Louis J. Luzbetak Lectures,* edited by Stephen Bevans, 275–90. Maryknoll, NY: Orbis, 2012.

Sedmak, Clemens. *Doing Local Theology: A Guide for Artisans of a New Humanity.* Maryknoll, NY: Orbis, 2002.

Shepherd, David. *Bias to the Poor.* London: Hodder and Stoughton, 1983.

Sinus. "What Are Sinus-Milieus®?" https://www.sinus-institut.de/en/sinus-milieus .

Sison, Antonio D. *The Art of Indigenous Inculturation: Grace on the Edge of Genius.* Maryknoll, NY: Orbis, 2021.

Spencer, Stephen. *SCM Study Guide to Christian Mission: Historic Types and Contemporary Expressions.* London: SCM, 2007.

Spencer, Stephen, with Mwita Akiri. *Growing and Flourishing: The Ecology of Church Growth.* London: SCM, 2019.

Spracklen, Karl. "Theorising Northernness and Northern Culture: The North of England, Northern Englishness, and Sympathetic Magic." *Journal for Cultural Research* 20.1 (2016) 4–16.

The Susanna Wesley Foundation. "A Northern Gospel." March 23, 2020. https://susannawesleyfoundation.org/researching-church-gospel-culture-rooms/.

Taylor, Charles. *A Secular Age,* Cambridge, MA: Harvard University Press, 2007.

Thiselton, Anthony C. *New Horizons in Hermeneutics.* London: HarperCollins, 1992.

Unlock Democracy. "About Unlock Democracy." https://unlockdemocracy.org.uk/about-us.

Veling, Terry A. *Practical Theology: "On Earth as it is in Heaven."* Maryknoll, NY: Orbis, 2005.

Wakefield, Gavin, and Nigel Rooms. *Northern Gospel, Northern Church: Reflections on Identity and Mission.* Durham, UK: Sacristy Press, 2016.

Walls, Andrew F. "The Gospel as Prisoner and Liberator of Culture." In *New Directions in Mission and Evangelization 3: Faith and Culture,* edited by James A. Scherer and Stephen B. Bevans, 17–28. Maryknoll, NY: Orbis, 1999.

Walter, Gregory. *Being Promised: Theology, Gift and Practice.* Grand Rapids, MI: Eerdmans, 2013.

Wells, Samuel. *Improvisation: The Drama of Christian Ethics.* London: SPCK, 2004.

Wessels, Anton. *Europe: Was It Ever Really Christian?* Translated by John Bowden. London: SCM, 1994.

Whiteman, Darrell. "Anthropology and Mission: The Incarnational Connection." In *Mission and Culture: The Louis J. Luzbetak Lectures,* edited by Stephen B. Bevans, 59–98. Maryknoll, NY: Orbis, 2012.

———. "The Conversion of a Missionary: A Missiological Study of Acts 10." *Missiology: An International Review* 51.1 (2022) 19–30.

The Work of the People. "Go to Hell." https://www.theworkofthepeople.com/go-to-hell.

Wrogemann, Henning. *Intercultural Hermeneutics.* Intercultural Theology 1, translated by Karl E. Böhmer. Downers Grove, IL: IVP Academic, 2016.

York St. John University. "Is God Northern?" https://www.yorksj.ac.uk/news/2021/is-god-northern/.

Index

adoptionism, 62
African epistemology, 59–60
agency, 58–59, 66, 147, 156, 159–60, 176, 180–83
Akiri, Mwita, 140–41
Allen, Roland, 31
Alpha course, 165
Angel of the North, 104
Arbuckle, Gerald, 13
asset-based community development, 159, 220
Augustine (of Canterbury), 18
authenticity, 105–6, 129–30, 198–99

Beckford, Robert, 22–23
Berkhof, Hendrikus, 68–69, 71
Bevans, Steve, 9, 17, 63, 205
Bible translation, 13, 55, 59
Bickley, Paul, 200–201
boma approach, 33, 35
Boniface, 18
Bosch, David, 8, 9
Boucher Chisale, Claude, 27–30
Bowen, John, 33
Brazil, 206
Bunting, Basil, 93, 97, 102
Bunyan, John, 198

Cameron, Helen, 154
Campbell, Ted, 73
Cardijn, Joseph, 12
Christ
    crucifixion, 24–25
    descent into hell, 186
    incarnation, 209–10
    presence of, 72–74
Christology, 69
church attendance, 115, 124
church growth, 140–74
church leadership, 117–20, 124, 130–31, 163–64
church as living organism, 151–52
church membership, 154–55
church planting, 144, 170–71
Colenso, John, 55–60
colonialism, 49–60, 206
coloniality, 183–84
    resistance to, 197–201
Columbus, 19
community, 106, 199
community service, 149–51, 158–59, 168–69
consumerism, 212–13
contextual theology, 70, 205
    emic critique, 11–40
    etic critique, 41–53
contextualization, 13, 219–20
conviviality, 208, 212–15, 219, 232
creation, 9–10
critical intersubjectivity, 48–49, 51–52
Crusades, 19
culture
    change and complexity, 29–30
    and faith, 2–3, 25–26
    and globalization, 39
    theology of, 40

Davison, Andrew, 9, 10

De Mesa, José, 25–26
discipleship, 145–46, 149, 151, 159–61, 169–70
docetism, 62
Donovan, Vincent, 30–33
Dorling, Danny, 80
Dulles, Avery, 149–52

Eliot, T. S., 101
Epimetheus, 213
essentialism, 34–39, 77–88, 106
ethnography, 297
Eucharist, 182
evangelism, 32–35, 146–49, 156–57, 173
Ewell, Sam, 203–21

faith, and culture, 2–3, 25–26, 62
Filipino culture, 26
Flett, John, 9
"flourishing" churches, 113–17, 140–74
Food Banks, 216–18
Fox, Kate, 46–47, 85–88, 93, 105, 107
freedom, 131–32, 145, 149, 208–9, 215, 219
Freire, Paulo, 12
Fresh Expressions, 171–72, 174

Gadamer, Hans-Georg, 38
garden imagery, 220–21
Gehalt, 88–94, 103–10
Gentiles, 14–15, 63–64, 67
Good Samaritan parable, 213, 216
Gormley, Anthony, 104
Gorringe, Tim, 40, 92
gospel, not static, 65
Goto, Courtney, 41–53, 135–38, 179, 184
Gregory the Great, 18
Gunton, Colin, 68–69, 71

Heaney, Robert, 4, 23–24, 47, 176–84, 192
Heath, Elaine, 185–86
Hodgson, Dorothy, 34–38
holiness, 89
Holy Saturday, 186
Holy Spirit, 14, 64–67
home, 106, 199
honesty, 129–30
hope, 94–96, 102–3, 107–10, 131–32, 200–201
hospitals, 216
Hull, John, 17
human rights, 11, 12
humility, 66–67, 182, 198
humor, 107–10, 131–32, 200–201
Hunt, Robert, 15
hybridization, 192–97

Illich, Ivan, 115, 204, 206–10, 221
incarnation, 183, 208–10, 212
    prolonging, 212–19
inculturation, 13–21, 25–26, 212
    dynamic, 30, 34
    projects in Africa, 27–38
individualizing, 35–36

Jennings, Willie James, 20, 53–67, 179–81, 204
Jesuits, 20–21
Joh, Wohnee Anne, 23–25
Justin Martyr, 16

kenosis, 9, 50
Kes (film), 108
kingdom of God, 89, 91–92, 95, 103, 104, 197
Korean culture, 24–25
Kraft, Charles, 13
Kwiyani, Harvey, 141

Las Casas, Bartolomé de, 19–20
Leopando, Irwin, 12
Liberation Theology, 12
liminality, 191–92, 196, 198
listening, 38
Loach, Ken, 107–10
Luzbetak, Louis, 12–13

Maasai, 30–38
McGilchrist, Iain, 213
Maconie, Stuart, 81–82
Malawi, 27–30
Maritain, Jacques, 12
Marley, Bob, 22
Marsh, Clive, 88–92

Milbank, Alison, 188
mimicry, 196
missio Dei, 8–10, 48, 49–60, 74–76
Missio Munich, banner, 27–30
missiology, 2
mission
  origins in God, 9
  polycentric, 141
  reverse, 25, 58, 67, 182, 204
Moon, W. Jay, 13
multicultural/intercultural, 212
mystery, of Christ, 72–74, 77

nativism, 49–51
Newbiggin, Lesslie, 9
Nida, Eugene, 13
Niven, Alex, 80, 82, 93–105
Nobili, Robert de, 21
North of England, 40, 43, 45, 47, 63
  culture, 83–110, 184, 200
  geography, 79–82, 184
  "grim," 94–95, 104–6, 191, 198
  North–South divide, 175–76, 178–79
  Northern Powerhouse, 98
  Northernness, 5–7, 46–47, 51, 81–94, 104–10, 129–30

The Old Oak (film), 107–10
Origen, 16

parishes
  English historic, 154, 188
  in Tanzania, 144, 148, 155
  transition, 189–90, 219
participation, 8–9
particular vs. universal, 38–39
particularity, 176–80
Paul, Apostle, 144
phronesis, 1–4, 186
pilgrim principle, 15, 25, 29, 36, 61, 76, 87, 92, 146–47
Plekon, Michael, 189–90
poesis, 1, 4, 5, 26, 67
post-Christian west, 67–69, 113, 155, 185–88
post-colonial theology, 4, 6, 175–202
practical theology, 41–53, 205
prophetic tradition, 44
presence of God, 72–74, 90
Prometheus, 213
promise of God, 65–66, 181, 218–19

race, 20, 53–67
Raiser, Konrad, 9
Rastafarians, 21
realism, 105–6, 198–99
refugees, 108–9
regional theology, 40, 215, 221
relationality, 103–4, 165, 208, 211–13
research methods, 48–51
resistance, 197–201
Rhodes, Alexandre de, 21
Ricci, Matteo, 21
Robin Hood, 98, 104
Roest, Gert-Jan, 68–76
Roman Empire, 17–18
Russell, Dave, 79–80, 83

sacraments, 149, 157–58, 166–68, 181–82
Sanneh, Lamin, 38, 58–59
Scharmer, Otto, 191, 198
schools, in Illich's thought, 212–13
Schreiter, Robert, 39
Schroeder, Roger, 9, 17, 63
Shepstone, Theophilus, 55–56
Sison, Antonio, 26
slave trade, 20, 54
Spencer, Stephen, 140–60, 170–72, 282
Spiritans, 32–38
Spracklen, Karl, 83–84, 104
stories, 200–201
supersessionism, 54–55, 59, 61, 64–65
Sydney Opera House, 1–2
symbol, compared with sign, 43–44

Tanzania, 59–60, 140–71
Taylor, Charles, 75, 190
Taylor, John V., 182–83
Tertullian, 15, 21
Theodosius, 17–18
theological anthropology, 17, 56, 218
theology in the vernacular, 22–26
Thomas Aquinas, 9–10
Tillich, Paul, 88–91

translation, 59–62, 65

"U" theory of change, 191–92, 198, 202

Valignano, Alessandro, 21
Vatican Council (2nd, 1962–65), 12
Venn, Henry, 159–60

Walls, Andrew, 15, 61
Walter, Gregory, 66, 181
Whiteman, Daniel, 13
will, divine, 26
Willingen, Conference on International Missions, 9
witness, 53, 133, 205–6
women, spirituality, 34–37, 39
Wort, Elli, 2–3, 111–12, 128, 136

Xavier, Francis, 21

Zulus, 55–58
Zurara (chronicler), 20, 54

www.ingramcontent.com/pod-product-compliance
Lightning Source LLC
LaVergne TN
LVHW050622100826
845148LV00011B/1699

9798385265039